Pasta e Verdura

Also by Jack Bishop

Lasagna
Something Sweet

Pasta e Verdura

140 VEGETABLE SAUCES

FOR SPAGHETTI, FUSILLI, RIGATONI, AND ALL OTHER NOODLES

JACK BISHOP

HarperCollins*Publishers*

HarperCollins books may be purchased for educational, business, or sales promotional use. For information please write: Special Markets Department, HarperCollins Publishers, Inc., 10 East 53rd Street, New York, NY 10022.

FIRST EDITION

Designed and illustrated by Barbara Balch

Library of Congress Cataloging-in-Publication Data

Bishop, Jack.
    Pasta e verdura: 140 vegetable sauces for spaghetti, fusilli, rigatoni, and all other noodles / Jack Bishop.
        p.   cm.
    Includes index.
    ISBN 0-06-017402-1
    1. Sauces. 2. Cookery (Vegetables) 3. Cookery (Pasta) 4. Cookery, Italian. I. Title.
    TX819.A1B53   1996
    641.8'14—dc20   95-49009

96 97 98 99 00 ❖/RRD 10 9 8 7 6 5 4 3 2 1

To Lauren, with love

~

Contents

~

~

Acknowledgments

~

No author works alone. This project was supported by many friends and family who deserve my thanks.

My agent, Angela Miller, helped get this book off the ground and encouraged me throughout its writing with her sharp insights and good humor.

For many years now, a cadre of professional friends and colleagues has helped sustain my efforts with their advice and thoughtful examples. Thank you to Pam Anderson, Mark Bittman, Stephanie Lyness, Chris Kimball, Anne Tuomey, and John Willoughby for their continued friendship.

Susan Friedland's sound editing sharpened my writing and made this a better book. My thanks to the entire team at HarperCollins, especially Jennifer Griffin, Sue Llewellyn, Estelle Laurence, and Joseph Montebello for their contributions on my behalf.

My parents, Jack and Judith Bishop, my in-laws, Martin and Marilyn Chattman, and my siblings, Dana Bishop and Doug Bishop, have all eaten at my table and served up their own suggestions and praises for my cooking. Thanks also to the legion of friends who have passed through my kitchen and faithfully eaten the pasta of the day.

Lauren Chattman, best friend, partner, traveling companion, fellow Italophile, and wife, made all this work enjoyable.

Introduction

As I sat in a working-class trattoria in Rome a year ago, enjoying a bowl of tagliatelle tossed with sautéed radicchio, caramelized onions, and Parmesan cheese, I was once again amazed at the simplicity of great Italian cooking. Italians place the highest value on delicious everyday dishes, really nothing more than well-prepared peasant food. Italian cooking is also accessible and straightforward, which helps to explain its popularity in this country. As Italy's number-one crossover hit, pasta exemplifies the sensible Italian approach to food. It's quick, inexpensive, and satisfying.

While most Americans understand the virtues of pasta, not all comprehend its unrivaled diversity. Many of us are trying to change our daily kitchen routines and eat more grains and vegetables. Pasta is a natural ally. Unfortunately, the Italian pasta dishes we first came to love, the ones that still enjoy the greatest recognition in this country—fettuccine Alfredo, pesto, Bolognese meat sauce—are high in fat and low in vegetables and fiber. The trick then is to learn how to utilize the vast array of vegetables at the supermarket when making sauces for pasta. The source for this information is back in Italy, where cooks have turned basic vegetables into extraordinary but simple pasta sauces for centuries.

Pasta e Verdura provides endless ideas for cooks who love pasta and want to eat healthy meals based on grains and greens. This book offers simple yet satisfying sauce ideas for common supermarket items that many shoppers ignore such as kale, beets, escarole, and leeks. Of course, there are plenty of recipes using popular vegetables like broccoli, asparagus, peppers, spinach, carrots, and tomatoes as well as Italian staples like eggplant, zucchini, radicchio, endive, fava beans, fennel, and artichokes.

The book begins with introductory sections on pantry items you should keep on hand to create impromptu meals as well as a step-by-step guide to cooking pasta. The body of the book consists of twenty-seven alphabetical entries with information about individual vegetables ranging from asparagus to zucchini. Entries tell shoppers what to look for at the market and give tips on how to store and prepare each vegetable. Depending on the popularity of a specific vegetable, entries are followed by as many as twelve or as few as two recipes that demonstrate simple ways to turn the vegetable into a pasta sauce.

My philosophy as a cook has always been to choose naturally healthy recipes rather than attempting tortured approximations of fatty dishes. Recipes in this book convey my respect for ingredients and Italian traditions. Most rely on olive oil, although butter and cream make occasional appearances in small quantities when appropriate. As for cheese, many recipes contain small amounts for flavor—a shaving or two of Parmesan or a swirl of ricotta to give a sauce body.

All recipes are written to sauce one pound of pasta, enough for four main-course servings. Of course, there are times when one pound of pasta may only feed three especially hearty eaters, while the same pound can feed six as a first course. However, I have designed every recipe in this book to be a complete meal for four when served with some salad and bread.

Each recipe ends with an estimate of total preparation and cooking time. Most of the recipes in this book can be on the table in thirty minutes or less. A few recipes, especially those that rely on slow-cooking methods like roasting potatoes or boiling beans, may have long preparation times. However, most of the time is for unattended cooking and does not necessarily indicate especially difficult or lengthy kitchen work for the cook.

Throughout this book my approach is one of moderation and sensibility. Although I lost seven pounds from my already lean frame while testing these recipes, this is by no means a "diet" cookbook beholden to artificial guidelines and numerical games. My food is simple, delicious, easy to prepare, and naturally good for you. In other words, *buon appetito!*

Perfect Pasta Every Time

Never has so much been written about such simple food. Information about how to cook pasta has filled hundreds of books and magazines in recent years. Much of what has been written is wrong, especially "tips" like adding oil to the water as pasta cooks or rinsing drained noodles to prevent sticking. I am going to add to the written record on the subject with some brief comments based on years of experience. Read this section once, follow my suggestions when you cook, and I guarantee you will enjoy perfect pasta every time.

• FRESH • VS. • DRIED • PASTA •

"Fresh" pasta is an American marketer's dream come true. We all have been trained, and properly so, to choose fresh products over frozen or processed foods. Riding this wave, American companies are selling "fresh" pasta in refrigerated cases to shoppers who want to buy the best. The problem is that this pasta is neither "fresh" nor "the best."

In Italy there are two kinds of pasta. Fresh pasta, with just eggs and all-purpose flour, is something made at home for special occasions and used that day. Fresh pasta is essential when making filled pastas like ravioli and tortellini. Fresh strands of fettuccine are also wonderful when tossed with a delicate cream sauce. Most Italian towns and villages have a *pastificio* where fresh fettuccine, ravioli, and tortellini are sold. These pastas are prepared fresh every day and are never refrigerated for weeks before being sold. Fresh pasta has rather limited uses in the Italian kitchen.

For the most part, Italians rely on the myriad shapes of commercially produced dried pasta manufactured by an industry that dates back more than one hundred years. Water and semolina flour are kneaded together in a machine to form a smooth dough and then extruded through brass forms into one of a hundred possible shapes. The extruded pasta is dried in ovens, packaged, and then shipped. Because most of the moisture has been removed from dried pasta, it is shelf-stable and should stay "fresh" for months if not years.

Every recipe in this book was tested with dried pasta. Since most Americans don't live near a pasta shop that makes its own fresh pasta every day (if you live in a big city or one with a large Italian community this may not be true) and don't have the time to make their own fresh pasta for dinner, dried pasta is the logical choice. Fresh fettuccine would be nice in some of the recipes that follow and by all means use it if you like. However, dried pasta is just as good and should not be thought of as a compromise; it is merely different, not worse. Dried pasta has properties, such as its firm texture, that fresh can never possess. And if you do choose to use fresh pasta, please buy or make the real thing.

•CHOOSING THE RIGHT• •SHAPE AND BRAND•

How do you match a dried pasta shape with a particular sauce and which brand of pasta should you buy? Let me tackle the second question first. As recently as ten or fifteen years ago, American dried pastas were decidedly inferior. They often were made with inferior grades of flour and cooked up mushy and limp. This is no longer the case. As our appetite for pasta has grown (annual per-capita consumption is up to twenty pounds and growing rapidly), so has the quality of American pasta. Although I still prefer the De Cecco brand (the leading import from Italy) sold in bright blue boxes, I don't run from American pastas as I once did. My advice is to try several brands and see which one you like best. As long as it is made from 100 percent semolina and comes from Italy or the United States, the pasta is bound to be good if not great.

Choosing the right shape for a particular sauce is a bit more complicated. In general, the consistency of the sauce, rather than specific ingredients, determines the pasta shape I use. For instance, a chunky tomato sauce with large pieces of zucchini would overwhelm thin spaghetti but works nicely with large rigatoni that can trap the chunks of vegetables inside individual pieces of pasta.

I find it easier to divide various shapes into several categories and offer the following general guidelines. There are no right and wrong choices here, only more appropriate and less appropriate ones.

Thin, long noodles like linguine or spaghetti marry well with smooth sauces like pesto or those with relatively small chunks of vegetables.

Wide, long noodles like fettuccine or tagliatelle are wonderful when coated with creamy sauces. Again, this long shape is better with smaller rather than larger chunks of vegetables.

Short, narrow, tubular shapes like penne or small ziti are good with sauces that have small-to-medium pieces of vegetables. These pieces will become trapped inside the noodles, making the marriage of sauce and pasta complete.

Farfalle, butterfly-shaped pasta with deep crevices, and small shells can be used interchangeably with penne since all of these shapes have spaces that will trap and hold small pieces of vegetables and sauce.

Large, open shells or wide, tubular shapes like rigatoni are best with very chunky, hearty sauces.

·HOW TO COOK PASTA·

Pasta is one of those foods that is easy to cook but hard to cook exactly right. Certainly no Italian words inspire as much fear or confusion among American cooks as *al dente*. Simply translated as "to the tooth," the term refers to properly cooked pasta—tender not mushy, firm not hard, chewy not crunchy. Such a vague culinary definition inevitably leads to passionate disagreements. One woman's al dente is another man's mushy. Even within Italy, there is a split between north and south, with residents of Naples serving chewier pasta than their fellow countrymen in Bologna and Milan.

At some level, pasta is done when it tastes right to you. That said, there is only a window of a minute or so when I find that pasta is properly cooked. What follows are my recommendations for perfect pasta.

First of all, pasta should be cooked in plenty of water. I recommend four quarts of cold water for one pound of pasta. Six quarts is right for one and one half pounds of pasta, while larger amounts of pasta should be cooked in two pots. Choose an eight- to ten-quart pot for cooking pasta.

Once the water comes to a full rolling boil, I add a generous amount of salt, usually one tablespoon of clean-tasting kosher salt for one pound of pasta. Although this amount may seem high, remember that most of the salt goes down the drain with the cooking water. Pasta cooked without salt is bland and will never taste right no matter how much salt is added to the sauce, so make sure to add enough salt to the cooking water.

Once the salt has been added, I add the noodles (never breaking long strands in half) and stir several times to separate them. Cover the pot until the water returns to a boil. Remove the cover and stir several times. After the first minute or so, you can stir less frequently. The agitation of the boiling water will keep most strands separate. But to be on the safe side, stir the pasta once every minute or two.

Many cooks insist on adding oil to the cooking water, but I don't recommend it. Oil does reduce foaming and can reduce the chance of boil-overs (the oil coats the side of the pot and makes it harder for the foam to climb over the top), but it also makes the pasta slick. When properly cooked, pasta has a light film of starch that helps bind the sauce to the noodles. When pasta is cooked with oil, slickness can prevent the pasta from marrying properly with the sauce. If boil-overs are a concern, a better solution is to use a larger pot or lower the heat slightly once the pasta has been added to the boiling water.

As soon as pasta hits the boiling water, it starts to rehydrate and expand. Fresh pasta, which already contains much moisture, is sometimes fully hydrated as soon as the water returns to a boil, if it is quite thin, or more likely after a minute or two of cooking at a boil, if it is homemade and thicker. Basically, all you want to do is soften and heat fresh pasta. This takes just a few minutes, never more. Note that fresh pasta will never be as al dente as dried pasta. Dried pasta, of course, takes much longer to cook through.

After several minutes of cooking, dried pasta will be tender on the outside but still hard in the middle. At this stage, the partially cooked strands no longer snap easily in half, but will break if firmly squeezed. The inner core of each piece of pasta is white—not pale yellow like the exterior.

The next stage, which occurs a minute or two before the pasta is fully cooked, is what I call the "rubber band stage." At this point (which may occur after five minutes for thin spaghettini or ten minutes for thick, curly shapes like fusilli), the center begins to soften, the white core disappears, and the strand becomes elastic enough to quiver when gently pulled.

This is when personal taste comes into play. Southern Italians often drain pasta as soon as it quivers, leaving the pieces chewy enough that they sometimes stick slightly to back teeth when eaten. I cook pasta for another minute or two, to the stage preferred in northern Italy.

If you let pasta go three or four minutes, it still quivers but is now mushy and no longer al dente by anyone's definition. Overcooked pasta begins to taste watery and does not stand up as well to the sauce. Prolonged cooking washes away too much of the gelatinized starch (you can feel and see this white covering on just-drained pasta) that helps the sauce cling to the pasta.

My advice is to begin tasting dried pasta after it has cooked for four or five minutes for thin noodles and after seven or eight minutes for curly shapes. This is the earliest that the rubber band stage might begin. Once the pasta quivers you know it is almost done. Keep checking the pasta every minute or so from then on. As soon as the noodles seem almost al dente— they should still have some chewiness, but the center should no longer be hard or gummy—remove the pot from the heat and drain the pasta. The pasta continues to cook after it is drained so you need to compensate for this by draining the pasta when it is a little underdone. One final note: Cooking times on pasta boxes are often wrong so ignore them altogether.

• D R A I N I N G • S A U C I N G • • A N D   S E R V I N G •

Never shake pasta bone-dry as it drains. Instead, pour the pasta and cooking liquid into a large colander, allow the water to flow out, and then shake the colander once or twice to remove the excess liquid. For recipes that say "drain pasta, making sure that some liquid still clings to the noodles," this is the point at which the pasta and sauce should be combined. The small amount of cooking water remaining on the pasta helps spread the sauce and is especially useful when tossing pasta with relatively dry oil-based sauces. In general, tomato sauces contain more liquid, so you can shake the pasta several more times to remove most but not all of the water. To moisten particularly dry sauces, reserve one-quarter cup to one-half cup of the cooking liquid before draining the pasta and add this hot water as needed during the saucing process.

Some cookbook authors recommend adding a glass of cold water to the pot as soon as the pasta is done in order to stop the cooking process. I find this trick is not nearly as effective as immediate draining, and it can cause you to overcook the pasta. Other sources suggest rinsing drained pasta under cold, running water to prevent clumping. This only cools the pasta down, makes it taste watery, and removes the starchy coating that helps bind the sauce to the pasta. In short, never rinse cooked pasta.

Once the pasta has been drained, you have less than a minute to sauce it; otherwise, even premium brands may stick together. If your sauce is not done (I never throw pasta into the boiling water until the sauce is almost cooked), toss the drained pasta with a tablespoon or two of oil to slow down the clumping. Consider this an emergency measure.

To keep pasta piping hot, return it to the empty pot it was cooked in and add the sauce or add the drained pasta to the pan used to make the sauce if that pan is large enough. Also, use a minimum of strokes to coat the pasta evenly with sauce. Lifting noodles high above the pot may look good to guests buts cools the pasta down. If you want to add a tablespoon of top-quality olive oil or butter now, go ahead. It will help the sauce spread evenly and delivers a last-minute flavor boost. If you are watching fat intake, skip this step.

As you cook your way through this book, you will notice that my pastas are not swimming in sauce. Excessive saucing is a decidedly American tradition. In Italy, pasta is usually sauced quite meagerly and served as a light first course followed by chicken, fish, or meat. I have taken a middle road, knowing that Americans like to eat pasta as a main course. Saucing is generous in my recipes but not so excessive that the pasta is drowned out.

After mixing the sauce and pasta together, immediately transfer portions to warm bowls. (Place bowls in a 200° F. oven for several minutes while the pasta is cooking and use oven mitts to bring them to the table.) Don't use flat dinner plates. I like to serve pasta in wide, shallow soup bowls that trap heat and provide an edge against which long noodles can be twirled.

Despite my lengthy explanations, the whole process of draining, saucing, and serving should be accomplished as quickly as possible—no more than two minutes. Great pasta waits for no one.

Pasta Lover's Pantry

Spur-of-the-moment cooking is possible as long as you keep your pantry and refrigerator well stocked. The following ingredients are those I find most essential for preparing vegetarian pasta sauces. In addition to these staples, make sure to keep a good supply of olives, canned tomatoes, and garlic, onions, and shallots on hand. See their individual entries for information on buying and storing each of these vegetables, which can double as seasonings in smaller quantities in pasta sauces or as "main vegetables" in larger amounts.

Once you have stocked your pantry and refrigerator with the necessary items, add a good supply of dried pastas, in a variety of shapes, and some fresh, seasonal vegetables. Nothing more is required to make every recipe in this book.

~

•BREAD•CRUMBS• Plain bread crumbs can be used in place of grated cheese as a final complement to many pasta dishes. In southern Italy, where culinary economy has always been necessary and cheese is fairly scarce, many oil-based sauces are tossed with cooked pasta and toasted bread crumbs. I prefer to make my own bread crumbs from stale bread. Simply cut the bread—use white or whole-wheat as desired—into small chunks and grind them in a food processor until quite fine. Bread crumbs can be stored in an airtight container in the refrigerator for many weeks or in the freezer for several months.

Toasting heightens the flavor of the bread crumbs and is recommended before their use. Place the bread crumbs in a small skillet set over medium heat. Shake the pan occasionally to redistribute the crumbs and toast until golden brown. Fresh herbs, spices, even olive oil or melted butter can be used to season toasted bread crumbs.

~

•BUTTER• There are two types of butter sold in most supermarkets, lightly salted and unsalted (also called sweet). I prefer the clean, sweet flavor of unsalted butter and use it in all my cooking and baking. Some salted butter tastes fine but even then you never know how much salt has been added by the manufacturer. I like to add the salt myself so that I know how much is in a particular dish.

Although I use very little butter, I still buy it by the pound, often purchasing several pounds at a time when it goes on sale. Butter can be stored in the freezer. In fact, I keep all my butter, except for perhaps one stick, in the freezer. When I use up the stick in the refrigerator, I simply pull another stick from the freezer to take its place.

~

•CAPERS• These tiny unopened flower buds come from a bush that grows throughout the Mediterranean. The buds are pickled and packed in vinegar. I like Italian varieties packed in balsamic vinegar, which is not as harsh as white vinegar. Capers can be quite small (no larger than a sesame seed) or quite large (the size of a fleshy pea). I generally purchase small capers but larger capers can be used as long as they are chopped. Unopened jars can be stored indefinitely in the pantry. Store opened jars in the refrigerator, making sure to keep the capers covered with vinegar. They will keep for months, if not a year or two.

~

•CHEESES• Italy is known the world over for its cheeses. The following list includes those I find most useful when serving pasta. Of course, wrap all cheeses in plastic and store them in the refrigerator to prolong freshness. A soft cheese may last only days or a week; a piece of Parmesan will stay fresh for weeks if not months. Although I generally trim and discard any mold that appears on hard grating cheeses and then proceed to use the remainder, I discard soft cheeses at the first sign of mold.

Bel Paese: This creamy, almost runny cheese is really more for eating than for cooking, although its mild flavor and rich texture can be useful in some pasta sauces. Fontina can be used in its place if desired.

Fontina: This semisoft cheese has a gentle, nutty flavor and melts beautifully over hot pasta.

Goat Cheese: Fresh goat cheese is one of my favorites. Its light, creamy texture is similar to that of good ricotta, but the flavor is tangy and sometimes even pleasantly sharp. American goat cheese is just as good as French chèvre and there are even some low-fat versions on the market that are quite good. Regular goat cheese is relatively low in fat, as cheese goes, so don't worry about adding a few tablespoons to enrich a pasta sauce.

Gorgonzola: There are numerous varieties of this Italian blue cheese, ranging from aged, crumbly versions to those that are creamy and relatively mild. I prefer the latter for pasta sauces since extremely pungent Gorgonzola will overwhelm other flavors. Look for Gorgonzola that is labeled *dolcelatte* ("sweet milk") and appears creamy rather than crumbly. Other blue cheeses, like Saga, can be used as a substitute for Gorgonzola but may lack the creaminess and sweetness of the Italian cheese.

Mozzarella: Although the standard for many other Italian preparations like pizza, mozzarella has fairly limited uses in pasta sauces. A few recipes call for fresh or smoked mozzarella that is shredded in a food processor or by hand. When buying fresh mozzarella, choose cheese that is packed in water and avoid rubbery, shrink-wrapped versions.

Parmesan: Parmesan is the king of Italian cheeses. Authentic Parmesan comes from Parma in northern Italy and is called Parmigiano-Reggiano. When buying Parmesan, look for these words stenciled on the golden rind to assure that you are buying the highest-quality cheese. Since so little Parmesan is required in pasta recipes, I suggest that you splurge. If you are on a budget, there are other Parmesan cheeses from Italy of slightly lower quality. Grana Padano is a fine Italian alternative that is widely available. However, Parmesan made in Argentina, Switzerland, or the United States will not have the same creamy, nutty flavor as the real thing and is not recommended. Never purchase grated cheese in a bottle. It has only slightly more flavor than salted sawdust.

Although Americans tend to think that every pasta dish can be improved by the addition of some grated Parmesan cheese, this simply is not true. As anyone who has visited Italy knows, waiters will often refuse to bring cheese to patrons who have ordered linguine and clams. For the most part, I agree with Italian traditions regarding the use of cheese in pasta dishes. Although few dishes would be ruined by the addition of Parmesan, many won't be helped so I would rather leave it out.

Pecorino Romano: This pungent sheep's milk cheese is hard and a bit crumbly and is usually reserved for grating, although there are some softer versions that can be eaten out of hand. I generally call for Pecorino when I think its strong, tangy flavor is needed. Pecorino and Parmesan can be used interchangeably, but the results will be a bit different.

Ricotta: The quality of most ricotta cheese sold in supermarkets is so inferior that Italian cooks would not even recognize this product. Fresh ricotta should have a light, creamy consistency like goat cheese. Instead, it is often watery and curdy and seems more like cottage cheese. There are some good brands out there, especially those made locally by small firms that specialize in Italian products, and they should be used for the best results.

A lesser-known type of ricotta, called ricotta salata—a pressed and lightly salted sheep's milk cheese—has recently become available in this country. This imported, aged cheese has a wonderful creamy quality that is particularly good with tomato sauces. Ricotta salata looks like feta cheese—it is bright white and crumbly, just dry enough to stand up to the grater yet still moist—but it is much less salty. Italian delicatessens, gourmet stores, and better supermarkets now stock this cheese, for which there is no real substitute.

~

•CITRUS•FRUITS•   The rinds and juices of fresh lemons and oranges lend a bright, acidic component to pasta sauces. The colored rind contains numerous volatile oils that are released when cooked briefly in hot oil. Use a fine-tooth grater or peeler to remove the rind, making sure to leave behind the bitter white pith.

~

•CREAM•   A little cream goes a long way when properly used. A number of recipes in this book call for small amounts, usually just a few tablespoons, to enrich a sauce. Only the real thing can work such culinary wonders. If you are on a low-fat diet, choose another recipe rather than trying to find a substitute—there is none.

~

•HERBS•   I cannot overemphasize the importance of fresh herbs in Italian vegetarian cooking. When I moved out of the city several years ago and began tending my own herb garden, my cooking started to change. I found I was able to make simpler food with fewer ingredients that actually tasted better. The reason was clear—great herbs. Luckily, you don't have to be a gardener to enjoy fresh herbs at any time of the year. Most supermarkets now stock a wide array. While fresh flat-leaf parsley is a staple in my home (I always have some in the refrigerator to perk up pasta sauces or most anything), I also regularly use basil, mint, cilantro, chives, oregano, thyme, rosemary, sage, marjoram, and tarragon.

Rather than driving to three stores to find a specific herb, I want people who cook from my book to use what's on hand. For the most part, herbs are fairly interchangeable. I find it helpful though to recognize that some are more potent than others. Therefore, you may need to use more or less when making a substitution. Parsley and basil are the mildest, followed by mint, chives, cilantro, and tarragon, and finally by oregano, marjoram, thyme, sage, and rosemary. The order of this list is very tentative but is still useful. For example, if a recipe calls for one tablespoon of thyme, I might use an equal amount of oregano or sage but double or even triple the amount of parsley or basil. My best advice is to taste as you cook in order to add the proper amount.

A word about dried herbs. With one exception, I find that their flavor is dull and lifeless. Dried bay leaves have a gentle aromatic quality that comes out when a leaf is added to beans as they cook. (Remember to discard the bay leaf before serving.) Otherwise, I do not recommend dried herbs in my recipes.

•LEGUMES• Beans and lentils are natural partners for vegetable-based pasta sauces since they are so rich in protein, fiber, and other nutrients. Italians are particularly fond of white navy and cannellini beans as well as chick-peas. I prefer to keep a stock of dried beans on hand and then soak and cook them as needed. Although this requires some planning (you must soak beans for at least six hours), I find canned beans are mushy and a distant second in quality. Lentils have the advantage of not requiring presoaking and will soften after just 25 minutes of cooking.

•NUTS• Pine nuts, walnuts, and almonds (both sliced or whole) are used in this book. To make the most of these nuts, toast them to bring out their full flavor. Nuts can be placed on a baking sheet and toasted in a warm oven for five minutes or added to a skillet and toasted, shaking the pan occasionally to turn them, until fragrant and golden. In either case, make sure to keep an eye on the nuts and do not let them burn. The oils in all kinds of nuts will turn rancid fairly quickly at room temperature so store nuts in the refrigerator. Most nuts will keep at least several months if not longer.

*OLIVE*OIL*   The cooking of Italy, especially the southern region, relies on the oil pressed from olives. There are two levels of quality sold in this country—extra-virgin and pure. Extra-virgin olive oil has a richer flavor that will stand out in a salad dressing or when oil is drizzled over warm vegetables. Pure olive oil has less flavor but is fine for sautéing or frying. I use an inexpensive extra-virgin oil for most of my cooking. I reserve pricy extra-virgin oils for raw sauces or other dishes where the flavor of the oil will be quite noticeable.

RAISINS   The use of sweet items like raisins in savory pasta sauces dates back to the Middle Ages. Although once quite common, this pairing of sweet and savory is now rather rare. However, there are a number of occasions when a handful of raisins, either golden or black, are appropriate. Many of these recipes come from southern Italy, where the Arab influence from the Middle Ages can still be traced in the local cuisine.

SALT   Salt is the most important ingredient in my kitchen. I can find a substitute for most everything except for salt. You don't need to use it by the shovelful, but you do need to use it. There, I have said it!

As you might expect, I am picky about the kind of salt I buy. I find that coarse-grained kosher salt has a superior flavor to regular table salt and it is my first choice. Sea salt is also quite good, although it is much more expensive than kosher salt and is therefore my second choice. The lack of additives in kosher salt (some chemicals are added to table salt to keep it from clumping) allows the true salt flavor to shine through without any harshness. Because kosher salt has such large crystals, a teaspoon contains less salt than a teaspoon of table salt. All of my recipes were tested with kosher salt, so I suggest using less table salt if you decide to ignore my advice. In any case, it is imperative that you taste as you cook to determine the proper amount of salt that is required for any dish.

·SHERRY· Dry sherry can be used much like white wine in pasta sauces. Sherry has a richer, deeper flavor more reminiscent of wood than flowers or fruit but the effect will be similar.

·SPICES· Italian food does not rely on spices as much as some of the world's other great cuisines. However, I do find uses for a few key spices. Black pepper is the "hot" seasoning of choice in Italian kitchens. Grinding pepper in a mill as needed is the best way to capture the peppery flavor of this tiny dried berry. Fresh chile peppers are rarely used in Italy. Most Italian cooks rely on hot red pepper flakes, the dried seeds from mildly hot red chiles, when they want to add some heat. Ground cumin, ground cinnamon, and saffron threads also are used to a limited degree.

·SUN·DRIED·TOMATOES· Despite their trendy reputation, sun-dried tomatoes have a long history in Italy, especially in pasta sauces. For centuries, farmers dried summer tomatoes for the express purpose of using them in winter sauces. Many farmers still do this. Traditional Italian cooks would be surprised to see sun-drieds in everything from American salads to pizzas, but not pasta sauces.

When it comes to sun-dried tomatoes, American companies have been able to match the quality of their Italian competitors. Look for sun-dried tomatoes packed in olive oil from either country. Taste various brands to find one that you like. Good sun-dried tomatoes will be only mildly salty with a soft but not mushy texture. If they are too stiff or leathery, do not buy them again.

·VINEGARS· Despite what the chef at your local restaurant thinks, balsamic vinegar is not Italy's answer to soy sauce and should not be used indiscriminately. However, there are plenty of fine uses for this rich, dark elixir and many of them are in pasta sauces. Given the tremendous hype surrounding this vinegar, it is not surprising that much of what is sold in this country is dreck. Good balsamico must be aged for years and therefore will always cost more than three dollars a bottle. Expect to spend at least six to ten dollars for decent balsamic vinegar, and much more, up to thirty dollars, for something truly outstanding. Balsamic vinegar should be mild and sweet, never harsh and bitter. If you balk at the high prices, remember that most recipes call for just a tablespoon or two of vinegar.

In addition to balsamico, I make frequent use of aged red wine vinegar. The flavor is sharper than that of balsamico, but this vinegar lacks the sweetness that may be out of place in some recipes. For instance, I like the bite of red wine vinegar in raw tomato sauces.

• WINE •   A little red or white wine can add a pleasing acidic note to many sauces. Simmering the wine for several minutes will cause most of the alcohol to burn off, leaving behind just the flavor of the wine itself. As some wise cook once wrote, don't cook with any wine you would not drink.

Finding the Right Recipe

Recipes in this book are organized by the main vegetable component in the sauce. If asparagus is in season and in your refrigerator, you need only turn to the section on asparagus for six recipe ideas. Likewise, if you have some zucchini in the garden, turn to that entry and choose among seven recipes.

Some sauces rely on more than one vegetable. In these cases, recipes are organized by the main vegetable with cross-references for important supporting vegetables. For instance, a sauce with one head of broccoli, a small red bell pepper, and a handful of mushrooms would be found in the broccoli section with cross-references listed in the sections on peppers and mushrooms.

In addition, some sauces can be made with a vegetable other than the one indicated in the recipe. Headnotes discuss possible substitutions, while a cross-reference for the original recipe is listed in the section devoted to the alternate vegetable. For example, an asparagus recipe that could also be made with green beans will be cross-referenced in the green beans chapter.

There are times when you may wish to choose a recipe based on considerations other than what vegetables are on hand or in season. Below, I have listed recipes in their appropriate categories: low-fat sauces, dairy-free sauces, and quick sauces. These lists should help weekday cooks who need to get dinner on the table fast, as well as people on special diets, find the right recipes.

• L O W – F A T • S A U C E S •

Since the recipes in this book rely on vegetables and pasta, most are low in fat. Occasionally, recipes do call for a little heavy cream, a fair amount of cheese, or a heavy hand with the oil. For this reason, I have chosen to recognize those recipes that are especially low in fat.

The following sauces rely exclusively on olive oil and do not contain any butter, cream, or cheese added directly to the pasta or sauce. Some of the following recipes may call for grated cheese passed separately at the table, but you can use as much or as little as desired. You can forgo sprinkling these pastas with cheese at the table, but the fat savings are fairly small. I have limited this list to sauces that do not contain more than one-quarter cup oil, one tablespoon per person if the pasta and sauce are eaten as a main course for four people. I have also limited this list to sauces that do not contain any high-fat ingredients such as olives or nuts.

Braised Artichokes with Tomatoes and Thyme (page 27)
Braised Artichokes with Garlic, Lemon, and White Wine (page 28)
Arugula with Cucumbers, Mint, and Lemon Juice (page 38)
Sautéed Arugula with Fresh Tomatoes and Garlic (page 41)
Boiled Beets and Wilted Beet Greens with Garlic and Lemon (page 58)
Roasted Beets and Red Onion with Balsamic Vinegar and Rosemary (page 59)
Broccoli Rabe and Leeks Braised in White Wine and Tomatoes (page 73)
Broccoli Rabe with White Beans and Tomatoes (page 76)
Red Cabbage Smothered with Onions and Red Wine (page 81)
Blanched Carrots and Slow-Cooked Endive with Chives (page 88)
Hearty Carrot and Lentil Sauce with Tomatoes (page 91)
Roasted Eggplant and Red Bell Pepper Puree (page 106)
Roasted Eggplant with Tomatoes and Fresh Herbs (page 107)
Sautéed Endive with Red Bell Peppers, Shallots, and White Wine (page 124)
Braised Fava Beans with Tomatoes and Pecorino Romano (page 129)
Peeled Fava Beans with Red Onion, White Wine, and Mint (page 130)
Sautéed Fennel with Quick Tomato Sauce and Parmesan (page 136)
Oven-Roasted Garlic with Tomatoes and Basil (page 145)
Green Beans with Bell Peppers, White Wine, and Tarragon (page 158)
Haricots Verts with Raw Tomatoes and Mint (page 163)
Red Swiss Chard with Wild Mushrooms and Sherry (page 172)

• DAIRY-FREE • SAUCES •

The following recipes do not use butter, cream, or cheese (including grated cheese passed at the table) and are appropriate for vegans and any others who want to avoid dairy products.

Sautéed Arugula with Fresh Tomatoes and Garlic (page 41)

Raw Arugula with Chick-Pea Salsa (page 42)

Asparagus with Toasted Bread Crumbs, Lemon, and Garlic (page 53)

Boiled Beets and Wilted Beet Greens with Garlic and Lemon (page 58)

Roasted Beets and Red Onion with Balsamic Vinegar and Rosemary (page 59)

Steamed Broccoli with Sun-Dried Tomatoes and Lemon Zest (page 66)

Blanched Broccoli with Spicy Black Olive Vinaigrette (page 67)

Broccoli Rabe with Garlic and Hot Red Pepper (page 72)

Broccoli Rabe and Leeks Braised in White Wine and Tomatoes (page 73)

Broccoli Rabe with Caramelized Onions (page 74)

Shredded Brussels Sprouts with Orange and Almonds (page 83)

Blanched Carrots and Slow-Cooked Endive with Chives (page 88)

Sautéed Cauliflower with Garlic, Raisins, and Pine Nuts (page 95)

Roasted Eggplant and Red Bell Pepper Puree (page 106)

Grill-Roasted Eggplant with Tahini, Lemon, and Parsley (page 109)

Braised Fennel with Raisins and Toasted Pine Nuts (page 139)

Salsa Verde with Garlic, Herbs, Green Olives, Capers, and Lemon (page 146)

Garlic Sautéed in Olive Oil with Parsley and Lemon (page 148)

Roasted Pearl Onions and Carrots with Thyme (page 149)

Caramelized Vidalia Onions with Black Olives and Rosemary (page 152)

Steamed Green Beans with Roasted Potatoes and Pesto (page 161)

Haricots Verts with Raw Tomatoes and Mint (page 163)

Sautéed Escarole with Black Olives and Oregano (page 176)

Spicy Collard Greens with Garlic and Chile Flakes (page 181)

Dandelion Greens with Lemon Oil and Toasted Pine Nuts (page 183)

Braised Leeks with Yellow Bell Peppers and Fresh Tomatoes (page 191)

Sautéed White Mushrooms with Carrots and Oregano (page 200)

Sautéed White Mushrooms Scented with Orange and Marjoram (page 201)

Grilled Portobello Mushrooms with Raw Tomato Sauce (page 203)

Sautéed Shiitake Mushrooms with Garlic and Lemon (page 207)

Marinated Black and Green Olives with Mixed Fresh Herbs (page 215)

Green Olive Tapenade with Spinach, Shallot, and Orange Zest (page 218)

Grilled Peppers with Red Wine Vinegar and Tarragon (page 241)

Crunchy Potato Croutons with Tomatoes and Parsley Pesto (page 245)

Roasted New Potatoes with Herbs, Garlic, and Balsamic Vinegar (page 248)

Wilted Spinach with Golden Raisins and Pine Nuts (page 261)

Sautéed Spinach and Chick-Peas with Lemon and Thyme (page 267)

• QUICK • SAUCES •

Each recipe ends with an indication of how long it will take to get dinner on the table from the moment you walk into the kitchen. The following sauces can be made in twenty minutes, the time it takes to bring water to a boil and cook the pasta. There are dozens more recipes that can be made in twenty-five or thirty minutes and are almost as fast. With very few exceptions, the recipes in this book require less than forty-five minutes from start to finish. However, this list will direct you to those sauces that require the least time and effort to prepare.

Raw Tomato Sauce with Smoked Mozzarella and Basil (page 293)
Raw Tomato Sauce with Black Olive Paste (page 294)
Quick Tomato Sauce with Fresh Basil and Garlic (page 297)
Salsa Cruda with Zucchini, Tomatoes, Red Onion, and Lemon (page 311)

Vegetarian Pasta Sauces, A to Z

Artichokes

My mother never made artichokes, which may explain why I can remember so vividly my first culinary adventure with this flower bud from a Mediterranean thistle plant. I did not sample this delectable if unusual vegetable until I was 20 years old and visiting Paris for the first time. Knowing how passionate I was about food, the friend I was visiting was determined to impress me with a home-cooked meal. Although the rest of my first Parisian supper has slipped from memory, I clearly recall the first course. He steamed two artichokes in a hot pot and served them with melted butter—surely there could be no better introduction to Paris or French cuisine.

Of course, it was the Italians who introduced the artichoke to Paris and the world. Artichokes are now grown in warm, dry climates around the globe, including the small California town of Castroville, which is known as the "artichoke capital of America." They crown an artichoke queen every year in Castroville and past wearers of the tiara have included a soon-to-be-discovered Marilyn Monroe.

Despite such star attractions, Americans have warmed slowly to this exotic vegetable. However, in Italy artichokes are deep-fried (for the famous *carciofi alla Giudia*), steamed, boiled, braised, stewed, roasted, grilled, and even eaten raw in salads. Although artichokes can be found in markets at many times of the year, supply and quality are at their peak during spring.

• S E L E C T I O N •

Artichokes the size of grapefruits as well as those the size of walnuts often grow on the same plant. Size is not a function of age—hence the term "baby" artichoke is really a misnomer—but location on the plant. In general, I like to work with artichokes that are about 8 ounces each, what is usually called "medium-sized." If you can find smaller artichokes, buy them. Preparation may take slightly longer when repeated on more items, but their flavor is usually superb and the texture is always tender. Note that smaller artichokes may cook more quickly than the times given in the following recipes, which can compensate for the longer preparation time. In any case, avoid massive artichokes that weigh more than ½ pound; their flavor is muted and the texture is often stringy or woody.

Look for artichokes with an even green color and few if any blemishes or soft spots. Artichokes that feel heavy for their size generally have more meaty flesh and should be selected when possible. Most important, pick artichokes with tightly closed leaves. If the leaves have unfurled it is a sure sign that the artichoke has been off the plant for some time. Also, try bending back an outer leaf. If it snaps rather than tears, the artichoke is fresh. Although some cooks discard the stems, I find them quite delectable once peeled. Therefore, buy artichokes with stems, which also protect the leaves from drying out and are a good indication that the artichokes have been properly handled during shipping.

• S T O R A G E •

Artichokes should stay fresh for several days in the refrigerator. To prevent them from drying out, stand stem ends in a glass of water. Remember an artichoke is a flower and will respond if treated as such.

• P R E P A R A T I O N •

While artichokes may be cooked whole and served as is for a first course or side dish, they must trimmed before use in pasta sauce. Since cut artichokes will immediately turn gray (much like a cut apple turns brown, only faster), they must be kept in acidulated water until you are ready to use them. Begin by squeezing a lemon into a large bowl filled with cold water. Add the lemon halves to the bowl. Work with just one artichoke at a time and dip it into the water bath if it starts to discolor as you proceed.

To begin actual preparation, bend back and snap off the tough outer leaves on the artichoke. Remove several layers until you reach leaves that are mostly pale green or yellow except for the tips. Cut off the pointed leaf tops that are dark green. (Trim about 1 inch from a medium artichoke.) Trim the base of the stem and use a vegetable peeler to remove the dark green outside layer of skin from the stem. Use a knife or the vegetable peeler to remove any dark green leaf bases that may still encircle the top of the stem.

The next step is to quarter the artichoke lengthwise, leaving part of the stem attached to each piece. Beginning at the stem end of each quarter, slide a small, sharp knife under the fuzzy choke and cut toward the leaf tips. Discard the choke. Cut the cleaned quarters as directed in individual recipes and drop the pieces into the bowl with the acidulated water. Once one artichoke has been completely trimmed, repeat the procedure with the next artichoke.

• U S E   I N   S A U C E S •

The tender leaves, hearts, and stems can be cooked in several ways. Boiling is certainly the fastest cooking method—it takes less than 10 minutes to soften medium artichoke quarters. Trimmed artichokes can be boiled until very tender, then pureed with olive oil and seasonings and thinned with some of the cooking liquid for a quick sauce. Artichokes can also be boiled until crisp-tender (about 8 minutes) and then sautéed with other vegetables to finish the softening process.

Trimmed artichokes may also be braised over low heat in a covered pan. Because artichokes used in pasta sauces must be completely tender (and not crisp), braising takes anywhere from 20 to 45 minutes depending on the size of the artichokes and their freshness. Braising also requires some sort of flavorful cooking liquid. Possible choices include canned tomatoes and their juice, white wine, lemon juice, or water flavored with herbs, garlic, and/or onion.

Braised Artichokes with Tomatoes and Thyme

• SERVES 4 •

TIME: 70 minutes

BEST PASTA CHOICE: Linguine or other long, thin shape

Artichokes take a basic tomato sauce to new culinary heights. Thin wedges of trimmed artichokes slowly soften in a thyme-scented tomato broth for a rich but low-fat sauce. Serve this substantial pasta with a light salad and some peasant bread to soak up every drop of the sauce. Feel free to substitute oregano or marjoram for the thyme.

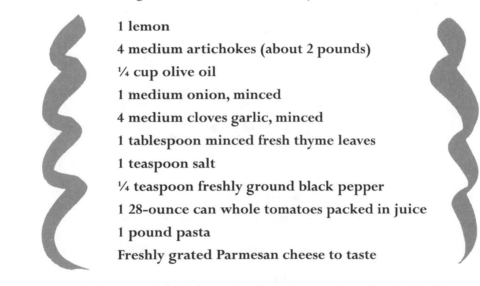

1 lemon

4 medium artichokes (about 2 pounds)

¼ cup olive oil

1 medium onion, minced

4 medium cloves garlic, minced

1 tablespoon minced fresh thyme leaves

1 teaspoon salt

¼ teaspoon freshly ground black pepper

1 28-ounce can whole tomatoes packed in juice

1 pound pasta

Freshly grated Parmesan cheese to taste

1. Cut the lemon in half and squeeze the juice into a large bowl of cold water. Add the lemon halves to the bowl. Prepare the artichokes as directed on page 25. Cut the cleaned artichoke quarters into ¼-inch-thick wedges. Drop the wedges into the bowl with the acidulated water.

2. Heat the oil in a large sauté pan with a cover. Add the onion and sauté over medium heat until translucent, about 5 minutes. Stir in the garlic and sauté for 1 minute. *continued*

3. Drain the artichokes and add them to the pan along with the thyme, salt, pepper, and 1 cup water. Simmer briskly until most of the water in the pan has evaporated, about 10 minutes.

4. Coarsely chop the tomatoes and add them to the pan along with all of their packing juice. Cover the pan and simmer gently, occasionally using a spoon to break apart the tomatoes, until the sauce thickens and the artichokes soften completely, about 35 minutes. Taste for salt and pepper and adjust seasonings if necessary.

5. While preparing the sauce, bring 4 quarts of salted water to a boil in a large pot. Cook and drain the pasta. Toss the hot pasta with the artichoke sauce. Mix well and transfer portions to warm pasta bowls. Serve immediately with grated cheese passed separately.

Braised Artichokes with Garlic, Lemon, and White Wine

• SERVES 4 •

TIME: 60 minutes

BEST PASTA CHOICE: Linguine or other long, thin shape

Artichoke wedges soften in a covered skillet filled with white wine that is perfumed with slivered garlic and lemon zest. Total cooking time is fairly high for this dish but actual hands-on work can be completed in about 20 minutes. Serve the pasta with the same dry white used in the sauce. Choose a not overly oaky Chardonnay or refreshing Pinot Grigio or sauvignon blanc. Accompany with plenty of bread to soak up the sauce.

1 lemon

4 medium artichokes (about 2 pounds)

¼ cup olive oil

6 medium cloves garlic, cut into thin slivers

1 teaspoon salt

2 cups dry white wine

¼ cup minced fresh parsley leaves

1 pound pasta

1. Grate 1 teaspoon zest from the lemon and reserve. Cut the lemon in half and squeeze the juice into a large bowl of cold water. Add the lemon halves to the bowl. Prepare the artichokes as directed on page 25. Cut the cleaned artichoke quarters into ¼-inch-thick wedges. Drop the wedges into the bowl with the acidulated water.

2. Heat the oil in a large sauté pan with a cover. Add the garlic and sauté over medium heat until lightly colored, about 2 minutes. Stir in the reserved lemon zest and salt. Drain the artichokes and add them to the pan along with the wine.

3. Cover the pan and simmer gently until the artichokes are tender and offer little resistance when pierced with a fork, about 40 minutes. Stir in the parsley. Taste for salt and adjust seasonings if necessary.

4. While preparing the sauce, bring 4 quarts of salted water to a boil in a large pot. Cook and drain the pasta. Toss the hot pasta with the artichoke sauce. Mix well and transfer portions to warm pasta bowls. Serve immediately.

Artichokes, Mushrooms, and Roasted Red Peppers with Parmesan

● SERVES 4 ●

TIME: 40 minutes

BEST PASTA CHOICE: Penne or other short, tubular shape

This sauce is a mélange of colors, textures, and flavors, including two kinds of peppers—hot red chile pepper flakes and roasted red bell peppers. Although I usually roast my own bell peppers, prepared versions are adequate in sauces where the peppers are merely an accent. Look for roasted red peppers packed in extra-virgin olive oil. The amount of hot red pepper flakes can be increased or decreased, as desired.

1 lemon

3 medium artichokes (about 1½ pounds)

2 teaspoons salt

1 pound fresh white mushrooms

¼ cup olive oil

1 medium onion, minced

2 medium cloves garlic, minced

½ teaspoon hot red pepper flakes or to taste

½ cup dry white wine

2 small red bell peppers (about ½ pound),
    roasted (see page 232) and sliced thin,
    or 6 ounces roasted red pepper packed
    in olive oil, drained and sliced thin

¼ cup minced fresh parsley leaves

1 pound pasta

> **¼ cup freshly grated Parmesan cheese,
> plus more to taste**

1. Bring 4 quarts of salted water to a boil in a large pot for cooking the pasta. Bring 3 quarts of water to a boil in another pot for cooking the artichokes.

2. Cut the lemon in half and squeeze the juice into a large bowl of cold water. Add the lemon halves to the bowl. Prepare the artichokes as directed on page 25. Cut the cleaned artichoke quarters into ¼-inch-thick wedges. Drop the wedges into the bowl with the acidulated water.

3. Drain the artichokes and add them to the pot along with the lemon halves and 1 teaspoon salt. Simmer until the artichokes are tender but not mushy, about 8 minutes. Drain the artichokes and discard the lemon halves. Set the artichokes aside.

4. Wipe the mushrooms with a paper towel to loosen and remove any dirt. Trim and discard a thin slice from the stem end of each mushroom. Thinly slice the mushrooms and set them aside.

5. Heat the oil in a large sauté pan. Add the onion and sauté over medium heat until translucent, about 5 minutes. Stir in the garlic and hot red pepper flakes and cook for 1 minute.

6. Add the mushrooms, raise the heat to medium-high, and cook until they have released their juices, about 4 minutes. Add the wine and 1 teaspoon salt. Simmer until the liquid has reduced and thickened a bit, about 2 minutes.

7. Add the artichokes to the sauce along with the roasted peppers and parsley. Toss several times to heat the vegetables through. Taste for salt and hot pepper and adjust seasonings if necessary.

8. While preparing the sauce, cook and drain the pasta, making sure that some water still clings to the noodles. Toss the hot pasta with the sauce and ¼ cup Parmesan. Mix well and transfer portions to warm pasta bowls. Serve immediately with more grated cheese passed separately.

Artichoke Puree with Sun-Dried Tomatoes

• SERVES 4 •

TIME: 30 minutes

BEST PASTA CHOICE: Linguine or other long, thin shape

Trimmed artichokes can be blanched and then pureed with garlic and olive oil for a quick, creamy sauce. Toss the hot pasta with the puree as well as sun-dried tomatoes and minced parsley, which add both flavor and color to this sauce.

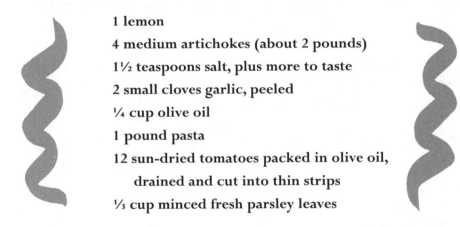

1 lemon

4 medium artichokes (about 2 pounds)

1½ teaspoons salt, plus more to taste

2 small cloves garlic, peeled

¼ cup olive oil

1 pound pasta

12 sun-dried tomatoes packed in olive oil,
 drained and cut into thin strips

⅓ cup minced fresh parsley leaves

1. Bring 4 quarts of salted water to a boil in a large pot for cooking the pasta. Bring 3 quarts of water to a boil in another pot for cooking the artichokes.

2. Cut the lemon in half and squeeze the juice into a large bowl of cold water. Add the lemon halves to the bowl. Prepare the artichokes as directed on page 00. Drop the cleaned quarters into the bowl with the acidulated water.

3. Drain the artichokes and add them to the pot along with the lemon halves and 1 teaspoon salt. Simmer until the artichokes can be easily pierced with a fork, about 10 minutes.

4. Drain the artichokes, reserving ⅓ cup of the cooking liquid and discarding the lemon halves. Transfer the artichokes to the work bowl of a food processor and puree along with the garlic, oil, and ½ teaspoon salt until smooth. Scrape the puree into a bowl and stir in the reserved cooking liquid to thin the mixture to a sauce consistency. Taste for salt and adjust seasonings if necessary.

5. Cook and drain the pasta, making sure that some water still clings to the noodles. Toss the hot pasta with the thinned artichoke puree, the sun-dried tomatoes, and the parsley. Mix well and transfer portions to warm pasta bowls. Serve immediately.

Artichoke Puree with Olives, Capers, and Oregano

● SERVES 4 ●

TIME: 30 minutes

BEST PASTA CHOICE: Linguine or other long, thin shape

Here, pureed artichokes are combined with the Mediterranean flavors of black olives, capers, and oregano. I like meaty (and not terribly salty) Kalamata olives in this dish. Niçoise or other olives in brine (as opposed to oil-cured versions that tend to be saltier and more leathery) can also be used.

1 lemon

4 medium artichokes (about 2 pounds)

1½ teaspoons salt

2 medium shallots, chopped

¼ cup olive oil

15 large black olives such as Kalamatas (about 4 ounces), pitted and chopped

2 tablespoons drained capers, minced

2 tablespoons minced fresh oregano leaves

1 pound pasta

continued

1. Bring 4 quarts of salted water to a boil in a large pot for cooking the pasta. Bring 3 quarts of water to a boil in another pot for cooking the artichokes.

2. Cut the lemon in half and squeeze the juice into a large bowl of cold water. Add the lemon halves to the bowl. Prepare the artichokes as directed on page 25. Drop the cleaned quarters into the bowl with the acidulated water.

3. Drain the artichokes and add them to the pot along with the lemon halves and 1 teaspoon salt. Simmer until the artichokes can be easily pierced with a fork, about 10 minutes.

4. Drain the artichokes, reserving ⅓ cup of the cooking liquid and discarding the lemon halves. Transfer the artichokes to the work bowl of a food processor and puree along with the shallots, oil, and ½ teaspoon salt until smooth. Scrape the puree into a bowl and stir in the reserved cooking water to thin the mixture to a sauce consistency. The puree should be a bit bland since the olives and capers are salty.

5. Combine the olives, capers, and oregano in a small bowl and set them aside.

6. Cook and drain the pasta, making sure that some water still clings to the noodles. Toss the hot pasta with the thinned artichoke puree as well as the olives, capers, and oregano. Mix well and transfer portions to warm pasta bowls. Serve immediately.

Arugula

Arugula has grown wild in southern Italy at least since the time of Romans. However, until the last decade or so it was virtually unknown in this country and had limited acceptance even in northern Italy. Unlike other wild greens that are often tough and require long cooking, arugula leaves are generally quite tender and small. Although wild arugula is usually very pungent, cultivated strains vary in intensity from faintly peppery to downright spicy.

Arugula goes by a number of names including *rucola, arucola, arugola,* and rocket, an appellation that is especially common on the West Coast. Although arugula is now available year-round at most supermarkets, you can substitute watercress in a pinch. These leaves are generally rounder and smaller but have a similar peppery bite.

• S E L E C T I O N •

Look for crisp, dark green leaves with stems and roots still attached. Avoid bunches with many yellow or limp leaves.

• S T O R A G E •

Arugula will wilt and bruise in just a day or two so it is best to buy this green as needed. Since arugula will also bruise when cut, do not slice the leaves or detach them from their stems and roots until the last possible moment.

Refrigerate arugula in a loosely sealed bag. To prolong freshness, wrap roots in a damp paper towel and refresh the towel as needed, at least once a day.

• P R E P A R A T I O N •

Trim the tough stems and roots and wash and dry the leaves thoroughly before use. Minimally sandy, arugula can be washed and dried in a salad spinner. If the leaves are very muddy, soak them in successive batches of cold water until no grit appears on the bottom of the bowl. Small leaves should be left whole; they will wilt to a fraction of their original size when tossed with hot pasta. Larger leaves can be left whole or sliced crosswise into strips just before they are needed to prevent excessive bruising.

• U S E   I N   S A U C E S •

Arugula leaves are so tender that they will be "cooked" after just 30 seconds of gentle tossing with drained pasta and a hot sauce. The leaves can also be briefly sautéed, but cooking tends to reduce their bite. For a full peppery punch, puree the raw leaves into a pesto-like sauce.

• R E L A T E D   R E C I P E S •

Blanched Peas with Watercress, Basil Oil, and Parmesan Curls (page 228)
Sautéed Red Peppers with Escarole and Garlic (page 235)

Arugula with Black Olive–Tomato Sauce

● SERVES 4 ●

TIME: 20 minutes

BEST PASTA CHOICE: Fusilli or other short, curly shape

This potent sauce can be prepared in the time it takes to bring water to a boil and cook the pasta. Raw arugula is tossed with the quick tomato sauce and hot pasta just before serving. A few stirs (and no cooking) will wilt the greens. I prefer the intense flavor of oil-cured olives in this recipe but pitted olives packed in brine can be used in a pinch. Since these olives are usually much larger, reduce the number to just a dozen or so.

2 tablespoons olive oil

3 medium cloves garlic, minced

½ teaspoon hot red pepper flakes or to taste

1 28-ounce can crushed tomatoes

20 oil-cured black olives (about 2 ounces), pitted and chopped

Salt to taste

1 large bunch arugula (⅓ pound)

1 pound pasta

Freshly grated Parmesan cheese to taste

1. Bring 4 quarts of salted water to a boil in a large pot for cooking the pasta.

2. Heat the oil in a large skillet. Add the garlic and hot red pepper flakes and sauté over medium heat until the garlic starts to color, 1 to 2 minutes.

3. Add the tomatoes and olives to the pan and simmer until the sauce thickens a bit, about 10 minutes. Add salt to taste but use sparingly if the olives are particularly salty.

continued

4. Stem, wash, and partially dry the arugula. Set the damp arugula leaves aside.

5. While preparing the sauce, cook and drain the pasta. Toss the hot pasta with the tomato sauce and the arugula. Stir several times to wilt the arugula. Transfer portions to warm pasta bowls. Serve immediately with grated cheese passed separately.

Arugula with Cucumbers, Mint, and Lemon Juice

● SERVES 4 ●

TIME: 20 minutes

BEST PASTA CHOICE: Orecchiette or small shells

This light, refreshing sauce combines a number of assertive flavors and takes very little time to prepare. Since this sauce is not cooked, the flavor of the oil is particularly prominent. Therefore, choose the finest extra-virgin olive oil, preferably one that is more fruity than sharp. Ripe summer tomatoes, perhaps marinated with thinly sliced red onions, would be a perfect accompaniment to this pasta.

2 medium bunches arugula (about ½ pound)

1 medium cucumber (about ½ pound)

¼ cup minced fresh mint leaves

¼ cup extra-virgin olive oil

3 tablespoons lemon juice

1 teaspoon salt

¼ teaspoon freshly ground black pepper

1 pound pasta

1. Bring 4 quarts of salted water to a boil in a large pot for cooking the pasta.

2. Stem, wash, and dry the arugula. Coarsely chop the leaves and place them in a medium bowl.

3. Peel and halve the cucumber. Use a small spoon to scoop out the seeds from each half. Cut the seeded cucumber into ¼-inch pieces and add them to the bowl with the arugula.

4. Add the mint, oil, lemon juice, salt, and pepper to the bowl and toss gently. (The sauce can be covered and set aside at room temperature for up to 1 hour, if desired.)

5. Cook and drain the pasta, making sure that some water still clings to the noodles. Toss the hot pasta with the arugula sauce. Mix well until the arugula wilts slightly, about 30 seconds. Transfer portions to pasta bowls and serve immediately.

Arugula Puree with Walnuts and Goat Cheese

• SERVES 4 •

TIME: 25 minutes

BEST PASTA CHOICE: Linguine or other long, thin shape

Like basil, fresh arugula leaves can be transformed into a silky sauce with just a quick whir in a food processor. The rich flavor of toasted walnuts enhances this sauce, while creamy goat cheese mellows the strong arugula flavor. If you like, an equal amount of ricotta may be substituted for the goat cheese. Since this sauce is quite rich, serve the pasta with a simple side dish, like steamed asparagus or broccoli, or a marinated vegetable salad with an acid kick that will contrast nicely with the sauce.

continued

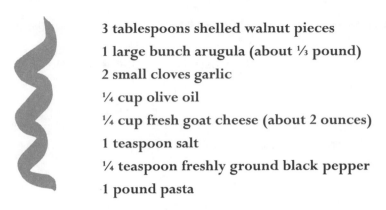

3 tablespoons shelled walnut pieces
1 large bunch arugula (about ⅓ pound)
2 small cloves garlic
¼ cup olive oil
¼ cup fresh goat cheese (about 2 ounces)
1 teaspoon salt
¼ teaspoon freshly ground black pepper
1 pound pasta

1. Bring 4 quarts of salted water to a boil in a large pot for cooking the pasta.

2. Preheat the oven to 350° F. Spread the walnuts in a single layer on a small baking sheet. Bake the nuts until lightly toasted, about 5 minutes. Do not let the walnuts burn. Set the toasted nuts aside to cool slightly.

3. Stem, wash, and dry the arugula. Place the leaves in the work bowl of a food processor. Add the toasted walnuts and the garlic and process, scraping down the sides of the bowl once, into a rough puree. With the motor running, slowly pour the oil through the feed tube and process into a smooth sauce.

4. Scrape the sauce into a small bowl. Stir in the goat cheese, salt, and pepper. (Don't worry if there are a few small lumps of cheese that cannot be incorporated into the sauce; they will melt when tossed with the pasta.) Taste for salt and pepper and adjust seasonings if necessary. A small amount of sauce must cover 1 pound of pasta so it should be well seasoned.

5. While preparing the sauce, cook and drain the pasta, making sure that some water still clings to the noodles. Toss the hot pasta with the arugula sauce. Mix well and transfer portions to warm pasta bowls. Serve immediately.

Sautéed Arugula with Fresh Tomatoes and Garlic

● SERVES 4 ●

TIME: 25 minutes

BEST PASTA CHOICE: Linguine or other long, thin shape

This quick sauce pairs chopped arugula with ripe summer tomatoes and plenty of garlic for a lively, fresh sauce. Peeled and seeded tomatoes make a more elegant sauce—there are no pieces of tomato skin. Skins will slip right off after the tomatoes have been dropped into boiling water for about 20 seconds (or slightly longer if the tomatoes are not quite ripe). Use the same water to then cook the pasta. The sauce is fairly juicy so serve the pasta with plenty of bread.

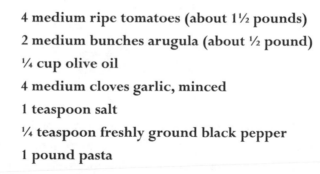

4 medium ripe tomatoes (about 1½ pounds)
2 medium bunches arugula (about ½ pound)
¼ cup olive oil
4 medium cloves garlic, minced
1 teaspoon salt
¼ teaspoon freshly ground black pepper
1 pound pasta

1. Bring 4 quarts of salted water to a boil in a large pot for cooking the pasta. Add the tomatoes and turn them several times to resubmerge the parts of the tomatoes that bob to the surface. Keep the tomatoes in the water for 20 seconds. Use a slotted spoon to transfer the tomatoes to a work surface. Cool the tomatoes slightly and peel the skins with your fingers. Core the peeled tomatoes and cut them in half. Working over the sink, gently squeeze the seeds and excess liquid out of the tomatoes. Cut the tomatoes into ½-inch cubes and set them aside. Reserve the water in the pot for cooking the pasta.

2. Stem, wash, and dry the arugula. Coarsely chop the leaves and set them aside.

continued

3. Heat the oil in a large skillet. Add the garlic and sauté over medium heat until golden, about 2 minutes. Add the tomatoes, salt, and pepper and cook until the tomatoes just begin to lose their shape, about 3 minutes.

4. Stir the arugula into the pan. Cook until the arugula is just wilted, about 2 minutes. Taste for salt and pepper and adjust seasonings if necessary.

5. While preparing the sauce, cook and drain the pasta. Toss the hot pasta with the sauce. Mix well and transfer portions to warm pasta bowls. Serve immediately.

Raw Arugula with Chick-Pea Salsa

• SERVES 4 •

TIME: 60 minutes, plus time for soaking the chick-peas

BEST PASTA CHOICE: Orecchiette or small shells

Chopped fresh arugula is tossed with hot pasta and a cumin-flavored chick-pea salsa for an unusual pasta dish that takes its cues from the Arab-influenced cooking of Sicily. Dried chick-peas are much firmer when reconstituted than mushy canned versions and I recommend that you take the time to prepare them. The process is quite simple and rehydrated chick-peas will keep for up to 2 days in the refrigerator.

1 cup dried chick-peas
2 medium cloves garlic, peeled, plus
   1 medium clove, minced
1 bay leaf
15 large black olives such as Kalamatas
   (about 4 ounces)

2 tablespoons lemon juice

½ teaspoon ground cumin

1 teaspoon salt

6 tablespoons olive oil

1 large bunch arugula (about ⅓ pound)

1 pound pasta

1. Place the dried chick-peas in a medium bowl and cover with at least 2 inches of water. Soak overnight and drain. Place the chick-peas, the 2 whole garlic cloves, and the bay leaf in a medium pot and cover with several inches of water. Bring the water to a boil and simmer gently until the chick-peas are tender, 35 to 40 minutes. Drain the chick-peas and discard the garlic and bay leaf. Place the chick-peas in a medium bowl and set aside. (The chick-peas can be covered and refrigerated for up to 2 days.)

2. Bring 4 quarts of salted water to a boil in a large pot for cooking the pasta.

3. Pit and coarsely chop the olives. Add them to the bowl with the chick-peas.

4. Whisk together the lemon juice, minced garlic, cumin, and salt. Slowly whisk in ¼ cup oil until the dressing is thick and emulsified. Drizzle the vinaigrette over the chick-peas and olives and toss gently. Taste for salt and adjust seasonings if necessary. (The salsa can be covered and set aside at room temperature for up to 4 hours, if desired.)

5. Stem, wash, and dry the arugula. Coarsely chop the leaves and set them aside.

6. Cook and drain the pasta, making sure that some liquid still clings to the noodles. Toss the hot pasta with the chick-pea salsa, the chopped arugula, and the remaining 2 tablespoons oil. Mix well until the arugula wilts. Transfer portions to pasta bowls and serve immediately.

Asparagus

This member of the lily family reaches its peak in early spring but is available during most of the year. Originally cultivated in the eastern Mediterranean, asparagus has a long history of use throughout Europe, and was even prescribed as an aphrodisiac by Renaissance physicians.

Rare white stalks, grown under soil to prevent photosynthesis, are quite expensive and should be reserved for salads and side dishes. Because of their more robust flavor and greater availability, green asparagus are my first choice for pasta sauces. However, if you run across pricey purple-tinged spears, they can be used in sauces alone or with some green spears to cut the cost. Although their brilliant color is quite attractive, the flavor is fairly close to that of regular asparagus. Asparagus is an excellent source of vitamins A and C and takes well to numerous preparations.

• SELECTION •

Look for firm stalks with tightly closed, compact buds. Limp stalks or open buds mean that the asparagus is past its prime. There is considerable debate about size—some people prefer fat, juicy asparagus, while other cooks (myself included) favor thinner stalks. Fatter stalks can be stringy and tough and may require peeling. In addition, they must be cut into thin strips for pasta sauces. Therefore, look for asparagus that are no larger than your pinkie or ring finger.

Since asparagus are sold by the pound, I take off the rubber band that usually surrounds them and weed out any inferior spears. There is no sense buying less-than-perfect produce. This also allows you to select spears of uniform thickness, which will make preparation and cooking easier.

• S T O R A G E •

Refrigerate unwashed asparagus in a vegetable drawer to maintain crispness for a day or two. To store them longer, wrap the ends in a wet paper towel and dampen the towel as needed. Wash the asparagus only when ready to use them.

• P R E P A R A T I O N •

No matter how thin the asparagus, the tough ends must be removed. The stems will snap off in just the right place if you follow this method: With one hand, hold the asparagus about halfway down the stalk; with your other hand, hold the stem end between your thumb and index finger about 1 inch from the bottom and bend the stalk until it snaps. Discard the stem ends or save them for soup. Unless the stalks are quite thin, slice the remaining asparagus in half lengthwise and then cut them on the bias into 1-inch pieces for sauces.

• U S E   I N   S A U C E S •

I usually steam asparagus until crisp-tender (about 2 minutes is the right cooking time) before use in pasta sauces. Asparagus can also be boiled in lightly salted water but it is easier to overcook the spears. Asparagus also loses a bit of its intensity as well as some nutrients when boiled. The one advantage to boiling is that some of the cooking liquid can be reserved to build a sauce. Asparagus calls out for fresh herbs, especially basil or mint. Asparagus also has an affinity for lemon, garlic, and shallots.

• R E L A T E D   R E C I P E S •

Steamed Green Beans with Basil and Gorgonzola (page 157)
Salsa Primavera with Tomatoes, Mushrooms, and Mixed Vegetables (page 298)

Steamed Asparagus with Mint Pesto and Goat Cheese

• SERVES 4 •

TIME: 20 minutes

BEST PASTA CHOICE: Penne or other short, tubular shape

Fresh goat cheese gives mint pesto a tangy flavor and creamy texture. The pairing of this light sauce with steamed asparagus celebrates the delicate flavors of spring. This elegant dish would make an excellent first course since the pesto and asparagus can be prepared in advance.

2 pounds asparagus

2 cups loosely packed fresh mint leaves

¼ cup shelled walnut pieces

2 small cloves garlic, peeled

6 tablespoons olive oil

¼ cup fresh goat cheese (about 2 ounces)

1 teaspoon salt

¼ teaspoon freshly ground black pepper

1 pound pasta

1. Bring 4 quarts of salted water to a boil in a large pot for cooking the pasta.

2. Snap off the tough ends from the asparagus spears. Cut the spears in half lengthwise (thicker spears should be quartered), then slice them on the bias into 1-inch pieces. Steam the asparagus until crisp-tender, about 2 minutes. Set the cooked asparagus aside but cover to keep warm.

3. Place the mint, walnuts, and garlic in the work bowl of a food processor and grind, scraping down the sides of the bowl once, into a rough puree. With the motor running, slowly pour the oil through the feed tube and process until the pesto comes together. Beat in the goat cheese until the

sauce is smooth. Scrape the pesto into a small bowl and stir in the salt and pepper. Set the pesto aside.

4. Cook and drain the pasta, making sure that some water still clings to the noodles. Toss the hot pasta with the pesto and the asparagus. Mix well and transfer portions to warm pasta bowls. Serve immediately.

Steamed Asparagus with Basil and Ricotta

● SERVES 4 ●

TIME: 20 minutes

BEST PASTA CHOICE: Penne or other short, tubular shape

Ricotta cheese makes a creamy sauce that is high in flavor and low in fat, especially if you use the part-skim version. As an added bonus, this sauce can be made in the time it takes to cook the pasta. Adding some of the pasta water thins the thick sauce to the right consistency.

2 pounds asparagus

1⅓ cups ricotta cheese

⅔ cup freshly grated Parmesan cheese

½ cup minced fresh basil leaves

1 teaspoon salt

½ teaspoon freshly ground black pepper

1 pound pasta

1. Bring 4 quarts of salted water to a boil in a large pot for cooking the pasta.

2. Snap off the tough ends from the asparagus spears. Cut the spears in half lengthwise (thicker spears should be quartered), then slice them on the bias into 1-inch pieces. Steam the asparagus until crisp-tender, about 2 minutes. Set the cooked asparagus aside.   *continued*

3. Combine the two cheeses with the basil, salt, and pepper in a medium bowl. Set the mixture aside.

4. While preparing the sauce, cook the pasta. Just before it is done, carefully remove ⅓ cup of the cooking liquid and stir it into the cheese mixture. The cheese sauce should be smooth and creamy.

5. Drain the pasta, making sure that some water still clings to the noodles. Toss the hot pasta with the ricotta mixture and asparagus. Mix well to coat the pasta with the sauce. Transfer portions to warm pasta bowls and serve immediately.

Asparagus and Fresh Peas in Orange-Saffron Sauce

• SERVES 4 •

TIME: 30 minutes

BEST PASTA CHOICE: Fettuccine or other long, wide shape

Don't be put off by saffron's reputation as the world's most expensive spice. Although worth its weight in gold, a little saffron goes a long way—as this sauce proves. Look for the real thing from Spain and avoid unlabeled products or those from Mexico or India. To get the most bang for your buck, toast the saffron in an empty skillet to release its full flavor. Fresh orange zest and juice are natural complements to this earthy spice. Frozen peas can be used in a pinch but cannot compare with the delicate flavor and firm texture of fresh.

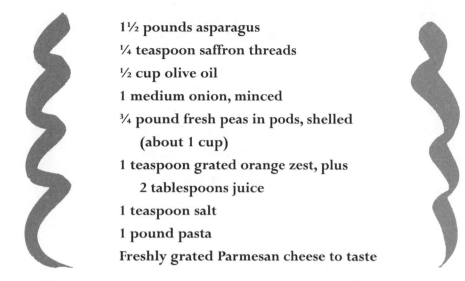

1½ pounds asparagus

¼ teaspoon saffron threads

½ cup olive oil

1 medium onion, minced

¾ pound fresh peas in pods, shelled
     (about 1 cup)

1 teaspoon grated orange zest, plus
     2 tablespoons juice

1 teaspoon salt

1 pound pasta

Freshly grated Parmesan cheese to taste

1. Bring 4 quarts of salted water to a boil in a large pot for cooking the pasta.

2. Snap off the tough ends from the asparagus spears. Cut the spears in half lengthwise (thicker spears should be quartered), then slice them on the bias into 1-inch pieces. Steam the asparagus until crisp-tender, about 2 minutes. Set the cooked asparagus aside.

3. Set a large skillet over medium heat. When the pan is hot, add the saffron and toast until the threads are brittle, about 1 minute. Use the back of a spoon to grind the saffron into a fine powder right in the pan.

4. Add the oil to the pan and heat briefly. Add the onion and sauté until translucent, about 5 minutes. Stir in the peas, orange zest, and salt and cook until the peas are tender, about 2 minutes. Stir in the orange juice and the asparagus and cook just until the asparagus is warmed through, no more than 1 minute.

5. While preparing the sauce, cook and drain the pasta, making sure that some water still clings to the noodles. Toss the hot pasta with the asparagus sauce. Mix well and transfer portions to warm pasta bowls. Serve immediately with grated cheese passed separately.

Asparagus with Mushrooms and Caramelized Shallots

● SERVES 4 ●

TIME: 30 minutes

BEST PASTA CHOICE: Linguine or other long, thin shape

Italian cooks are well known for their culinary economy. In this dish, some of the asparagus cooking water is reserved to make a pasta sauce. Although regular white mushrooms can be used, I prefer the meaty taste of cremini. This firm, medium brown variety is available at better supermarkets and has a rich, woodsy flavor.

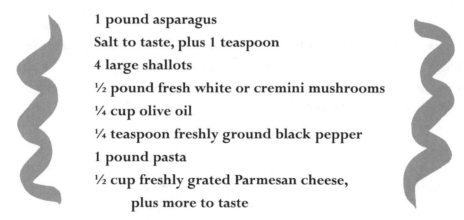

1 pound asparagus

Salt to taste, plus 1 teaspoon

4 large shallots

½ pound fresh white or cremini mushrooms

¼ cup olive oil

¼ teaspoon freshly ground black pepper

1 pound pasta

½ cup freshly grated Parmesan cheese,
plus more to taste

1. Bring 4 quarts of salted water to a boil in a large pot for cooking the pasta.

2. Bring several quarts of water to a boil in a medium saucepan. Snap off the tough ends from the asparagus spears. Cut the spears in half lengthwise (thicker spears should be quartered), then slice them on the bias into 1-inch pieces. Add the asparagus and salt to taste to the boiling water. Cook for 2 minutes, drain the asparagus, and reserve ¼ cup of the cooking liquid. Set the asparagus and cooking liquid aside separately.

3. Peel and slice the shallots crosswise into thin rings. Wipe the mushrooms with a paper towel to loosen and remove any dirt. Trim and discard a thin slice from the stem end of each mushroom. Thinly slice the mushrooms and set them aside.

4. Heat the oil in a large skillet. Add the shallots and sauté over medium heat, stirring occasionally to separate the rings, until crisp and light brown, about 10 minutes. Add the mushrooms, raise the heat to medium-high, and sauté until they have softened and thrown off their juices, about 5 minutes. Add 1 teaspoon salt and the pepper and stir briefly.

5. Add the asparagus and the reserved cooking liquid to the skillet. Simmer until the asparagus is heated through and the sauce has thickened a bit, about 2 minutes. Taste for salt and pepper and adjust seasonings if necessary.

6. While preparing the sauce, cook and drain the pasta. Toss the hot pasta with the asparagus sauce and ½ cup Parmesan. Mix well and transfer portions to warm pasta bowls. Serve immediately with more grated cheese passed separately.

Asparagus with Pink Tomato Sauce and Pine Nuts

● SERVES 4 ●

TIME: 30 minutes

BEST PASTA CHOICE: Spaghetti or other long, very thin shape

Plum tomatoes provide a dependable year-round source for fresh tomato flavor. They also are not terribly watery, which makes them a good candidate for quick sauces like this. Pine nuts can be omitted in a pinch but they are a natural complement to the other ingredients.

continued

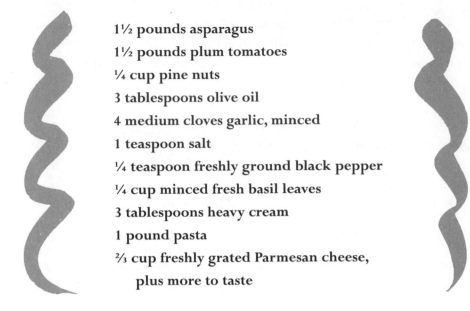

1½ pounds asparagus
1½ pounds plum tomatoes
¼ cup pine nuts
3 tablespoons olive oil
4 medium cloves garlic, minced
1 teaspoon salt
¼ teaspoon freshly ground black pepper
¼ cup minced fresh basil leaves
3 tablespoons heavy cream
1 pound pasta
⅔ cup freshly grated Parmesan cheese,
    plus more to taste

1. Bring 4 quarts of salted water to a boil in a large pot for cooking the pasta.

2. Snap off the tough ends from the asparagus spears. Cut the spears in half lengthwise (thicker spears should be quartered), then slice them on the bias into 1-inch pieces. Steam the asparagus until crisp-tender, about 2 minutes. Set the cooked asparagus aside.

3. Core and cut the tomatoes in half around the equator. Squeeze out the excess liquid and as many seeds as possible. (Do this over the sink.) Chop the tomatoes into ½-inch chunks and set them aside.

4. Set a large skillet over medium heat. Add the pine nuts and toast, shaking the pan occasionally to redistribute the nuts, until golden brown (about 5 minutes). Do not let the nuts burn. Set the toasted nuts aside.

5. Heat the oil in the empty skillet. Add the garlic and sauté over medium heat until lightly colored, about 2 minutes. Add the tomatoes, salt, and pepper. Cook until the tomatoes are just heated through, 2 to 3 minutes.

6. Stir the basil and cream into the pan and cook until the cream has thickened and reduced a bit, about 1 minute. Stir in the asparagus and mix well. Cook

until heated through, 1 to 2 minutes. Taste for salt and pepper and adjust seasonings if necessary.

7. While preparing the sauce, cook and drain the pasta. Toss the hot pasta with the asparagus sauce, the toasted pine nuts, and ⅔ cup Parmesan. Mix well and transfer portions to warm pasta bowls. Serve immediately with more grated cheese passed separately.

Asparagus with Toasted Bread Crumbs, Lemon, and Garlic

● SERVES 4 ●

TIME: 25 minutes

BEST PASTA CHOICE: Spaghetti or other long, very thin shape

In southern Italy economical cooks use toasted bread crumbs instead of expensive Parmesan cheese to enliven simple pasta dishes. I like the flavor of good bread crumbs, especially in dishes with strong components like lemon and garlic that don't always marry well with cheese. Try making your own bread crumbs from leftover bread—just grind stale bread in a food processor and keep the crumbs in the refrigerator or freezer.

2 pounds asparagus

⅓ cup plain bread crumbs

½ cup olive oil

4 medium cloves garlic, minced

¼ cup minced fresh parsley leaves

¼ cup lemon juice

1 teaspoon salt

1 pound pasta

continued

1. Bring 4 quarts of salted water to a boil in a large pot for cooking the pasta.

2. Snap off the tough ends from the asparagus spears. Cut the spears in half lengthwise (thicker spears should be quartered), then slice them on the bias into 1-inch pieces. Steam the asparagus until crisp-tender, about 2 minutes. Set the cooked asparagus aside.

3. Set a large skillet over medium heat. Add the bread crumbs and toast, shaking the pan occasionally to redistribute the crumbs, until golden brown, about 5 minutes. Do not let the bread crumbs burn. Set the toasted bread crumbs aside.

4. Heat the oil in the empty skillet. Add the garlic and sauté over medium heat until lightly colored, about 2 minutes. Stir in the parsley, lemon juice, and salt and cook for 30 seconds.

5. Add the asparagus to the pan and mix well. Taste for salt and adjust seasonings if necessary.

6. While preparing the sauce, cook and drain the pasta, making sure that some water still clings to the noodles. Toss the hot pasta with the asparagus sauce and the toasted bread crumbs. Mix well and transfer portions to warm pasta bowls. Serve immediately.

Beets

Most Americans have little idea how to handle beets. Given the fact that they are unusually sweet and incredibly messy to prepare, this is not really much of a surprise. However, beets deserve more recognition for their versatility. The bulbous dark red roots are the most familiar part of this vegetable. The red stems, which look a little like rhubarb, have no real culinary value. However, the red-veined leaves, which are sadly overlooked by many cooks, can be prepared much like any other leafy green. The leaves and roots can be prepared separately or together in salads, side dishes, or even pasta sauces.

While some purists may find spaghetti dyed fuchsia too jarring to contemplate, the flavor of beet-based sauces is undeniably delicious. If you are really adverse to purple pasta (no doubt kids will love it), use beets in salads and side dishes but reserve the leafy tops for pasta sauces. They can be used in any recipe that calls for Swiss chard or spinach. Smaller, younger leaves are more tender and less fibrous and should be chosen if at all possible.

As with all beet preparations, pasta sauces made with beets can take two tacks—either accentuate or tone down the sweet properties of this ruby-colored root. Roasting in the oven heightens the natural sugars, while combining boiled beets with their wilted leaves tends to balance the sweetness of the bulb with the bitterness of the tops.

• S E L E C T I O N •

Although beets are sometimes sold without their green tops, buying beets with their leaves is the best way to gauge overall freshness. If the leaves are crisp, not wilted; dark green, not yellowed; and do not show signs of decay, the beets are invariably fresh. Also, avoid beets with dry patches or obvious signs of age. If at all possible, choose medium or small beets. Large beets are often woody and will take much longer to soften properly when cooked. To ensure even cooking, it is also a good idea to buy beets that are similar in size, in any case no larger than an egg.

• S T O R A G E •

Beets can be refrigerated for several days, even a week, in a plastic bag. While it's fine if some moisture clings to the leaves, do not wash the beets until you are ready to use them. If you are planning on pairing the beets with their leafy greens, which will become limp fairly quickly, you need to use the beets sooner rather than later.

• P R E P A R A T I O N •

Beets have the potential to cause a great mess in your kitchen and on your hands. Preparation steps are intended to reduce but not eliminate the bleeding that can dye counters and clothes. The first task is to remove and reserve the leafy greens by snapping the stems at the point where the leaves begin. Next, trim all but the last inch of the stems from the beets them-selves—leaving some stem attached helps reduce bleeding. Dangling roots may be trimmed, again exercising care not to cut into the beet itself. Wash the beets to remove caked-on dirt but be careful not to scrape away the skin, which will cause the beets to bleed excessively. Once beets have been either boiled or roasted, the skin can be removed by rubbing the exterior with a paper towel. Cooked and peeled beets are ready to be sliced and added to a pasta sauce.

Even if the leaves are not used in a pasta sauce, do not discard them. They can be prepared much as you would handle any leafy green and are most similar to red-veined Swiss chard. As with other greens, beet leaves are usually quite sandy so place them in a large bowl and soak in several changes of cold water until no grit appears on the bottom of the bowl. Shake the leaves to remove excess moisture but do not dry them. Damp leaves can be sliced crosswise and wilted in just minutes in a covered pan.

• U S E   I N   S A U C E S •

Beets should be cooked separately and then added to pasta sauces. Oven-roasting beets that are wrapped in aluminum foil concentrates their sweet flavor. About an hour in a 400° F. oven is enough to soften small or medium beets. For quicker cooking, boiling is an excellent option, although the beets do lose a bit of their sweetness. Simmer beets for about 25 minutes or until a metal skewer glides easily through them. In general, I roast beets when I want to play up their sweetness and boil them when I am trying to tone down their natural sugars. Of course, pairing the bitter tops with the beets is the most efficient way to create a sauce that keeps the sweetness in check.

Boiled Beets and Wilted Beet Greens with Garlic and Lemon

● SERVES 4 ●

TIME: 40 minutes

BEST PASTA CHOICE: Fusilli or other short, curly shape

This sauce utilizes both the beets and their leafy tops, so freshness is paramount. Boiled and diced beets are added to a simple sauce of tender beet greens wilted in garlic and olive oil. A splash of lemon juice helps balance the sweetness in the beets, as does the gentle bitterness of the greens themselves.

4 medium beets with leafy greens still attached

Salt to taste, plus 1 teaspoon

¼ cup olive oil

4 medium cloves garlic, minced

1½ tablespoons fresh lemon juice

1 pound pasta

1. Bring 4 quarts of salted water to a boil in a large pot for cooking the pasta.

2. Slice the beet stems where the leaves begin and set the leaves aside. Trim all but the last inch of the stems from the beets themselves. Trim any dangling roots and wash the beets to remove any dirt. The trimmed beets should weigh about 1 pound.

3. Place the beets in a medium saucepan and cover with water. Bring the water to a boil and add salt to taste. Simmer until the beets are tender enough so that a metal skewer slides easily through them, about 25 minutes. Drain the beets and cool them slightly. Use paper towels to hold the beets and rub gently to slip off their skins. Trim and discard the remaining portion of the stem. Cut the peeled beets into ¼-inch cubes and set them aside.

4. While the beets are cooking, place the beet greens in a large bowl and soak in several changes of cold water until no grit appears on the bottom of the bowl. Shake the leaves to remove excess moisture but do not dry them. Slice the damp leaves crosswise into ½-inch-wide strips and set them aside. There should be about 5 cups of shredded beet greens.

5. Heat the oil in a large sauté pan with a cover. Add the garlic and sauté over medium heat until golden, about 2 minutes. Add the beet greens and 1 teaspoon salt. Stir several times to coat the leaves with the oil. Cover and cook, stirring several more times, until the beet greens have wilted, about 5 minutes.

6. Stir in the cubed beets and the lemon juice and cook until heated through, about 1 minute. Taste for salt and adjust seasonings if necessary.

7. While preparing the sauce, cook and drain the pasta. Toss the hot pasta with the beet sauce. Mix well and transfer portions to warm pasta bowls. Serve immediately.

Roasted Beets and Red Onion with Balsamic Vinegar and Rosemary

• SERVES 4 •

TIME: 75 minutes

BEST PASTA CHOICE: Penne or other short, tubular shape

Beets are roasted in their skins, peeled, and then cut into thin strips to make the basis for a brilliant pasta sauce that will dye the noodles a shocking purple. The beets are roasted with a red onion and both vegetables are then combined with olive oil, balsamic vinegar, and rosemary to form a sweet-and-savory sauce that is extraordinarily tasty.   *continued*

8 medium beets (about 1½ pounds
when trimmed as directed)
1 large red onion (about ¾ pound)
¼ cup olive oil
2 teaspoons balsamic vinegar
1 tablespoon minced fresh rosemary leaves
1 teaspoon salt
¼ teaspoon freshly ground black pepper
1 pound pasta

1. Preheat the oven to 400° F. Bring 4 quarts of salted water to a boil in a large pot for cooking the pasta.

2. Trim all but the last inch of the stems from the beets. Trim any dangling roots and wash the beets to remove any dirt. Wrap the beets in aluminum foil and place them in a large baking dish. Place the unpeeled onion in the baking dish.

3. Roast the beets and the onion until tender enough so that a metal skewer slides easily through them, about 1 hour. Unwrap the beets and cool them slightly.

4. Use paper towels to hold the beets and rub gently to slip off their skins. Trim and discard the remaining portion of the stem. Cut the peeled beets into slices that are about 1 inch long and ¼ inch thick. Place the beets in a large bowl. Peel the onion and cut it into thin pieces about the same size as the beet strips. Add onion to bowl.

5. Drizzle the oil and vinegar over the beets and onions. Stir in the rosemary, salt, and pepper and mix gently. Taste for salt and pepper and adjust seasonings if necessary.

6. While preparing the sauce, cook and drain the pasta, making sure that some liquid still clings to the noodles. Toss the hot pasta with the beet sauce. Mix well and transfer portions to warm pasta bowls. Serve immediately.

Broccoli

The written record regarding broccoli dates back to ancient Rome, where it was widely enjoyed. Although first introduced to this country by Thomas Jefferson, broccoli did not become popular here until the early part of this century when Italian immigrant farmers in California began growing it commercially. Of course, broccoli is now tremendously popular, in part because of its long growing season and low cost.

As the most widely available member of the trendy crucifer family of vegetables, broccoli has been getting plenty of attention in the media for its high nutrition content, especially of vitamins A and C. If you're concerned about obtaining and then retaining the maximum amount of these nutrients, chose specimens with very dark green or purple florets (they have the most vitamin C) and keep cooking times to a minimum. Prolonged cooking, especially boiling in abundant water, will cause water-soluble compounds, such as vitamin C, to dissipate.

• SELECTION •

Color is the best way to pick broccoli. Deep green florets that are tinged with purple are an indication that the broccoli is fresh and full of nutrients. Avoid broccoli that is pale green or yellow, as well as any bunches with soft or decaying florets. Florets, which are actually the plant's blossoms, should be compact and without yellow flowers. If you plan on using the stalks, look for a bunch with relatively thin stalks that are medium green, not light green, in color. Thick stalks will invariably be woody and not terribly appetizing. Also give the broccoli a good whiff; it should smell fresh, not sour or musty.

• S T O R A G E •

Do not wash broccoli until you are ready to cook it, since dampness will cause florets to soften and become mushy. Keep broccoli in a plastic bag in the refrigerator. In general, it will stay fresh for at least several days, or maybe a week. Outer florets will begin to soften first so watch them carefully and use the broccoli as soon as this occurs.

• P R E P A R A T I O N •

With the exception of locally grown broccoli, I find the stalks on most supermarket broccoli very tough and difficult to incorporate into pasta sauces. Therefore, the preparation in most recipes begins with discarding the stalks. If you would like to eat the stalks, note that the outer layer is usually quite dry and should be removed using a combination of a vegetable peeler and small knife to trim any small offshoots from the stalks. Peeled stalks can then be thinly sliced or diced. As for the florets, break them apart with your hands and then slice them into small, bite-sized pieces.

• U S E   I N   S A U C E S •

Broccoli takes to a number of moist cooking methods. It can be cooked fully by boiling and used as is in a salad-like sauce with pesto or a vinaigrette. Boiled broccoli can also be added to a pan sauce with cream and tomatoes. Steaming for several minutes will leave broccoli a bit more crisp. However, a quick sauté in garlicky oil, for instance, will finish the cooking process and infuse the broccoli with flavor. While most cooking methods are fairly quick and try to retain the texture of the broccoli, it can also be boiled, chopped, and cooked down for a long time into a rough puree that can be spread on toasts or tossed with pasta.

• R E L A T E D   R E C I P E S •

Salsa Primavera with Tomatoes, Mushrooms, and Mixed Vegetables (page 298)

Broccoli in "Hot" Pink Tomato Sauce with Basil

• SERVES 4 •

TIME: 25 minutes

BEST PASTA CHOICE: Linguine or other long, thin shape

This festive sauce pairs bright green broccoli florets with a spicy pink cream sauce dotted with chunks of red ripe tomatoes and shredded fresh basil leaves. Although this classic sauce usually has substantially more cream as well as a good dose of butter, I still consider this lighter version a fairly rich sauce best served with just bread and salad for a simple but luxurious meal.

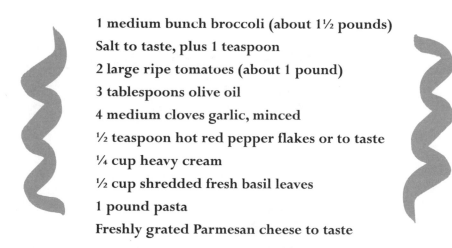

1 medium bunch broccoli (about 1½ pounds)
Salt to taste, plus 1 teaspoon
2 large ripe tomatoes (about 1 pound)
3 tablespoons olive oil
4 medium cloves garlic, minced
½ teaspoon hot red pepper flakes or to taste
¼ cup heavy cream
½ cup shredded fresh basil leaves
1 pound pasta
Freshly grated Parmesan cheese to taste

1. Bring 4 quarts of salted water to a boil in a large pot for cooking the pasta.

2. Bring several quarts of water to a boil in another pot. Trim and discard the broccoli stalks. Separate the florets and cut them into small, bite-sized pieces. There should be about 5 cups of florets. Add the broccoli and salt to taste to the boiling water. Cook until the broccoli is crisp-tender, about 2 minutes. Drain and set aside the broccoli.

continued

3. Core and cut the tomatoes into ½-inch cubes. Set them aside.

4. Heat the oil in a large skillet. Add the garlic and hot pepper flakes and sauté over medium heat until the garlic is lightly colored, about 2 minutes. Add the tomatoes and 1 teaspoon salt and cook, stirring often, until the tomatoes form a rough sauce, about 2 minutes.

5. Add the cream and basil to the pan. Simmer briefly until the cream thickens slightly, about 1 minute. Stir in the blanched broccoli and cook just long enough to heat the broccoli through. Taste for salt and hot pepper and adjust seasonings if necessary.

6. While preparing the sauce, cook and drain the pasta. Toss the hot pasta with the broccoli sauce. Mix well and transfer portions to warm pasta bowls. Serve immediately with grated cheese passed separately.

Chopped Broccoli Puree with Garlic

● SERVES 4 ●

TIME: 35 minutes

BEST PASTA CHOICE: Penne or other short, tubular shape

This recipe breaks most of the rules of broccoli preparation. I usually discard the stalks since they are often tough. I also generally cook the florets only until crisp-tender, no more than a couple of minutes. Here, sliced stalks and florets are cooked in a small amount of water until quite tender, almost mushy. The broccoli is then chopped and added to garlicky olive oil. The liquid used to cook the broccoli is added to the pan and reduced until the mixture becomes a coarse puree. Although I like the simple, clean flavors of just garlic, good olive oil, and broccoli, hot red pepper flakes can be added to spice things up if you like.

1 large bunch broccoli (about 2 pounds)
1 teaspoon salt, plus more to taste
6 tablespoons olive oil
4 medium cloves garlic, minced
Freshly ground black pepper to taste
1 pound pasta
Freshly grated Parmesan cheese to taste

1. Bring 4 quarts of salted water to a boil in a large pot for cooking the pasta.

2. Bring 2 quarts of water to a boil in another pot. Separate the broccoli florets from the stalks. Trim a thick slice from the base of the stalks and trim away any other particularly tough or woody parts. Use a combination of a small, sharp knife and a vegetable peeler to peel the stalks. Slice the peeled stalks into ¼-inch-thick disks. Separate the florets into small, bite-sized pieces. Add the broccoli and 1 teaspoon salt to the pot and simmer briskly until the broccoli is quite tender, about 10 minutes. Use a slotted spoon to transfer the broccoli to a cutting board. Reserve the cooking liquid separately. Cool the broccoli slightly and chop it fine.

3. Heat the oil in a large skillet. Add the garlic and sauté over medium heat until golden, about 2 minutes. Add the chopped broccoli and cook, stirring often, for about 1 minute.

4. Add 1 cup of the reserved cooking liquid to the skillet. Simmer briskly, adding more water as needed if the pan appears dry, until the broccoli forms a rough puree and is no longer soupy, about 15 minutes. Add salt and pepper to taste.

5. While preparing the sauce, cook and drain the pasta. Toss the hot pasta with the broccoli sauce. Mix well and transfer to warm pasta bowls. Serve immediately with grated cheese passed separately.

Steamed Broccoli with Sun-Dried Tomatoes and Lemon Zest

● SERVES 4 ●

TIME: 25 minutes

BEST PASTA CHOICE: Fusilli or other short, curly shape

My friend Bruce Hainley shared this extremely versatile sauce with me and it quickly became a standard in my kitchen. This pasta dish can be served immediately or cooled to room temperature and enjoyed as a summer salad. Either way the strong punch of garlic and bright lemon flavor are welcome contrasts to the broccoli and sun-dried tomatoes.

1 large bunch broccoli (about 2 pounds)

6 tablespoons olive oil

4 medium cloves garlic, minced

1 teaspoon grated lemon zest

15 sun-dried tomatoes packed in olive oil,
**   drained and cut into thin strips**

1 teaspoon salt

1 pound pasta

1. Bring 4 quarts of salted water to a boil in a large pot for cooking the pasta.

2. Trim and discard the broccoli stalks. Separate the florets and cut them into small, bite-sized pieces. There should be about 5 cups of florets. Steam the broccoli until almost tender, about 3 minutes. Set the broccoli aside.

3. Heat the oil in a large skillet. Add the garlic and sauté over medium heat until golden, about 2 minutes. Add the lemon zest, sun-dried tomatoes, and salt and continue cooking for another minute.

4. Stir in the steamed broccoli and toss well to coat the florets with the oil. Cook until the broccoli is heated through and tender, about 1 minute. Taste for salt and adjust seasonings if necessary.

5. While preparing the sauce, cook and drain the pasta, making sure that some water still clings to the noodles. Toss the hot pasta with the broccoli sauce. Mix well and transfer portions to warm pasta bowls. Serve immediately.

Blanched Broccoli with Spicy Black Olive Vinaigrette

● SERVES 4 ●

TIME: 25 minutes

BEST PASTA CHOICE: Fusilli or other short, curly shape

For this simple sauce, broccoli is boiled until tender and then tossed with black olives and a spicy vinaigrette. The pasta can be eaten immediately or cooled to room temperature and served as a salad, making this sauce a good summertime choice.

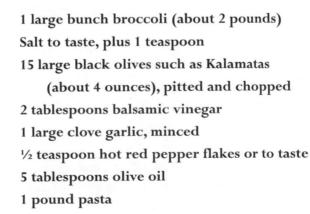

1 large bunch broccoli (about 2 pounds)

Salt to taste, plus 1 teaspoon

15 large black olives such as Kalamatas
    (about 4 ounces), pitted and chopped

2 tablespoons balsamic vinegar

1 large clove garlic, minced

½ teaspoon hot red pepper flakes or to taste

5 tablespoons olive oil

1 pound pasta

continued

1. Bring 4 quarts of salted water to a boil in a large pot for cooking the pasta.

2. Bring several quarts of water to a boil in another pot. Trim and discard the broccoli stalks. Separate the florets and cut them into small, bite-sized pieces. There should be about 5 cups of florets. Add the broccoli and salt to taste to the boiling water. Cook until the broccoli is tender, about 3 minutes. Drain the broccoli.

3. Toss the drained broccoli and the chopped olives in a large bowl.

4. Stir together the vinegar, garlic, hot red pepper flakes, and 1 teaspoon salt in a small bowl. Slowly whisk in the oil until the dressing is thick and emulsified. Taste for salt and hot pepper and adjust seasonings if necessary. Drizzle the vinaigrette over the broccoli and mix gently.

5. While preparing the sauce, cook and drain the pasta, making sure that some water still clings to the noodles. Toss the hot pasta with the broccoli sauce. Mix well and transfer portions to warm pasta bowls. Serve immediately.

Blanched Broccoli with Basil Pesto and Ripe Tomatoes

• SERVES 4 •

TIME: 30 minutes

BEST PASTA CHOICE: Shells or other open shape

This sauce is perfect for the early fall when tomatoes are still at their peak and broccoli is in season. The sauce is fairly juicy so make sure to serve some bread with the pasta.

1 large bunch broccoli (about 2 pounds)
Salt to taste
1 cup tightly packed fresh basil leaves
2 medium cloves garlic, peeled
2 tablespoons pine nuts
6 tablespoons olive oil
¼ cup freshly grated Parmesan cheese
2 medium ripe tomatoes (about ¾ pound)
1 pound pasta

1. Bring 4 quarts of salted water to a boil in a large pot for cooking the pasta.

2. Bring several quarts of water to a boil in another pot. Trim and discard the broccoli stalks. Separate the florets and cut them into small, bite-sized pieces. There should be about 5 cups of florets. Add the broccoli and salt to taste to the boiling water. Cook until the broccoli is tender, about 3 minutes. Drain and set aside the broccoli.

3. Place the basil, garlic, and pine nuts in the work bowl of a food processor and process, scraping down the sides of the bowl as needed, until smooth. With the motor running, slowly pour the oil through the feed tube and process until smooth.

4. Scrape the pesto into a large bowl. Stir in the cheese and additional salt to taste.

5. Core and cut the tomatoes into ½-inch cubes. Add the tomatoes to the bowl with the pesto and toss gently. Add the broccoli to the bowl and toss gently. Taste for salt and adjust seasonings if necessary.

6. While preparing the sauce, cook and drain the pasta. Toss the hot pasta with the broccoli sauce. Mix well and transfer portions to pasta bowls. Serve immediately.

Broccoli Rabe

Broccoli rabe grows wild throughout southern Italy and has long been a staple in many hardscrabble regions, in part because of its intense flavor and ability to satisfy even large appetites. In this country, broccoli rabe was until recently found only in Italian markets. However, this hardy vegetable has become more widely available during the past decade, no doubt because of our increasing interest in Italian cooking. In many supermarkets, it is available almost year-round, with only a slight break in supply during the height of summer.

As you might surmise from its name, broccoli rabe, which is also known as *rapini* or *broccoletti di rape,* is related to regular broccoli. While broccoli has compact florets that form a tight head, the florets in a bunch of broccoli rabe grow randomly on thinner leafy stalks. In fact, farmers call broccoli rabe a "nonheading" variety because of its appearance. The flavor of regular broccoli is reminiscent of cabbage, but broccoli rabe has more in common, at least in terms of flavor, with bitter leafy greens such as collards. Like leafy greens, broccoli rabe also cooks down quite a lot so you will need about 2 pounds to sauce 1 pound of pasta.

• SELECTION •

Look for broccoli rabe with firm, slender green stems and tightly closed, dark green buds. There should be no sign of wilting among the leaves and no yellow flowers on the buds. Broccoli rabe with thicker stalks can be purchased, but there will be more waste since thick stalks must be trimmed before cooking.

• S T O R A G E •

Broccoli rabe can be stored in a plastic bag in the refrigerator for several days. To prevent leaves from wilting, lightly mist them every day or two. At the first signs of softening, cook broccoli rabe.

• P R E P A R A T I O N •

Trim and discard any thick stalks since they tend to be tough and woody, even when cooked. Thinner stalks can be peeled if desired or left as is for a somewhat crisper texture. Remove any wilted leaves. Tear larger leaves in half and break florets into several pieces. Rinse the trimmed broccoli rabe under running water. If the broccoli rabe is sandy, soak it in several changes of cold water. Although broccoli rabe can be chopped quite small, I generally like to leave pieces fairly large, especially since the leaves will shrink considerably during cooking.

• U S E   I N   S A U C E S •

Broccoli rabe can be prepared using two basic methods, either a combination of blanching and sautéing, or wilting. Blanching leaches out some bitterness and ensures that the broccoli rabe is quite tender. Blanched broccoli rabe should be drained and then sautéed, perhaps in garlic-infused oil, until well flavored. Broccoli rabe can also be wilted in tomato sauce or white wine or with just the moisture that clings to the leaves after they have been washed. Wilting keeps the inherent bitterness in place and usually results in a firmer texture, especially if the cooking time is relatively short and the amount of moisture in the pan is minimal. Since broccoli rabe is so strongly flavored, pair it with other forceful ingredients, like garlic and hot red pepper flakes.

Broccoli Rabe with Garlic and Hot Red Pepper

● SERVES 4 ●

TIME: 20 minutes

BEST PASTA CHOICE: Rigatoni or other large, tubular shape

The strong, earthy flavor of broccoli rabe stands up beautifully to the healthy dose of garlic and hot red pepper flakes in this simple sauce. Use ¼ teaspoon more or less hot red pepper flakes depending on your tolerance for spicy foods.

2 small bunches broccoli rabe (about 2 pounds)

⅓ cup olive oil

6 large cloves garlic, cut into thin slivers

¾ teaspoon hot red pepper flakes or to taste

1 teaspoon salt

1 pound pasta

1. Bring 4 quarts of salted water to a boil in a large pot for cooking the pasta.

2. Bring several quarts of water to a boil in a medium saucepan. Discard the tough, thick stems from the broccoli rabe. Tear large leaves in half and break florets into several small pieces. Rinse the broccoli rabe under cold, running water. (If particularly sandy, soak the broccoli rabe in a large bowl of cold water, changing the water as needed until no grit appears on the bottom of the bowl.) Add the broccoli rabe to the boiling water and cook until tender, 2 to 3 minutes. Drain and set aside the broccoli rabe.

3. Heat the oil in a deep sauté pan. Add the garlic and hot red pepper flakes and sauté over medium heat until the garlic is golden brown, 2 to 3 minutes.

4. Add the damp broccoli rabe and salt to the pan. Turn the broccoli several times until it is well coated with the oil and heated through, about 2 minutes. Taste for salt and hot pepper and adjust seasonings if necessary.

5. While preparing the sauce, cook and drain the pasta, making sure that some liquid still clings to the noodles. Toss the hot pasta with the broccoli rabe sauce. Mix well and transfer portions to warm pasta bowls. Serve immediately.

Broccoli Rabe and Leeks Braised in White Wine and Tomatoes

● SERVES 4 ●

TIME: 35 minutes

BEST PASTA CHOICE: Spaghetti or other long, very thin shape

The sweetness of sautéed leeks and tomatoes is an excellent foil for the bitterness of the broccoli rabe. The wine adds a floral note that binds the various flavors together. Choose a white wine with some fruit but one that is still fairly dry. A Pinot Grigio or sauvignon blanc would be best.

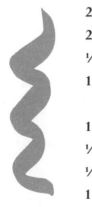

2 small bunches broccoli rabe (about 2 pounds)

2 medium leeks (about 1 pound)

¼ cup olive oil

1 cup drained canned whole tomatoes,
  juice discarded

1 teaspoon salt

¼ teaspoon freshly ground black pepper

½ cup dry white wine

1 pound pasta

1. Bring 4 quarts of salted water to a boil in a large pot for cooking the pasta.

2. Discard the tough, thick stems from the broccoli rabe. Rinse the broccoli rabe under cold, running water. (If particularly sandy, soak the broccoli rabe in a large bowl of cold water, changing the water until no grit appears on the bottom of the bowl.) Roughly chop the broccoli rabe and set it aside.

continued

3. Discard the dark green tops and tough outer leaves from the leeks. Trim a thin slice from the root ends and cut each leek in half lengthwise. Wash the leeks under cold, running water, gently spreading apart but not separating the inner layers to remove all traces of soil. If the leeks are particularly sandy, soak them in several changes of clean water. Lay the leeks flat side down on a work surface and cut them crosswise into very thin half circles.

4. Heat the oil in a large sauté pan. Add the leeks and sauté over medium heat until the leeks have wilted and are beginning to brown, about 7 minutes.

5. Finely chop the tomatoes. Add the tomatoes, salt, and pepper to the pan and cook until the tomatoes have softened, about 2 minutes.

6. Add the broccoli rabe and wine to the pan and stir several times to coat the broccoli rabe with the tomato-leek mixture. Cover and cook, stirring occasionally, until the broccoli rabe is quite tender, about 15 minutes. Taste for salt and pepper and adjust seasonings if necessary.

7. While preparing the sauce, cook and drain the pasta. Toss the hot pasta with the broccoli rabe sauce. Mix well and transfer portions to warm pasta bowls. Serve immediately.

Broccoli Rabe with Caramelized Onions

● SERVES 4 ●

TIME: 30 minutes

BEST PASTA CHOICE: Linguine or other long, thin shape

The sweetness of caramelized onions balances the bitterness in broccoli rabe for a simple but richly flavored sauce. Cooking onions over medium heat slowly changes their color to golden brown and causes the natural sugars to caramelize. As long as you make sure not to cook the onions too quickly, the process is quite simple. This hearty sauce is especially nice with whole-wheat pasta.

**¼ cup olive oil, plus more
    for drizzling over pasta
2 large onions (about 1 pound),
    peeled and sliced thin
2 small bunches broccoli rabe
    (about 2 pounds)
4 medium cloves garlic, minced
1 teaspoon salt
¼ teaspoon freshly ground black pepper
1 pound pasta**

1. Bring 4 quarts of salted water to a boil in a large pot for cooking the pasta.

2. Heat the oil in a large sauté pan. Add the onions and sauté over medium heat, stirring occasionally, until golden brown, about 20 minutes. If the onions start to burn, lower the heat. They should be richly colored to bring out their sweetness.

3. While the onions are caramelizing, bring several quarts of water to a boil in a medium saucepan. Discard the tough, thick stems from the broccoli rabe. Tear large leaves in half and break florets into several small pieces. Rinse the broccoli rabe under cold, running water. (If particularly sandy, soak the broccoli rabe in a large bowl of cold water, changing the water as needed until no grit appears on the bottom of the bowl.) Add the broccoli rabe to the boiling water and cook for 2 minutes. Drain and set aside the broccoli rabe.

4. Add the garlic to the pan with the onions and cook for 1 minute. Add the broccoli rabe, salt, and pepper and cook, stirring occasionally, until the broccoli rabe is tender, about 5 minutes. Taste for salt and pepper and adjust seasonings if necessary.

continued

5. While preparing the sauce, cook and drain the pasta, making sure that some liquid still clings to the noodles. Toss the hot pasta with the broccoli rabe sauce. Mix well and transfer portions to warm pasta bowls. Drizzle each bowl with olive oil to taste and serve immediately.

Broccoli Rabe with White Beans and Tomatoes

• SERVES 4 •

TIME: 30 minutes, after soaking and cooking the dried beans

BEST PASTA CHOICE: Orecchiette or small shells

A spicy tomato sauce is built around broccoli rabe that has been briefly wilted in hot oil. The addition of cooked white beans makes the sauce particularly hearty, perfect for a cold winter's night. Prepare your own white beans, soaked in advance as directed in this recipe, or use canned beans that have been drained and rinsed under running water to remove the gelatinous packing liquid.

1 cup dried navy or cannellini beans or
    2 cups canned beans, drained and rinsed

2 medium cloves garlic, peeled, plus
    3 medium cloves, minced

1 bay leaf

1 large bunch broccoli rabe (about 1½ pounds)

¼ cup olive oil

½ teaspoon hot red pepper flakes or to taste

2 cups drained canned whole tomatoes,
   juice reserved

1 teaspoon salt

1 pound pasta

Freshly grated Parmesan cheese to taste

1. If using dried beans, soak them in water to cover for at least 6 hours or overnight. Drain the beans and place them in a small pot. Add enough cold water to cover the beans by at least 2 inches. Add the whole garlic cloves and the bay leaf. Simmer gently over medium heat until the beans are tender, 45 minutes to 1 hour. Drain, discard the garlic and bay leaf, and set the beans aside. (The beans can be covered and refrigerated for several days. Bring the beans to room temperature before use.)

2. Bring 4 quarts of salted water to a boil in a large pot for cooking the pasta.

3. Discard the tough, thick stems from the broccoli rabe. Tear large leaves in half and break florets into several small pieces. Rinse the broccoli rabe under cold, running water. (If particularly sandy, soak the broccoli rabe in a large bowl of cold water, changing the water as needed until no grit appears on the bottom of the bowl.) Set the damp broccoli rabe aside.

4. Heat the oil in a deep sauté pan. Add the minced garlic and hot red pepper flakes and sauté over medium heat until the garlic is lightly colored, about 1 minute. Add the damp broccoli rabe and sauté, stirring occasionally, until slightly wilted, about 4 minutes.

5. Coarsely chop the tomatoes and add them to the pan along with ½ cup of their packing juice and the salt. Use a spoon to gently break apart the tomatoes as they cook. Simmer until the sauce thickens, about 10 minutes.

6. Add the beans to the sauce and heat through for several minutes. Taste for salt and hot pepper and adjust seasonings if necessary.

7. While preparing the sauce, cook and drain the pasta. Toss the hot pasta with the sauce. Mix well and transfer portions to warm pasta bowls. Serve immediately with grated cheese passed separately.

Cabbage and Brussels Sprouts

Cabbage is much maligned in this country, mostly because it is often over-cooked. That strong, sulfur-like smell and flavor that so many children and adults find objectionable comes from boiling cabbage for too long. Other cooking methods, notably slow-cooking in some garlic-flavored oil until tender, can accentuate the mild, sweet, earthy flavor of cabbage and brussels sprouts, a close relative that is also considered in this chapter.

Both cabbages and brussels sprouts are members of the crucifer family of vegetables that has been recently linked with so many health benefits. Like their more famous cousins broccoli and cauliflower, these vegetables deserve more attention from Americans. Italians, especially in the north, are partial to green cabbages. The crinkly Savoy cabbage is a special favorite in risotto and pasta sauces, and as a side dish. As long as you remember not to over-cook cabbage, you will enjoy the several varieties.

Although available in American markets for most of the year, cabbage is considered winter fare in Italy. A touch of frost is said to sweeten their flavor, so wait until fall or winter to enjoy the following recipes.

• SELECTION •

Look for cabbage with few signs of wilting or decay. A couple of dry or loose outer leaves are fine but the cabbage should be tightly closed, not open or falling apart. The color of the cabbage, whether green or red, should be deep, not anemic. Cabbage should be firm to the touch and there should be no decay or browning at the stem end. Most of these traits apply to brussels sprouts as well. Leaves should be tightly compacted and dark green with no yellowing. If at all possible, purchase brussels sprouts still attached to the long stalk on which they grow.

• S T O R A G E •

Store whole heads of cabbage unwashed in a plastic bag in the refrigerator. They should stay fresh for at least 1 week, if not longer. As time goes by, outer layers may dry out and have to be discarded. However, inner leaves will remain crisp for some time. Loose brussels sprouts should be stored the same way. If purchased on a stalk, store them on the stalk and remove them just before cooking to maintain freshness and full flavor.

• P R E P A R A T I O N •

Cabbage requires minimal preparation before cooking. Remove any dried-out or loose outer leaves, peeling back several layers on most heads of cabbage. Discard the stem and core and then shred with a knife or the shredding blade of a food processor. Heads of cabbage can first be cut into wedges and then sliced crosswise to facilitate the shredding process. Brussels sprouts require the same stemming and shredding preparation for use in pasta sauces.

• U S E   I N   S A U C E S •

In the end, I find that all cabbages are best suited to pasta sauces when prepared in one of two methods—blanching and then sautéing in an open pan or slow-cooking in a covered pan. Shredded cabbages need to cook down to concentrate the flavors and cause some browning. Blanching the cabbage before sautéing shortens the cooking time and leaches out some of the harsh flavor that some people find objectionable. Slow-cooking over low heat in a covered pan with liquid (wine or stock is best) is also a good option, especially with red cabbage, which contains a fair amount of natural sweetness.

Browned Savoy Cabbage with Garlic and Parmesan

• SERVES 4 •

TIME: 35 minutes

BEST PASTA CHOICE: Fettuccine or other long, wide shape

Savoy cabbage has tender, frilly leaves that are light green in color. The flavor of this cabbage, which is especially popular in northern Italy, is quite rich and even a bit sweet. Blanching and then browning the cabbage accentuate these characteristics. If Savoy cabbage is unavailable, this recipe can be made with regular green cabbage.

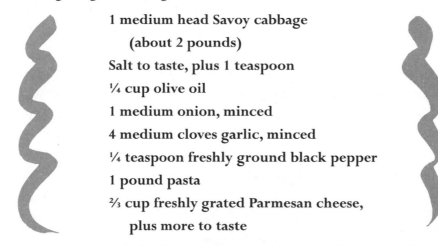

**1 medium head Savoy cabbage
   (about 2 pounds)**
Salt to taste, plus 1 teaspoon
¼ cup olive oil
1 medium onion, minced
4 medium cloves garlic, minced
¼ teaspoon freshly ground black pepper
1 pound pasta
**⅔ cup freshly grated Parmesan cheese,
   plus more to taste**

1. Bring 4 quarts of salted water to a boil in a large pot for cooking the pasta.

2. Bring several quarts of water to a boil in a large saucepan. Remove and discard any tough, dry outer leaves from the cabbage. Discard the stem. Cutting through the stem end, slice the cabbage into four thick wedges. Remove and discard the portion of the core that is attached to each wedge. Slice the wedges crosswise into very thin strips. Add the cabbage and salt to taste to the boiling water. Cook until the cabbage is tender, about 5 minutes. Drain and set aside the cabbage.

3. Heat the oil in a large sauté pan. Add the onion and sauté over medium heat until translucent, about 5 minutes. Stir in the garlic and cook until lightly colored, about 1 minute.

4. Add the cabbage, 1 teaspoon salt, and the pepper to the pan. Raise the heat to medium-high and stir to coat the cabbage with the oil. Cook, stirring often, until the cabbage has completely wilted and is just beginning to brown, about 15 minutes. Taste for salt and pepper and adjust seasonings if necessary.

5. While preparing the sauce, cook and drain the pasta, making sure that plenty of liquid still clings to the noodles. Toss the hot pasta with the cabbage sauce and ⅔ cup grated Parmesan. Mix well and transfer portions to warm pasta bowls. Serve immediately with more grated cheese passed separately.

Red Cabbage Smothered with Onions and Red Wine

● SERVES 4 ●

TIME: 40 minutes

BEST PASTA CHOICE: Penne or other short, tubular shape

For this wintery sauce, red cabbage is cooked until exceedingly tender. The sweetness of the cabbage is accentuated by the sautéed onions, while the red wine provides a fruity yet slightly acidic contrast. Choose a relatively young Chianti or similar wine for this sauce. Although even the smallest head of red cabbage weighs 3 pounds, this recipe requires only 1 pound of trimmed cabbage, which can be shredded with a knife or in a food processor fitted with the shredding disk.

⅓ **small head red cabbage**
    (about 1 pound when trimmed)
¼ **cup olive oil**

continued

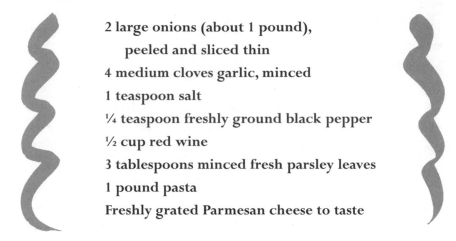

2 large onions (about 1 pound),
peeled and sliced thin
4 medium cloves garlic, minced
1 teaspoon salt
¼ teaspoon freshly ground black pepper
½ cup red wine
3 tablespoons minced fresh parsley leaves
1 pound pasta
Freshly grated Parmesan cheese to taste

1. Bring 4 quarts of salted water to a boil in a large pot for cooking the pasta.

2. Remove and discard any tough, dry outer leaves from the cabbage. Discard the stem. Cut the cabbage into ½-inch-thick wedges. Slice the wedges crosswise into very thin strips. There should be about 5 cups of shredded cabbage. Set the cabbage aside.

3. Heat the oil in a large, deep sauté pan. Add the onions and sauté over medium heat until golden, about 10 minutes. Stir in the garlic and continue cooking for another minute or so.

4. Add the cabbage, salt, and pepper to the pan. Stir several times to coat the cabbage with the oil. Cook, turning occasionally, until the cabbage is wilted, about 5 minutes.

5. Add the wine to the pan. Cover and cook, stirring occasionally, until the cabbage is extremely tender, about 20 minutes. Stir in the parsley. Taste for salt and pepper and adjust seasonings if necessary.

6. While preparing the sauce, cook and drain the pasta. Toss the hot pasta with the cabbage sauce. Mix well and transfer portions to warm pasta bowls. Serve immediately with grated cheese passed separately.

Shredded Brussels Sprouts with Orange and Almonds

● SERVES 4 ●

TIME: 30 minutes

BEST PASTA CHOICE: Fusilli or other short, curly shape

Brussels sprouts undergo a two-step cooking process in order to reduce their strong flavor. They are first blanched until almost tender and then sautéed until crisp. The sweetness from the browned onions and the orange juice also helps tame their strong flavor. Toasted, sliced almonds add a pleasing textural contrast.

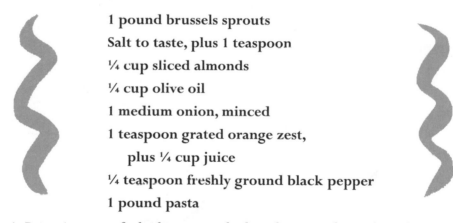

1 pound brussels sprouts

Salt to taste, plus 1 teaspoon

¼ cup sliced almonds

¼ cup olive oil

1 medium onion, minced

1 teaspoon grated orange zest,
    plus ¼ cup juice

¼ teaspoon freshly ground black pepper

1 pound pasta

1. Bring 4 quarts of salted water to a boil in a large pot for cooking the pasta.

2. Bring several quarts of water to a boil in a medium saucepan. Trim and discard a layer or two of loose outer leaves from each brussels sprout. Trim a thin slice from the stem end of each brussels sprout. Add the trimmed brussels sprouts and salt to taste to the boiling water. Cook until the brussels sprouts are almost tender but not soft, about 4 minutes. Drain the brussels sprouts and cool them slightly. Slice the brussels sprouts, cutting parallel to the stem end, into thin strips. Set the shredded brussels sprouts aside.

continued

3. Set a large skillet over medium heat. Add the almonds and cook, shaking the pan occasionally to turn the nuts, until lightly toasted (about 5 minutes). Do not let the nuts burn. Set the toasted nuts aside.

4. Add the oil to the empty skillet. Add the onion and sauté over medium heat until lightly browned, about 10 minutes.

5. Add the orange zest to the pan with the browned onions and cook for 1 minute. Raise the heat to medium-high and add the shredded brussels sprouts, 1 teaspoon salt, and the pepper to the pan. Cook, stirring occasionally, until the brussels sprouts have wilted and begun to brown, about 4 minutes.

6. Add the orange juice and toasted almonds to the pan and cook for 1 minute to blend flavors. Taste for salt and pepper and adjust seasonings if necessary.

7. While preparing the sauce, cook and drain the pasta, making sure that some liquid still clings to the noodles. Toss the hot pasta with the brussels sprouts sauce. Mix well and transfer portions to warm pasta bowls. Serve immediately.

Carrots

Carrots are often the first vegetable that children in this country will eat without coercion. No doubt their popularity with toddlers has something to do with their natural sweetness. Luckily, parents of small children don't have to worry about their kids eating too many carrots. They are rich in nutrients, especially vitamins A and C, and are a good source of fiber.

Carrots should be a favorite vegetable for the cook in a hurry since they require so little preparation and have a relatively long shelf-life in the refrigerator. I always keep a bag of carrots tucked in a produce drawer for "emergency" meals. When using carrots in pasta sauces, the idea is to play off their sweetness. This can take the form of a simple sauce of buttered carrots with fresh herbs or something more complex with the sweetness of carrots acting as a foil for the pleasant bitterness of braised kale or endive. Carrots also have a natural affinity for acidic tomatoes and are a wonderful addition to simple marinara sauces.

• SELECTION •

Look for small or medium carrots (about 8 per pound) rather than mammoth carrots that often have woody centers and very little sweetness. Carrots should be quite firm and should not exhibit any signs of age, especially dried-out patches or desiccated ends. Also avoid carrots with cracks or sprouting white rootlets—indications that the carrots have been out of the ground for a long time. Fresh carrots will be deep orange in color and crisp with a good moisture content. Never buy carrots that are limp or bendable. I often buy carrots with their greens still attached—fresh-looking tops mean that the carrots have been recently dug and have not been warehoused for weeks. You should discard the tops as soon as possible since over time they can rob flavor and moisture from the carrots. The quality of bagged carrots is often quite good, so don't hesitate to buy them as long as they meet the requirements I have outlined, except of course the fresh-looking tops.

• S T O R A G E •

Carrots can be stored in the refrigerator for at least a week, often longer without damage. As carrots age, they sprout tiny white hairlike roots and must be used before this happens.

• P R E P A R A T I O N •

Unlike so many other vegetables, carrots require little advance work. Simply trim the tops and tips and then remove the skin with a vegetable peeler. Carrots can be cut into numerous shapes from small dice to long matchsticks. Remember that because of their firmness, carrots will retain whatever shape you cut them into even when cooked for a long time.

• U S E   I N   S A U C E S •

Carrots must be cooked in some liquid and are therefore braised or blanched in all of my recipes. For braising, slow-cook the carrots in water, stock, or tomato sauce. Covering the pan allows the carrots to cook in a relatively small amount of liquid and concentrates their flavor. Many pasta sauces rely on blanched carrots. They may be fully cooked and then just tossed with other elements (because of its sweet dairy flavor, butter is a natural partner for carrots) or partially cooked and then added to a skillet and sautéed with other ingredients until tender.

• R E L A T E D   R E C I P E S •

Roasted Pearl Onions and Carrots with Thyme (page 149)
Sautéed White Mushrooms with Carrots and Oregano (page 200)
Spinach in Tomato Sauce with Shallots and Carrots (page 263)

Carrots Braised in Tomato Sauce with Shallots

• SERVES 4 •

TIME: 45 minutes

BEST PASTA CHOICE: Linguine or other long, thin shape

Diced carrots soften in a slow-simmering tomato sauce that is sparked by the addition of shallots and parsley. Half of the cooked sauce is pureed to give the sauce a smooth base. The final mixture is also enriched with a small amount of butter. While I like the gentle flavor of shallots in this sauce, a minced small onion can be used in their place.

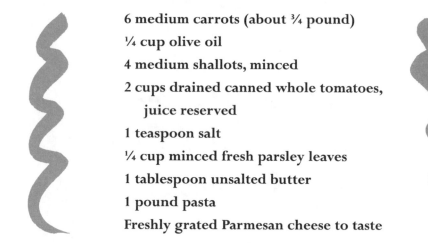

6 medium carrots (about ¾ pound)

¼ cup olive oil

4 medium shallots, minced

2 cups drained canned whole tomatoes, juice reserved

1 teaspoon salt

¼ cup minced fresh parsley leaves

1 tablespoon unsalted butter

1 pound pasta

Freshly grated Parmesan cheese to taste

1. Bring 4 quarts of salted water to a boil in a large pot for cooking the pasta.

2. Peel and trim the ends from the carrots. Cut the carrots into ¼-inch dice. Set the carrots aside.

3. Heat the oil in a large skillet. Add the carrots and shallots to the pan and sauté over medium heat until the shallots are golden, about 6 minutes.

continued

4. Coarsely chop the tomatoes and add them to the pan along with 1 cup of their packing liquid and the salt. Simmer gently, uncovered, occasionally using the back of a spoon to break apart the tomatoes, until the sauce thickens and the carrots become quite tender, about 30 minutes. Stir in the parsley.

5. Puree half of the sauce in a food processor or blender until smooth. Mix the pureed sauce and the butter back into the skillet with the remaining sauce, stirring over low heat until the butter melts. Taste for salt and adjust seasonings if necessary.

6. While preparing the sauce, cook and drain the pasta. Toss the hot pasta with the carrot sauce. Mix well and transfer portions to warm pasta bowls. Serve immediately with grated cheese passed separately.

Blanched Carrots and Slow-Cooked Endive with Chives

● SERVES 4 ●

TIME: 35 minutes

BEST PASTA CHOICE: Penne or other short, tubular shape

The carrots undergo two cooking processes for this sauce. They are first blanched until just tender and then added to the skillet with the partially caramelized endive strips and cooked until they turn light brown around the edges and the endive is fully caramelized.

6 medium carrots (about ¾ pound)

Salt to taste, plus 1 teaspoon

2 large heads Belgian endive (about ¾ pound)

¼ cup olive oil

1 small onion, minced

¼ teaspoon freshly ground black pepper

2 tablespoons snipped fresh chives

1 pound pasta

1. Bring 4 quarts of salted water to a boil in a large pot for cooking the pasta.

2. Bring several quarts of water to a boil in a medium saucepan. Peel and trim the ends from the carrots. Slice the carrots into matchstick pieces that are about 1 inch long and ¼ inch thick. Add the carrots and salt to taste to the boiling water. Cook until the carrots are tender but not mushy, about 5 minutes. Drain and set aside the carrots.

3. Remove and discard any tough or blemished outer leaves from the endive. Trim a thin slice from the root end. Slice the endive in half lengthwise. Slice the halves crosswise into ½-inch-wide strips and set them aside.

4. Heat the oil in a large sauté pan. Add the onion and cook over medium heat until translucent, about 5 minutes. Stir in the endive, 1 teaspoon salt, and the pepper. Cook, stirring occasionally, until the endive has cooked down substantially and is light brown in color, about 12 minutes.

5. Add the blanched carrots to the pan. Cook until the carrots have browned slightly around the edges and the endive is a rich brown color, about 10 minutes. Stir in the chives. Taste for salt and pepper and adjust seasonings if necessary.

6. While preparing the sauce, cook and drain the pasta, reserving ⅓ cup of the cooking liquid. Toss the hot pasta with the vegetables. Mix well, adding as much of the reserved cooking liquid as needed to moisten the pasta. Transfer portions to warm pasta bowls and serve immediately.

Blanched-and-Buttered Carrots with Garlic and Mixed Fresh Herbs

● SERVES 4 ●

TIME: 25 minutes

BEST PASTA CHOICE: Fusilli or other short, curly shape

This basic sauce pairs blanched carrots with butter, garlic, and an array of garden-fresh herbs. Use several herbs for maximum interest. Good choices include oregano, thyme, marjoram, chives, basil, mint, and tarragon.

8 medium carrots (about 1 pound)

Salt to taste, plus 1 teaspoon

1 cup tightly packed mixed fresh herb leaves

 (see headnote above)

6 tablespoons unsalted butter

4 medium cloves garlic, minced

 1 pound pasta

1. Bring 4 quarts of salted water to a boil in a large pot for cooking the pasta.

2. Bring several quarts of water to a boil in a medium saucepan. Peel and trim the ends from the carrots. Cut the carrots into ¼-inch dice. Add the carrots and salt to taste to the boiling water. Cook until the carrots are tender but not mushy, about 5 minutes. Drain and set aside the carrots.

3. Wash and pat dry the herbs. Leave small leaves like oregano or thyme whole; shred or chop larger leaves like basil or mint. Set the herbs aside.

4. Melt the butter in a large skillet. When the butter foams, add the garlic and sauté over medium heat until golden, about 2 minutes. Add the carrots

and cook, stirring occasionally, until heated through, about 2 minutes. Stir in the herbs and 1 teaspoon salt.

5. While preparing the sauce, cook and drain the pasta, making sure that some liquid still clings to the noodles. Toss the hot pasta with the carrot sauce. Mix well and transfer portions to warm pasta bowls. Serve immediately.

Hearty Carrot and Lentil Sauce with Tomatoes

• SERVES 4 •

TIME: 40 minutes

BEST PASTA CHOICE: Penne or other short, tubular shape

This sturdy sauce relies on sautéed carrots and onions as well as canned tomatoes and lentils. Unlike other legumes, lentils do not require soaking. They will become tender after just 20 to 25 minutes of cooking. Follow this dish with a lively salad perhaps with artichoke hearts or maybe raw fennel.

¾ cup brown lentils

1 bay leaf

1 medium clove garlic, peeled

3 medium carrots (about ⅓ pound)

3 tablespoons olive oil

1 small onion, minced

1½ cups drained canned whole tomatoes, juice reserved

1 teaspoon salt

¼ teaspoon freshly ground black pepper

1 pound pasta

Freshly grated Parmesan cheese to taste

continued

1. Bring 2 quarts of water to a boil in a medium saucepan. Add the lentils, bay leaf, and whole garlic clove and simmer over medium heat until the lentils are tender but not mushy, about 20 to 25 minutes. Drain, discard the bay leaf and garlic, and set the lentils aside.

2. Bring 4 quarts of salted water to a boil in a large pot for cooking the pasta.

3. Peel and trim the ends from the carrots. Cut the carrots into ¼-inch dice. Set the carrots aside.

4. Heat the oil in a large skillet. Add the onion and sauté over medium heat until translucent, about 5 minutes. Add the carrots and cook until they have softened, about 10 minutes.

5. Coarsely chop the tomatoes and add them to the pan along with ½ cup of their packing liquid and the salt and pepper. Simmer gently, occasionally using the back of a spoon to break apart the tomatoes, until a rough sauce forms, 10 to 15 minutes.

6. Add the lentils to the tomato sauce and heat through for a minute or two. Taste for salt and pepper and adjust seasonings if necessary.

7. While preparing the sauce, cook and drain the pasta. Toss the hot pasta with the carrot sauce. Mix well and transfer portions to warm pasta bowls. Serve immediately with grated cheese passed separately.

Cauliflower

Cauliflower is a member of the crucifer family of vegetables that includes broccoli and cabbage. Despite its family tree, cauliflower is relatively mild-tasting and sometimes even sweet. The unique color and gentle flavor are the result of some tricky field work.

Soon after the first leaves poke through the soil, a tiny bud forms. When this bud is quite small, the dark green leaves, which are still attached to many heads of cauliflower at the market, are wrapped up and around the plant. The head is actually a collection of densely packed unopened flower buds, hence the term flowerets or florets. Because the florets are deprived of sunlight, they do not become green and keep their milky white color as they grow. At harvesttime, the leaves are pulled back and whole head is shipped to market. While cauliflower greens are quite tough and bitter, they are edible and can be prepared like collards or any other winter greens.

· SELECTION ·

Cauliflower should be creamy white in color with no black spots or discoloration. The florets should be firm to the touch and tightly packed. The green leaves should be firm not limp. The head should feel relatively heavy for its size, an indication that the cauliflower has not lost too much moisture during shipping.

• S T O R A G E •

Cauliflower is a relatively sturdy vegetable and it should stay fresh for several days in the refrigerator.

• P R E P A R A T I O N •

Trimming a head of cauliflower into bite-sized florets requires the use of your hands and a knife. Begin by snapping off and discarding the green leaves that surround the core. With the core now exposed, it is fairly easy to make a circular incision around the core, leaving about ½ inch of the stem attached to the florets. Once the incision is complete, lift the core out and use your hands to break the head into several smaller pieces. At this point, I usually slice florets into small, bite-sized pieces.

• U S E   I N   S A U C E S •

The quickest and easiest way to cook cauliflower is in boiling water. Florets can be boiled until crisp-tender, drained, and then braised in a covered pan, perhaps in tomato sauce, until completely tender. Florets can also be boiled until completely tender and then tossed with flavoring agents. Instead of blanching, I sometimes sauté florets over low heat for a relatively long time. This causes the florets to become golden and concentrates their natural sugars. To finish cooking, add liquid to the pan, cover, and braise until tender.

Sautéed Cauliflower with Garlic, Raisins, and Pine Nuts

● SERVES 4 ●

TIME: 25 minutes

BEST PASTA CHOICE: Linguine or other long, thin shape

Bite-sized pieces of cauliflower are partially cooked in boiling water, drained, and then cooked in a covered sauté pan until tender. Raisins, toasted pine nuts, and a healthy dose of garlic give this sauce its southern Italian character.

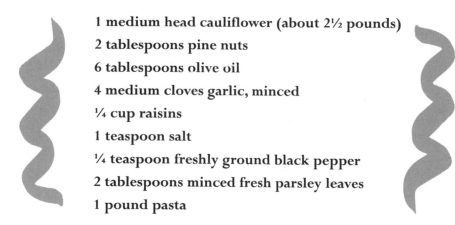

1 medium head cauliflower (about 2½ pounds)

2 tablespoons pine nuts

6 tablespoons olive oil

4 medium cloves garlic, minced

¼ cup raisins

1 teaspoon salt

¼ teaspoon freshly ground black pepper

2 tablespoons minced fresh parsley leaves

1 pound pasta

1. Bring 4 quarts of salted water to a boil in a large pot for cooking the pasta.

2. Bring several quarts of water to a boil in a medium saucepan. Trim and discard the leaves from the cauliflower. Remove the core and stalks and break the cauliflower into small florets. Slice the florets into small, bite-sized pieces. There should be about 5 cups of florets. Add the cauliflower to the boiling water and cook until crisp-tender, about 4 minutes. Drain and set aside the cauliflower.

continued

3. Set a large sauté pan over medium heat. Add the pine nuts and toast, shaking the pan occasionally to turn the nuts, until golden (about 5 minutes). Do not let the nuts burn. Set the toasted nuts aside.

4. Heat the oil in the empty pan. Add the garlic and sauté over medium heat until golden, about 2 minutes. Add the cauliflower and cook for a minute or two, turning often, until well coated with the oil.

5. Add the toasted pine nuts, raisins, salt, and pepper to the pan. Cover and cook over low heat, stirring occasionally, until the cauliflower is tender, about 10 minutes. Stir in the parsley. Taste for salt and pepper and adjust seasonings if necessary.

6. While preparing the sauce, cook and drain the pasta, making sure that some liquid still clings to the noodles. Toss the hot pasta with the cauliflower sauce. Mix well and transfer portions to warm pasta bowls. Serve immediately.

Cauliflower with Tomatoes, Green Olives, and Capers

● SERVES 4 ●

TIME: 35 minutes

BEST PASTA CHOICE: Fusilli or other short, curly shape

Cauliflower is blanched and then braised in tomato sauce for this Sicilian-inspired recipe with green olives and capers. Choose any large green olives packed in brine, especially Sicilian colossals. Add salt sparingly to this sauce, which already has a number of salty ingredients.

2 tablespoons olive oil

4 medium cloves garlic, minced

2 cups drained canned whole tomatoes,
    juice reserved

1 small head cauliflower (about 2 pounds)
12 large green olives (about 3 ounces),
    pitted and chopped
1 tablespoon drained capers
2 tablespoons minced fresh parsley leaves
Salt to taste
1 pound pasta
Freshly grated Pecorino Romano cheese
    to taste

1. Bring 4 quarts of salted water to a boil in a large pot for cooking the pasta.

2. Heat the oil in a large sauté pan. Add the garlic and sauté over medium heat until golden, about 2 minutes. Coarsely chop the tomatoes and add them to the pan along with 1 cup of their packing juice. Simmer gently, occasionally using a spoon to break apart the tomatoes, until the sauce thickens slightly, about 10 minutes.

3. While the sauce is simmering, bring several quarts of water to a boil in a medium saucepan. Discard the leaves from the cauliflower. Remove the core and stalks and break the cauliflower into small florets. Slice the florets into small, bite-sized pieces. There should be about 4 cups of florets. Add the cauliflower to the boiling water and cook until crisp-tender, about 4 minutes. Drain and set aside the cauliflower.

4. When the tomato sauce has thickened, add the cooked cauliflower along with the olives and capers. Simmer gently until the cauliflower softens and the flavors are blended, about 15 minutes. Stir in the parsley. Taste and add salt sparingly.

5. While preparing the sauce, cook and drain the pasta. Toss the hot pasta with the cauliflower sauce. Mix well and transfer portions to warm pasta bowls. Serve immediately with grated cheese passed separately.

Blanched Cauliflower with Basil and Toasted Walnuts

• SERVES 4 •

TIME: 25 minutes

BEST PASTA CHOICE: Farfalle or other small shape with crevices

In this simple sauce, the cauliflower is boiled until tender, drained, and then tossed with garlic-infused butter, a generous handful of basil, and toasted walnuts. The whole process takes just a few minutes and the result is a rich, nutty sauce with a fragrant undertone provided by the basil.

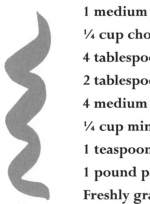

1 medium head cauliflower (about 2½ pounds)

¼ cup chopped walnuts

4 tablespoons unsalted butter

2 tablespoons olive oil

4 medium cloves garlic, minced

¼ cup minced fresh basil leaves

1 teaspoon salt

1 pound pasta

Freshly grated Parmesan cheese to taste

1. Bring 4 quarts of salted water to a boil in a large pot for cooking the pasta.

2. Bring several quarts of water to a boil in a medium saucepan. Trim and discard the leaves from the cauliflower. Remove the core and stalks and break the cauliflower into small florets. Slice the florets into small, bite-sized pieces. There should be about 5 cups of florets. Add the cauliflower to the boiling water and cook until tender, about 7 minutes. Drain and set aside the cauliflower.

3. Set a large skillet over medium heat. Add the walnuts and toast, shaking the pan occasionally to turn them, until fragrant (about 5 minutes). Do not let the nuts burn. Set the nuts aside.

4. Add the butter and oil to the empty skillet. When the mixture is hot, add the garlic and sauté over medium heat until golden, about 2 minutes.

5. Stir in the cauliflower, toasted walnuts, basil, and salt. Mix well to coat the cauliflower with the butter and oil. Cook until the cauliflower is heated through, no more than a minute or two. Taste for salt and adjust seasonings if necessary.

6. While preparing the sauce, cook and drain the pasta, making sure that some liquid still clings to the noodles. Toss the hot pasta with the cauliflower sauce. Mix well and transfer portions to warm pasta bowls. Serve immediately with grated cheese passed separately.

Blanched Cauliflower with Spicy Tomato-Cream Sauce

● SERVES 4 ●

TIME: 25 minutes

BEST PASTA CHOICE: Penne or other short, tubular shape

A bright pink tomato sauce sparked by hot red pepper flakes is the perfect medium for blanched cauliflower. Canned tomatoes are used in this substantial fall or winter sauce but are prepared like fresh. Instead of coarsely chopping the tomatoes and adding them to the pan with some of the packing juice, in this recipe the tomatoes are removed from their packing juice and cut into small dice. Since no packing juice is added and the tomatoes are cooked briefly, they retain their shape and the sauce is not too thick.

continued

1 small head cauliflower (about 2 pounds)
¼ cup olive oil
4 medium cloves garlic, minced
½ teaspoon hot red pepper flakes or to taste
1½ cups drained canned whole tomatoes,
**   juice discarded**
1 teaspoon salt
¼ cup heavy cream
1 pound pasta
Freshly grated Parmesan cheese to taste

1. Bring 4 quarts of salted water to a boil in a large pot for cooking the pasta.

2. Bring several quarts of water to a boil in a medium saucepan. Trim and discard the leaves from the cauliflower. Remove the core and stalks and break the cauliflower into small florets. Slice the florets into small, bite-sized pieces. There should be about 4 cups of florets. Add the cauliflower to the boiling water and cook until crisp-tender, about 4 minutes. Drain and set aside the cauliflower.

3. Heat the oil in a large sauté pan. Add the garlic and hot red pepper flakes and sauté over medium heat until the garlic is golden, about 2 minutes.

4. Finely chop the tomatoes. Add them to the pan along with the cauliflower and salt. Cook until the tomatoes soften but do not lose their shape, about 3 minutes.

5. Add the cream to the pan. Simmer until the sauce thickens a bit, about 3 minutes. Taste for salt and hot pepper and adjust seasonings if necessary.

6. While preparing the sauce, cook and drain the pasta. Toss the hot pasta with the cauliflower sauce. Mix well and transfer portions to warm pasta bowls. Serve immediately with grated cheese passed separately.

Golden Cauliflower in Spicy Tomato Sauce

● SERVES 4 ●

TIME: 55 minutes

BEST PASTA CHOICE: Spaghetti or other long, very thin shape

Sautéing small pieces of cauliflower for a relatively long time (15 to 20 minutes) allows them to develop a rich, golden color and a pleasant sweetness, which is further complemented by a small amount of butter. Caramelized onions add depth to the spicy tomato sauce.

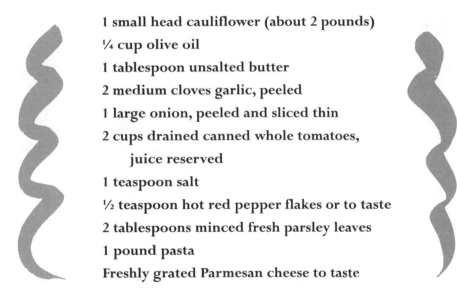

1 small head cauliflower (about 2 pounds)
¼ cup olive oil
1 tablespoon unsalted butter
2 medium cloves garlic, peeled
1 large onion, peeled and sliced thin
2 cups drained canned whole tomatoes,
**   juice reserved**
1 teaspoon salt
½ teaspoon hot red pepper flakes or to taste
2 tablespoons minced fresh parsley leaves
1 pound pasta
Freshly grated Parmesan cheese to taste

1. Bring 4 quarts of salted water to a boil in a large pot for cooking the pasta.

2. Discard the leaves from the cauliflower. Remove the core and stalks and break the cauliflower into small florets. Slice the florets into small, bite-sized pieces. There should be about 4 cups of florets.

continued

3. Heat 2 tablespoons oil and the butter in a large sauté pan. Add the cauliflower and whole garlic cloves. Sauté over medium heat, turning the vegetables several times to promote even cooking, until the cauliflower is golden, 15 to 20 minutes. Remove the cauliflower from pan and set it aside.

4. Add the remaining oil to the pan that still contains the whole garlic cloves. Add the onion and cook over medium heat until the thin slices have wilted and turned golden brown, about 12 minutes. Remove and discard the garlic cloves.

5. Coarsely chop the tomatoes and add them to the pan along with ½ cup of their packing juice, the salt, and the hot red pepper flakes. Simmer gently, occasionally using a spoon to break apart the tomatoes, until the sauce thickens, 10 to 15 minutes.

6. Return the cooked cauliflower to the pan. Simmer just until the cauliflower is heated through and the flavors are well combined, about 5 minutes. Stir in the parsley. Taste for salt and hot pepper and adjust seasonings if necessary.

7. While preparing the sauce, cook and drain the pasta. Toss the hot pasta with the cauliflower sauce. Mix well and transfer portions to warm pasta bowls. Serve immediately with grated cheese passed separately.

Eggplant

Eggplant has a long history of being misunderstood. As a member of the nightshade family (relatives include tomatoes, potatoes, and tobacco), eggplant was long associated with madness and was avoided until the seventeenth or eighteenth century. Perhaps this assessment came after someone tried to eat raw eggplant. Unlike most other vegetables, there is no use for eggplant unless it is cooked.

How to cook eggplant has been equally confusing. Many sources recommend salting to remove "bitter" juices. While there are indeed many inferior eggplant in the market that might benefit from salting, careful shopping usually makes salting unnecessary.

The other issue that confronts eggplant lovers is the tendency of this fleshy vegetable to soak up oil like a sponge. I get around this problem by relying on such cooking methods as grilling and roasting, which require only moderate amounts of fat. The result is an astonishing variety of recipes, some where the smoky flavor of eggplant dominates and others where the spongelike character is used to advantage to soak up the flavors of other ingredients in the sauce.

• SELECTION •

Eggplant come in an array of colors, including white, pinkish purple, purplish black, and even alternating stripes of mauve and white. Eggplant also come in an array of sizes—anywhere from the size of an egg to a football. In general, I prefer smaller eggplant since I find that they have fewer seeds and are therefore less bitter. The flesh of smaller eggplant also tends to be firmer and creamier. Even in cases where I call for larger specimens, avoid eggplant that weigh much more than 1¼ pounds; a 2- or 3-pound eggplant may be impressive-looking but the flavor is bound to be second-rate.

If the eggplant will be sliced and grilled, choose a small ¼-pound variety of any color. I especially like thin, delicate Japanese eggplant, but a small Italian variety is delicious as well. If roasting the eggplant whole in either the oven or on the grill, a larger globe variety (about 1¼ pounds) is your best choice. Medium or large eggplant can be used in recipes that called for stewing cubes or frying slices.

No matter the size, eggplant should have firm, taut skins and feel heavy for their size. Wrinkled skin or unusual lightness is a sure sign that the eggplant has lost much of its moisture and is old. Fresh eggplant should not give too easily to light pressure from your thumb and the cap, if present, should be bright green in color.

• S T O R A G E •

Eggplant does not stand up especially well during long storage. After a few days in the refrigerator, the skin starts to wrinkle and the flesh softens. To keep eggplant as fresh as possible, store them loose at room temperature or in a paper bag in the refrigerator and do not wash them until just before use. Moisture speeds the softening process and is the reason why eggplant should not be stored in plastic bags where condensation can occur.

• P R E P A R A T I O N •

In most recipes, I find that the skin offers a welcome color and textural contrast to the soft flesh. Even in cases where the skin is to be removed, this is much easier to accomplish once the eggplant has been roasted and the skin blisters. Therefore, preparation requires no more than trimming the stem end and either slicing the eggplant into long, lengthwise thin strips for grilling or frying (or crosswise into circles if the eggplant is large) or cutting into cubes for stewing.

While I usually do not salt eggplant before cooking, there is one exception. Salting eggplant before frying releases some of its moisture, which helps reduce spattering and oil absorption.

• USE IN SAUCES •

Since eggplant can act as a sponge for oil, I avoid sautéing and prefer grilling, roasting, or stewing. Despite their obvious differences, grilling slices of eggplant or roasting a whole eggplant have much in common. Both techniques reduce the moisture level in the eggplant and concentrate its sweet, smoky flavor. Slices of eggplant need only be brushed lightly with oil and sprinkled with salt and pepper before charring over hot coals. I generally pair grilled eggplant with raw sauces like pesto. Roasting the eggplant in its skin can be accomplished in the oven or on the grill. The roasted eggplant is peeled and the pulp is used as the basis for a smooth sauce.

On top of the stove, I either stew or fry eggplant. Cubes can be cooked in a covered pan with plenty of liquid (tomato sauce is perfect) for a chunky sauce. I find that thin slices actually absorb less fat when deep-fried rather than sautéed, in part because the temperature of the oil is so much higher and cooking is accomplished in much less time. Simply slide slices into a skillet filled with about ½ inch of oil and fry, turning once, until golden and crisp, about 3 minutes per side. Drain on paper towels.

Roasted Eggplant and Red Bell Pepper Puree

• SERVES 4 •

TIME: 60 minutes

BEST PASTA CHOICE: Fusilli or other short, curly shape

Oven-roasted eggplant and peppers are peeled and then pureed with garlic, olive oil, lemon juice, and hot red pepper flakes for a versatile sauce that can be made several days in advance of serving. Just toss the chunky red puree with hot pasta and freshly minced basil leaves. To balance the rich, sweet flavor of the sauce, serve with a salad of mixed bitter greens.

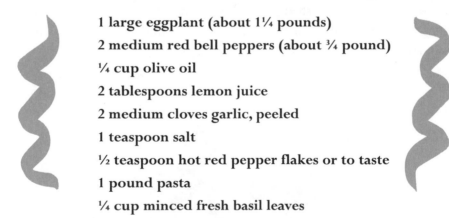

1 large eggplant (about 1¼ pounds)

2 medium red bell peppers (about ¾ pound)

¼ cup olive oil

2 tablespoons lemon juice

2 medium cloves garlic, peeled

1 teaspoon salt

½ teaspoon hot red pepper flakes or to taste

1 pound pasta

¼ cup minced fresh basil leaves

1. Preheat the oven to 400° F. Bring 4 quarts of salted water to a boil in a large pot for cooking the pasta.

2. Place the eggplant and bell peppers on a small baking sheet and brush them lightly with 1 tablespoon oil. Bake, turning several times, until the eggplant is quite soft and the peppers are charred, about 35 minutes.

3. Place the peppers in a paper bag and steam for 5 minutes to loosen the skins. Peel, core, and seed the peppers. Place the flesh in the work bowl of a food processor. Briefly cool the eggplant until it is just warm to the touch.

Trim the stem and peel away the skin with your fingers. Place the flesh in the work bowl with the peppers.

4. Add the remaining 3 tablespoons oil, lemon juice, garlic, salt, and hot red pepper flakes to the food processor and puree until the mixture is smooth. Taste for salt and hot pepper and adjust seasonings if necessary. (The puree can be covered and refrigerated for several days. Bring the sauce to room temperature before tossing it with pasta.)

5. Cook and drain the pasta. Toss the hot pasta with the eggplant puree and the basil. Mix well and transfer portions to warm pasta bowls. Serve immediately.

Roasted Eggplant with Tomatoes and Fresh Herbs

● SERVES 4 ●

TIME: 70 minutes

BEST PASTA CHOICE: Rigatoni or other large, tubular shape

So many eggplant recipes are weighted down by excess oil because the porous flesh will absorb as much oil as is provided during cooking. This problem can be avoided if the eggplant is roasted whole in the oven. Just a teaspoon of olive oil will keep the skin from sticking to the baking sheet. The roasted eggplant is then peeled and the tender flesh is added to a tomato sauce brimming with the flavors of fresh herbs: oregano, which is cooked along with the tomato sauce; and basil, which is added just before the sauce is tossed with pasta. Fresh thyme or marjoram could be substituted for the oregano and parsley or even mint can be added in place of the basil. The sharpness of Pecorino Romano cheese is a welcome last-minute addition to the dish.

continued

1 large eggplant (about 1¼ pounds)

1 teaspoon olive oil, plus 3 tablespoons

1 small onion, minced

3 medium cloves garlic, minced

1½ cups drained canned whole tomatoes,
   juice reserved

1 tablespoon minced fresh oregano leaves

1 teaspoon salt

½ teaspoon freshly ground black pepper

2 tablespoons minced fresh basil leaves

1 pound pasta

Freshly grated Pecorino Romano or
   Parmesan cheese to taste

1. Preheat the oven to 400° F.

2. Place the eggplant on a small baking sheet and brush it very lightly with 1 teaspoon oil. Bake the eggplant, turning once, until the flesh is soft and the skin is wrinkled, about 30 minutes. Briefly cool the eggplant until it is just warm to the touch. Trim the stem and peel away the skin with your fingers. Cut the eggplant into ½-inch cubes and set them aside.

3. Bring 4 quarts of salted water to a boil in a large pot for cooking the pasta.

4. Heat the remaining 3 tablespoons oil in a large skillet. Add the onion and sauté over medium heat until translucent, about 5 minutes. Add the garlic and cook for 1 minute.

5. Coarsely chop the tomatoes and add them to the skillet along with ¾ cup of their packing juice. Cook for several minutes, occasionally using a spoon to break apart the tomatoes.

6. Stir in the eggplant, oregano, salt, and pepper. Simmer over medium heat until the sauce thickens, 20 to 25 minutes. Stir in the basil. Taste for salt and pepper and adjust seasonings if necessary.

7. While preparing the sauce, cook and drain the pasta. Toss the hot pasta with the eggplant sauce. Mix well and transfer portions to warm pasta bowls. Serve immediately with grated cheese passed separately.

Grill-Roasted Eggplant with Tahini, Lemon, and Parsley

● SERVES 4 ●

TIME: 45 minutes

BEST PASTA CHOICE: Spaghetti or other long, very thin shape

This sauce takes its cue from the Middle Eastern dip called baba ghanoush. The eggplant are roasted in their skins over hot coals and then peeled and pureed with sesame paste, lemon juice, and garlic. (The eggplant can be roasted in a 400° F. oven until soft, but the sauce will lack the smoky punch that grilling provides.) Garnish bowls of pasta with a spoonful of diced tomatoes, if desired.

4 medium eggplant (about 2 pounds)
2 medium cloves garlic, peeled
⅓ cup tahini (sesame paste)
¼ cup lemon juice
1 teaspoon salt
Freshly ground black pepper to taste
1 pound pasta
¼ cup minced fresh parsley leaves
2 tablespoons olive oil

1. Light the grill or make a charcoal fire. Bring 4 quarts of salted water to a boil in a large pot for cooking the pasta.

2. Prick the eggplant in several places with a fork. Use a stiff wire brush to scrape the hot grill clean. Place the eggplant on the grill and cook, turning

continued

several times, until the skins blacken and the eggplant soften and collapse, about 20 minutes. Briefly cool the eggplant until they are just warm to the touch. Trim the stem and peel away the skin with your fingers. Transfer the pulp to a colander to allow the juices to drain off. Mash the pulp with a fork and continue to allow the juices to drain off for several minutes.

3. Place the garlic, tahini, lemon juice, salt, and pepper in the work bowl of a food processor and pulse several times to combine. With the motor running, pour 2 tablespoons cold water through the feed tube to thin the mixture.

4. Add the eggplant pulp to the food processor and blend until smooth. Add more cold water, a tablespoon at a time, to thin the puree if it seems too thick to coat pasta. Taste for salt and pepper and adjust seasonings if necessary.

5. While preparing the sauce, cook and drain the pasta. Toss the hot pasta with the eggplant puree and the parsley. Mix well and transfer portions to warm pasta bowls. Drizzle some of the oil over each bowl of hot pasta and serve immediately.

Grilled Eggplant with Raw Tomato Sauce, Fresh Mozzarella, and Basil

● SERVES 4 ●

TIME: 25 minutes

BEST PASTA CHOICE: Fusilli or other short, curly shape

This summery room-temperature sauce matches grilled eggplant with raw tomatoes, cubed mozzarella, red wine vinegar, and basil. Shrink-wrapped mozzarella will not deliver the same creaminess as fresh mozzarella packed in water. Substitute other fresh herbs as desired.

4 small eggplant (about 1 pound)

¼ cup olive oil

Salt to taste, plus 1 teaspoon

Freshly ground black pepper to taste,
**   plus ½ teaspoon**

2 large ripe tomatoes (about 1 pound)

½ pound fresh mozzarella packed in water,
**   drained**

2 tablespoons red wine vinegar

2 medium cloves garlic, minced

15 large fresh basil leaves, shredded

1 pound pasta

1. Light the grill or make a charcoal fire. Bring 4 quarts of salted water to a boil in a large pot for cooking the pasta.

2. Trim the ends from the eggplant. Cut the eggplant lengthwise into ⅓-inch-thick slices. Brush both sides of the eggplant slices with 2 tablespoons oil and sprinkle them generously with salt and pepper.

3. Use a stiff wire brush to scrape the hot grill clean. Grill the eggplant, turning once, until both sides are marked with very dark stripes, about 7 minutes. Cool the eggplant slices slightly and cut them into 1-inch squares.

4. While the eggplant are cooking, core and cut the tomatoes into ½-inch cubes. Cut the mozzarella into ¼-inch cubes. Toss the tomatoes and mozzarella in a large bowl. Add the remaining 2 tablespoons oil, vinegar, garlic, basil, 1 teaspoon salt, and ½ teaspoon pepper. Mix gently and set aside for 10 minutes to allow flavors to blend. Taste for salt and pepper and adjust seasonings if necessary.

5. While the tomatoes are marinating, cook and drain the pasta. Toss the hot pasta with the tomato mixture. Add the eggplant and mix well until the cheese softens and starts to melt. Transfer portions to pasta bowls and serve immediately

Grilled Eggplant with Cilantro Pesto

● SERVES 4 ●

TIME: 30 minutes

BEST PASTA CHOICE: Linguine or other long, thin shape

Grilled eggplant is a perfect match for a cilantro pesto enriched with walnuts and Pecorino Romano cheese. Toasting the walnuts releases their natural oils and increases their intensity in the sauce. Pair this summery pasta sauce with a fresh tomato salad to round out the meal.

6 small eggplant (about 1½ pounds)

½ cup olive oil

Salt to taste, plus 1 teaspoon

Freshly ground black pepper to taste,
**   plus ½ teaspoon**

2 tablespoons shelled walnut pieces

1 cup tightly packed fresh cilantro leaves

2 medium cloves garlic, peeled

¼ cup freshly grated Pecorino Romano cheese

1 pound pasta

1. Light the grill or make a charcoal fire. Bring 4 quarts of salted water to a boil in a large pot for cooking the pasta.

2. Trim the ends from the eggplant. Cut the eggplant lengthwise into ⅓-inch-thick slices. Brush both sides of the eggplant slices with 3 tablespoons oil and sprinkle them generously with salt and pepper.

3. Use a stiff wire brush to scrape the hot grill clean. Grill the eggplant, turning once, until both sides are marked with very dark stripes, about 7 minutes. Cool the eggplant slices slightly and cut them into ½-inch squares.

4. Set a small skillet over medium heat and add the walnuts. Toast the nuts, shaking the pan occasionally to turn them, until fragrant, about 5 minutes. Do not let the nuts burn.

5. Place the nuts in the work bowl of a food processor. Add the cilantro and garlic and process, scraping down the sides of the bowl once, until the mixture is roughly ground. With the motor running, slowly pour the remaining 5 tablespoons oil through the feed tube and process until smooth.

6. Scrape the pesto into a large bowl. Stir in the grated cheese, 1 teaspoon salt, and ½ teaspoon pepper. Add the grilled eggplant to the bowl and mix gently. Taste for salt and pepper and adjust seasonings if necessary.

7. While preparing the sauce, cook and drain the pasta, making sure that some water still clings to the noodles. Toss the hot pasta with the eggplant sauce. Mix well and transfer portions to warm pasta bowls. Serve immediately.

Grilled Eggplant with Sun-Dried Tomato and Goat Cheese Puree

• SERVES 4 •

TIME: 30 minutes

BEST PASTA CHOICE: Linguine or other long, thin shape

A creamy sun-dried tomato sauce contrasts beautifully with slightly smoky slices of grilled eggplant. Although I like the tang that goat cheese gives this sauce, other soft cheeses like ricotta could be substituted, if desired.

continued

6 small eggplant (about 1½ pounds)

7 tablespoons olive oil

Salt to taste, plus 1 teaspoon

Freshly ground black pepper to taste, plus
¼ teaspoon

16 sun-dried tomatoes packed in olive oil,
drained

2 medium cloves garlic, peeled

2 tablespoons pine nuts

¼ cup fresh goat cheese (about 2 ounces)

1 pound pasta

1. Light the grill or make a charcoal fire. Bring 4 quarts of salted water to a boil in a large pot for cooking the pasta.

2. Trim the ends from the eggplant. Cut the eggplant lengthwise into ⅓-inch-thick slices. Brush both sides of the eggplant slices with 3 tablespoons oil and sprinkle them generously with salt and pepper.

3. Use a stiff wire brush to scrape the hot grill clean. Grill the eggplant, turning once, until both sides are marked with very dark stripes, about 7 minutes. Cool the eggplant slices slightly and cut them into ½-inch squares.

4. Place the sun-dried tomatoes, garlic, and pine nuts in the work bowl of a food processor and process, scraping down the sides of the bowl as needed, until finely ground. With the motor running, slowly pour the remaining 4 tablespoons oil through the feed tube and process until smooth.

5. Add the goat cheese, 1 teaspoon salt, and ¼ teaspoon pepper to the food processor. Process just until the cheese is incorporated. Scrape the sauce into a large bowl. Add the grilled eggplant and toss gently. Taste for salt and pepper and adjust seasonings if necessary.

6. While preparing the sauce, cook and drain the pasta, making sure that some water still clings to the noodles. Toss the hot pasta with the eggplant sauce. Mix well and transfer portions to warm pasta bowls. Serve immediately.

Crisp Eggplant Slices with Basic Tomato Sauce and Oregano

• SERVES 4 •

TIME: 60 minutes

BEST PASTA CHOICE: Linguine or other long, thin shape

Thin slices of eggplant can be fried until crisp and then used as a garnish for pasta tossed with a simple tomato sauce. A sprinkling of a sharp sheep's milk cheese, either crumbly ricotta salata or somewhat firmer Pecorino Romano, adds a welcome punch. Salting the eggplant slices helps remove some of their bitter juices and allows the eggplant to become especially crisp when fried.

1 large eggplant (about 1 pound)
Generous amount of salt, plus 1 teaspoon
2 tablespoons olive oil, plus more
    for frying the eggplant
1 medium onion, minced
4 medium cloves garlic, minced
2 cups drained canned whole tomatoes,
    juice reserved
½ teaspoon freshly ground black pepper
2 tablespoons minced fresh oregano leaves
1 pound pasta
Freshly grated ricotta salata or
    Pecorino Romano cheese to taste

1. Trim the ends from the eggplant and cut it lengthwise into ¼-inch-thick slices. Place the eggplant slices in a colander and sprinkle both sides generously with salt. Set the colander in the sink or over a plate and let the juices drain for about 40 minutes.

continued

2. Bring 4 quarts of salted water to a boil in a large pot for cooking the pasta.

3. While the salted eggplant is in the colander, heat 2 tablespoons oil in a large skillet. Add the onion and sauté over medium heat until translucent, about 6 minutes. Stir in the garlic and cook for 2 minutes.

4. Coarsely chop the tomatoes and add them to the pan along with 1 cup of their packing liquid. Add 1 teaspoon salt, the pepper, and the oregano. Simmer gently, occasionally using a spoon to break apart the tomatoes, until sauce thickens, about 20 minutes. Taste for salt and pepper and adjust seasonings if necessary.

5. While the tomato sauce is simmering, heat about ½ inch of oil in another large skillet. Wash and pat dry the eggplant slices. When the oil is very hot but not yet smoking, add as many eggplant slices as can comfortably fit in the pan. Fry the eggplant, turning once, until golden brown, about 3 minutes per side. Transfer fried eggplant to a platter lined with paper towels. Repeat with remaining slices. When the eggplant has cooled slightly, cut it into very thin strips that are about 2 inches long.

6. While the sauce is simmering and the eggplant is frying, cook and drain the pasta. Toss the hot pasta with the tomato sauce. Transfer portions to warm pasta bowls and top each serving with a handful of fried eggplant. Sprinkle generously with grated cheese and serve immediately.

Stewed Eggplant with Tomatoes, Mushrooms, and Green Olives

• SERVES 4 •

TIME: 40 minutes

BEST PASTA CHOICE: Rigatoni or other large, tubular shape

Diced eggplant, coarsely chopped canned tomatoes, sliced mushrooms, and chopped green olives cook together in a covered skillet until they are tender. The cover is then removed to allow some of the liquid to cook off. The result is a chunky sauce bursting with garden-fresh flavors. Although I like the aromatic quality of the bay leaf in this sauce, feel free to substitute fresh herbs like thyme, oregano, mint, or basil once the cover is removed.

1 large eggplant (about 1 pound)

½ pound fresh white mushrooms

¼ cup olive oil

1 medium onion, minced

4 medium cloves garlic, minced

2 cups drained canned whole tomatoes,
    juice reserved

12 large green olives (about 3 ounces),
    pitted and chopped

1 bay leaf

1 teaspoon salt

¼ teaspoon freshly ground black pepper

1 pound pasta

Freshly grated Parmesan cheese to taste

continued

1. Bring 4 quarts of salted water to a boil in a large pot for cooking the pasta.

2. Trim the ends from the eggplant and cut it into ½-inch cubes. Wipe the mushrooms with a paper towel to loosen and remove any dirt. Trim and discard a thin slice from the stem end of each mushroom. Thinly slice the mushrooms. Set the diced eggplant and the sliced mushrooms aside together.

3. Heat the oil in a deep sauté pan or Dutch oven with a cover. Add the onion and sauté over medium heat until softened, about 5 minutes. Stir in the garlic and continue cooking for another minute or two.

4. Coarsely chop the tomatoes and add them to the pan along with 1 cup of their packing juice. Stir in the eggplant, mushrooms, olives, bay leaf, salt, and pepper. Bring the sauce to a simmer, using the back of a spoon to break apart the tomatoes, and cover. Simmer gently, stirring occasionally, until the eggplant and mushrooms are almost tender, about 20 minutes.

5. Uncover the pan and continue cooking until the vegetables are soft and the sauce has thickened to the proper consistency, about 5 minutes. Taste for salt and pepper and adjust seasonings if necessary. Remove and discard the bay leaf.

6. While preparing the sauce, cook and drain the pasta. Toss the hot pasta with the sauce. Mix well and transfer portions to warm pasta bowls. Serve immediately with grated cheese passed separately.

Endive

As its name suggests, Belgian endive was first grown by farmers in Belgium. Although much of the endive in American markets still comes from Europe, some is grown domestically. However, even local endive is fairly expensive since the production is so labor-intensive.

Endive is a member of the chicory family of salad greens. Broad white leaves ringed with yellow grow in a compact, elongated head. Endive is produced by forcing chicory roots in the absence of light, much as you might force a bulb in a dark basement. Since endive is grown inside and requires constant attention, it is quite expensive. Endive is also quite perishable, which adds to the cost.

The flavor of raw endive can be best described as bittersweet. As endive cooks—it can be roasted, grilled, braised, or sautéed—the bitterness fades and the sweetness is accentuated. Endive is generally less bitter than magenta-tinged radicchio, another member of the chicory family. Endive and radicchio can be used as not-quite-equal substitutes for each other. Endive is a particularly good substitute for an elongated variety of radicchio that grows in Italy but is rarely found in American markets. In either case, the flavor and cooking properties of endive and radicchio are close enough to merit substitution in the majority of recipes, with the obvious differences in appearance.

• SELECTION •

Look for crisp heads without brown streaks or spots on the outer leaves or the root end. Heads should be compact, not open, and outer leaves should be crisp, not limp or dried out, even around the edges. The leaves should be milky white and ringed with some yellow but no green (a sign that they are old and/or were exposed to light). Squat, plump heads do a better job of keeping inner leaves crisp than long, thin heads and should be selected when possible.

• S T O R A G E •

Endive can be stored in a plastic bag in the refrigerator for several days. Do not wash endive until just before use. With time, outer leaves may brown or soften but inner leaves will remain crisp. You will need to discard more outer leaves from endive that has been stored for several days, but the inner leaves should still be fresh.

• P R E P A R A T I O N •

Like its cousin radicchio, endive requires little preparation. If the leaves look and feel clean, as is usually the case, there is no need to wash the endive. Simply discard any tough or blemished outer leaves and trim a thin slice from the root end. Slice the endive in half lengthwise and then slice crosswise to cut out thin half circles. If the endive feels gritty, briefly soak slices in a bowl of cold water and then drain and dry them.

• U S E   I N   S A U C E S •

Like other leafy vegetables, endive will shrink considerably when cooked. The leaves can be wilted in an open pan and then braised with some liquid, either wine, cream, or tomatoes, to make an excellent pasta sauce. If the endive is cooked long enough, the leaves will brown and caramelize, thus softening the bitter edge characteristic of raw endive.

• R E L A T E D   R E C I P E S •

Blanched Carrots and Slow-Cooked Endive with Chives (page 88)
Braised Radicchio with Spicy Tomato Sauce and Basil (page 253)
Caramelized Radicchio with Balsamic Vinegar (page 255)

Caramelized Endive with Parmesan and Cream

● SERVES 4 ●

TIME: 30 minutes

BEST PASTA CHOICE: Fettuccine or other long, wide shape

This sauce is incredibly basic but quite decadent. Endive is cooked slowly until golden brown and soft in order to highlight its sweetness, and then enriched with some heavy cream and a generous dusting of Parmesan cheese. This dish is perfect as a substantial first course to an elegant meal.

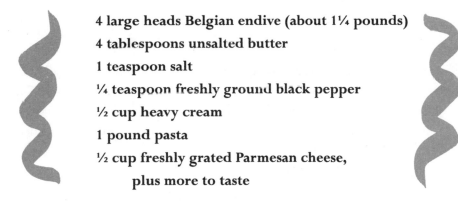

4 large heads Belgian endive (about 1¼ pounds)
4 tablespoons unsalted butter
1 teaspoon salt
¼ teaspoon freshly ground black pepper
½ cup heavy cream
1 pound pasta
½ cup freshly grated Parmesan cheese,
    plus more to taste

1. Bring 4 quarts of salted water to a boil in a large pot for cooking the pasta.

2. Remove and discard any tough or blemished outer leaves from the endive. Trim a thin slice from the root end. Slice the endive in half lengthwise. Slice the endive halves crosswise into very thin strips and set them aside.

3. Melt the butter in a large sauté pan. Add the endive, salt, and pepper and sauté over medium heat, stirring occasionally, until the endive is golden brown, 20 to 25 minutes.

4. Add the cream to the pan. Simmer gently until the sauce thickens, about 2 minutes. Taste for salt and pepper and adjust seasonings if necessary.

continued

5. While preparing the sauce, cook and drain the pasta, making sure that some liquid still clings to the noodles. Toss the hot pasta with the endive sauce and ½ cup grated Parmesan. Mix well and transfer portions to warm pasta bowls. Serve immediately with more grated cheese passed separately.

Braised Endive with Pink Tomato Sauce and Basil

● SERVES 4 ●

TIME: 30 minutes

BEST PASTA CHOICE: Penne or other short, tubular shape

Endive is partially wilted in garlicky olive oil to tame some but not all of its bitterness and then braised in a light tomato sauce with cream and basil. The slightly bitter endive is a perfect contrast to the sweet and acidic tomatoes. The small amount of cream in this sauce, just 4 tablespoons, adds richness and silkiness. Minced parsley can be substituted for the basil, if desired. This sauce can also be made with radicchio.

**3 medium heads Belgian endive
(about ¾ pound)**

¼ cup olive oil

3 medium cloves garlic, minced

**1 cup drained canned whole tomatoes,
juice discarded**

1 teaspoon salt

¼ teaspoon freshly ground black pepper

¼ cup heavy cream

¼ cup shredded fresh basil leaves

1 pound pasta

Freshly grated Parmesan cheese to taste

1. Bring 4 quarts of salted water to a boil in a large pot for cooking the pasta.

2. Remove and discard any tough or blemished outer leaves from the endive. Trim a thin slice from the root end. Slice the endive in half lengthwise. Slice the halves crosswise into very thin strips and set them aside.

3. Heat the oil in a large sauté pan. Add the garlic and sauté over medium heat until golden, about 2 minutes.

4. Add the endive to the pan and stir to coat the leaves with the oil. Cook, stirring occasionally, until the endive has wilted, about 5 minutes.

5. Finely chop the tomatoes. Add the tomatoes to the pan along with the salt and pepper. Cook, stirring occasionally, until the tomatoes begin to lose their shape, about 8 minutes.

6. Add the cream and basil to the pan and simmer gently until the sauce thickens, about 2 minutes. Taste for salt and pepper and adjust the seasonings if necessary.

7. While preparing the sauce, cook and drain the pasta, making sure that some liquid still clings to the noodles. Toss the hot pasta with the endive sauce. Mix well and transfer portions to warm pasta bowls. Serve immediately with grated cheese passed separately.

Sautéed Endive with Red Bell Peppers, Shallots, and White Wine

● SERVES 4 ●

TIME: 25 minutes

BEST PASTA CHOICE: Small shells or other small open shape

This sauce is one of contrasting flavors and colors. The bitterness of the endive is offset by the sweetness of the red peppers and sautéed shallots as well as by the bright, acidic flavor of the white wine. The colors in this sauce—white endive, bright red peppers, and green parsley—represent the Italian flag.

3 medium heads Belgian endive
   (about ¾ pound)
1 medium red bell pepper
¼ cup olive oil
4 medium shallots, peeled and sliced thin
1 teaspoon salt
¼ teaspoon freshly ground black pepper
½ cup dry white wine
¼ cup minced fresh parsley leaves
1 pound pasta
Freshly grated Parmesan cheese to taste

1. Bring 4 quarts of salted water to a boil in a large pot for cooking the pasta.

2. Remove and discard any tough or blemished outer leaves from the endive. Trim a thin slice from the root end. Slice the endive in half length-

wise. Slice the halves crosswise into very thin strips and set them aside. Core, halve, and seed the pepper. Slice the pepper into very thin strips that are about ½ inch long and set them aside.

3. Heat the oil in a large sauté pan. Add the shallots and sauté over medium heat until golden brown, about 6 minutes.

4. Add the endive to the pan and stir to coat the leaves with the oil. Add the salt and pepper and cook, stirring occasionally, until the endive has partially wilted, about 4 minutes. Add the peppers and cook for another 3 minutes.

5. Add the wine and the parsley to the pan and cook just until the aroma of the alcohol fades and the sauce is no longer soupy, about 3 minutes. Taste for salt and pepper and adjust seasonings if necessary.

6. While preparing the sauce, cook and drain the pasta. Toss the hot pasta with the endive sauce. Mix well and transfer portions to warm pasta bowls. Serve immediately with grated cheese passed separately.

Fava Beans

The arrival of fresh fava beans during the spring is widely anticipated in Italian markets. Like fresh peas, this legume comes in a long pod that contains several green beans, each about the size of a lima bean. Fresh favas have a sweet flavor tinged with a pleasant aura of bitterness. This is because the bean actually has two parts—a light green sheath or skin that is fairly bitter and a bright green internal flesh that is sweet. When favas are young, the outer part of the bean is still fresh and the contrast between sweet and lightly bitter is welcome in pasta sauces and other preparations. In fact, very fresh favas can be eaten raw. During the first part of the fava season, young pods are shelled and the beans are served on a platter perhaps drizzled with some olive oil and sprinkled lightly with salt.

However, if favas are not perfectly fresh, the outer skin on the bean can toughen and should be removed before the bean itself is cooked. To determine whether this step is necessary, taste several beans as you remove them from their cushiony pods. If they seem especially bitter or if the outer sheaths show any signs of dryness, drop the favas into boiling water for a minute or so to loosen this light-colored outer skin. Unfortunately, blanching only does part of the job and you will still have to peel the skin from each bean.

Because I enjoy the contrast between sweetness and bitterness in fresh favas, I do not peel them unless it is necessary. Of course, if you prefer to accent the sweet quality of favas, you can peel the outer sheaths even on very fresh samples. While I generally try to avoid this tedious step and compensate by pairing favas with sweet ingredients like tomatoes and cooked onions, some cooks might prefer to eliminate the bitter skins altogether.

• SELECTION •

Fava beans should be purchased while still in their pods so look to the pods to determine the quality of the beans. Pods should be bright green in color with no signs of dryness or decay. The insides of the pods are lined with a cushiony, foamlike material that is designed to protect the beans so expect the pods to feel soft or even squishy. However, pods should not be limp or old-looking.

• STORAGE •

As with fresh peas, the flavor of fresh favas begins to fade as soon as they are picked. Therefore, try to cook fava beans as soon as possible after purchasing them. If necessary, fava beans can be refrigerated for a day or two in a paper bag. However, the longer you store them, the more likely it becomes that you will need to boil them to remove the toughened outer sheaths around the beans before using them in pasta sauce.

• PREPARATION •

Fava beans should be shelled much as you would shell fresh peas. Simply tear the cushiony pod in half and remove the beans. If you want to remove the light green sheath that surrounds each bean, drop the shelled beans into boiling water for a minute. Drain the beans, refresh them in a bowl of cold water to stop the cooking process, and drain again. Use your fingers to scrape away part of the outer skin and reveal a bright green bean inside. I find it easiest to remove the skin from one end of the bean and then to squeeze gently to pop the inner meat out of the skin. In any case, this process can be a bit slow but is necessary if the favas are not absolutely fresh.

• USE IN SAUCES •

Cooking favas will mellow their bitterness, especially if they are paired with sweet ingredients like onions or tomato sauce. If favas are blanched and then peeled, they will be almost tender and require only minimal further cooking—perhaps a quick sauté in a splash of white wine. Unpeeled favas need to be cooked longer (between 4 and 8 minutes depending on their size and freshness) in a moist environment. I usually braise unpeeled favas, either in a covered pan filled with water and lemon juice or in a liquidy tomato sauce. If you blanch and peel favas and want to use them in a braising recipe, reduce their second cooking time considerably.

• RELATED RECIPES •

Blanched Peas with Quick Scallion Broth and Parmesan (page 223)
Blanched Peas with Yellow Bell Peppers and Tomatoes (page 226)
Blanched Peas with Watercress, Basil Oil, and Parmesan Curls (page 228)
Salsa Primavera with Tomatoes, Mushrooms, and Mixed Vegetables (page 298)

Braised Fava Beans with Tomatoes and Pecorino Romano

● SERVES 4 ●

TIME: 30 minutes

BEST PASTA CHOICE: Penne or other short, tubular shape

In this dish, fava beans are braised in a quick tomato sauce. The sweetness of the tomatoes contrasts nicely with the bitterness of the beans. A generous dusting of Italy's finest sheep's milk cheese, Pecorino Romano, adds sharpness, saltiness, and sweetness all at once.

2 pounds fresh fava beans in pods

¼ cup olive oil

1 medium onion, minced

2 cups drained canned whole tomatoes,
    juice reserved

1 teaspoon salt

¼ teaspoon freshly ground black pepper

1 pound pasta

Freshly grated Pecorino Romano cheese
    to taste

1. Bring 4 quarts of salted water to a boil in a large pot for cooking the pasta.

2. Shell the fava beans and rinse them briefly under cold, running water. There should be about 2 cups of shelled beans.

3. Heat the oil in a large skillet with a cover. Add the onion and sauté over medium heat until golden, about 7 minutes.

continued

4. Coarsely chop the tomatoes and add them to the pan along with ½ cup of their packing juice. Gently crush the tomatoes with the back of a spoon as you cook them for a minute or two to thicken the sauce a bit.

5. Add the fava beans, salt, and pepper to the pan. Bring the sauce to a simmer, reduce the heat to low, and cover. Cook, stirring once or twice, until the beans are tender, 4 to 8 minutes, depending on their freshness and size. Taste for salt and pepper and adjust seasonings if necessary.

6. While preparing the sauce, cook and drain the pasta. Toss the hot pasta with the fava bean sauce. Mix well and transfer portions to warm pasta bowls. Serve immediately with grated cheese passed separately.

Peeled Fava Beans with Red Onion, White Wine, and Mint

● SERVES 4 ●

TIME: 35 minutes

BEST PASTA CHOICE: Farfalle or other small shape with crevices

In this recipe I have chosen to peel the fava beans before adding them to the pasta sauce. A quick dip in boiling water loosens the skin on shelled beans and also partially cooks them. This technique should be used if the beans are not perfectly fresh or if the pasta sauce is fairly dry and does not contain enough moisture in which to braise the beans, which is the case here.

2 pounds fresh fava beans in pods

¼ cup olive oil

1 medium red onion, chopped

4 medium cloves garlic, minced

⅓ cup dry white wine

1 teaspoon salt

½ teaspoon freshly ground black pepper

¼ cup minced fresh mint leaves

1 pound pasta

Freshly grated Parmesan cheese to taste

1. Bring 4 quarts of salted water to a boil in a large pot for cooking the pasta.

2. Bring several quarts of water to a boil in a medium saucepan. Shell the fava beans. There should be about 2 cups of shelled beans. Add the beans to the boiling water and simmer for 1 minute. Drain the beans and refresh them in a bowl of cold water. Drain again and gently peel away and discard the thin, light green outer layer from the beans. Once the outer layer is partially peeled, try to pop the beans out with a gentle squeeze. Set the bright green peeled fava beans aside.

3. Heat the oil in a large skillet. Add the onion and sauté over medium heat until translucent, about 5 minutes. Stir in the garlic and continue cooking until golden, about 2 minutes.

4. Add the fava beans, wine, salt, and pepper to the pan. Cook, stirring occasionally, until the aroma of the alcohol fades and the beans are completely tender, about 2 minutes. Stir in the mint. Taste for salt and pepper and adjust seasonings if necessary.

5. While preparing the sauce, cook and drain the pasta, making sure that some water still clings to the noodles. Toss the hot pasta with the fava bean sauce. Mix well and transfer portions to warm pasta bowls. Serve immediately with grated cheese passed separately.

Fava Beans with Shallots, Fresh Herbs, and Goat Cheese

● SERVES 4 ●

TIME: 30 minutes

BEST PASTA CHOICE: Farfalle or other small shape with crevices

Young fava beans can be made tender in a matter of minutes by using a combination of cooking methods. The beans are first coated with oil that has been used to brown minced shallots. Lemon juice and water are added to the pan, which is covered to allow the fava beans to steam. When tender, the beans are seasoned with fresh herbs—parsley and basil are recommended in this recipe but a small amount of oregano, tarragon, or thyme would not be out of place. For a touch of creaminess, fresh goat cheese is tossed with the beans and pasta. The result is an elegant dish worthy of the finest spring meal.

2 pounds fresh fava beans in pods

¼ cup olive oil

2 medium shallots, minced

1 teaspoon salt

¼ teaspoon hot red pepper flakes
   or to taste

2 tablespoons lemon juice

2 tablespoons minced fresh parsley leaves

2 tablespoons minced fresh basil leaves

1 pound pasta

¼ cup fresh goat cheese
   (about 2 ounces)

1. Bring 4 quarts of salted water to a boil in a large pot for cooking the pasta.

2. Shell the fava beans and rinse them briefly under cold, running water. There should be about 2 cups of shelled beans. Set aside.

3. Heat the oil in a large skillet with a cover. Add the shallots and sauté over medium heat until golden brown, about 5 minutes. Add the fava beans, salt, and hot red pepper flakes and toss to coat the beans with the oil, cooking for about 30 seconds.

4. Add the lemon juice and ⅓ cup water to the pan, reduce the heat to low, and cover. Cook, stirring once or twice, until the beans are tender but still firm, 4 to 8 minutes, depending on their freshness and size. Stir in the herbs. Taste for salt and hot pepper and adjust seasonings if necessary.

5. While preparing the sauce, cook and drain the pasta, making sure that some water still clings to the noodles. Toss the hot pasta with the fava beans and cheese. Mix well until the cheese melts and evenly coats the pasta. Transfer portions to warm pasta bowls and serve immediately.

Fennel

This licorice-flavored bulb vegetable is common in Italian kitchens, where it is called *finocchio,* but is sadly unfamiliar to many American cooks. Luckily there is no need to search out fennel at specialty markets; it is probably right under your nose at the local supermarket. Grown throughout the Mediterranean and now in California among other places, this crisp vegetable is known for its faint sweetness and anise flavor. Although the anise flavor fades as fennel cooks, the sweetness lingers.

The fennel bulb is creamy white in color, the stems or stalks are light green (they look like thin ribs of celery), and the feathery medium-green leaves or fronds resemble dill. While you may be unfamiliar with fresh fennel, you undoubtedly would recognize the small pale green seed, which is used as an aromatic spice in most Italian sausages as well as in Indian cooking.

The crunchy, white bulb, which is actually the swollen base of the stems, has a texture akin to celery minus the annoying strings. The bulb is often eaten raw—thin slices can be seasoned with salt and pepper and served on a platter with a small bowl of the finest olive oil for dipping. A bowl of salty olives is the perfect partner for this light and refreshing antipasto. Fennel also lends itself to a number of cooking methods, including braising, blanching, sautéing, and grilling.

• SELECTION •

When shopping for fennel, make sure to purchase bulbs with stems and feathery fronds still attached. Even if you are not using the stems or fronds, their presence is a good indication that the bulb will have maximum flavor and freshness. Fennel can range in size from about ½ pound to 1½ pounds. I generally look for smaller bulbs, which are more tender and less woody. However, freshness is more important than size when shopping for fennel. Look for firm, white bulbs—there should be very little if any discoloring. The stems should also be firm and both the stems and fronds should look fresh, not dried out.

• STORAGE •

Fennel can be stored for several days in a plastic bag in the refrigerator without much harm. With time, the outer layer of the bulb will begin to dry out, and it should be removed before using the fennel in recipes.

• PREPARATION •

The first step is to cut off the stems at the top of the bulb and reserve the fronds. I often chop the fronds and use them as a garnish, much as one might use parsley, at the end of cooking. The stems can be discarded or reserved and used to flavor a vegetable stock or vegetable soup. Any dry or blemished parts of the bulb should be peeled away using a process similar to the peeling back of outer layers on a onion.

If you want the various layers to stay intact—this is important when grilling fan-shaped wedges of fennel—slice crosswise from top to bottom, making sure that each wedge contains a narrow piece of the base at the bottom. Before cutting fennel into thin strips for blanching, sautéing, or braising, trim away a thin slice from the base, including the small round knob. I usually cut the bulb in half, then rest the halves, flat side down, on the work surface and slice them as thinly as desired.

• USE IN SAUCES •

Braising fennel in water, white wine, or tomatoes softens the texture and mellows the intense flavor. Fennel also takes well to grilling—thin wedges still retain some crunchiness and the natural sugars caramelize over the intense heat. Very finely minced raw fennel can be used as an accent in summer sauces, especially those with raw tomatoes.

Sautéed Fennel with Quick Tomato Sauce and Parmesan

• SERVES 4 •

TIME: 35 minutes

BEST PASTA CHOICE: Fusilli or other short, curly shape

Thin strips of fennel are sautéed with garlic and then softened in a simple tomato sauce made with canned tomatoes and their juice. Finish this dish with a generous dusting of Parmesan at the table to balance the sweetness of the vegetables.

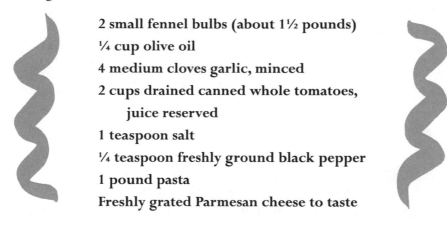

2 small fennel bulbs (about 1½ pounds)
¼ cup olive oil
4 medium cloves garlic, minced
2 cups drained canned whole tomatoes,
    juice reserved
1 teaspoon salt
¼ teaspoon freshly ground black pepper
1 pound pasta
Freshly grated Parmesan cheese to taste

1. Bring 4 quarts of salted water to a boil in a large pot for cooking the pasta.

2. Remove the green stems and the fronds from the fennel. Discard the stems. Chop the feathery fronds and reserve at least 1 tablespoon. Remove any blemished or tough layers from the fennel bulb and trim a thin slice from the base. Cut the bulb in half lengthwise through the base. Lay each half cut side down on a work surface and cut it into very thin slices. Set the fennel aside.

3. Heat the oil in a large sauté pan. Add the garlic and sauté over medium heat until lightly colored, about 1 minute. Stir in the sliced fennel and continue

cooking until the fennel has softened slightly and is just starting to become golden, about 8 minutes.

4. Coarsely chop the tomatoes and add them to the pan along with ½ cup of their packing juice, the salt, and the pepper. Use the back of a spoon to break apart the tomatoes. Simmer gently, stirring occasionally and continuing to break apart the tomatoes, until the fennel has softened completely and the sauce has thickened, about 20 minutes. Taste for salt and pepper and adjust seasonings if necessary.

5. While preparing the sauce, cook and drain the pasta. Toss the hot pasta with the fennel sauce and the chopped fennel fronds. Mix well and transfer portions to warm pasta bowls. Serve immediately with grated cheese passed separately.

Grilled Fennel and Red Onions with Sun-Dried Tomatoes and Basil

● SERVES 4 ●

TIME: 35 minutes

BEST PASTA CHOICE: Fusilli or other short, curly shape

This colorful sauce can hold for up to 60 minutes at room temperature before being tossed with hot pasta. Since this sauce is prepared without heating up the kitchen and allows for some advance work, it is the perfect choice on a hot summer's night when cooking might otherwise seem like a chore. As an accompaniment, serve bruschetta—slices of country bread brushed with olive oil, lightly grilled, and then briefly rubbed with a raw clove of garlic. Eat the bruschetta, Italy's version of garlic bread, as is or top it with slices of fresh tomato and herbs.   *continued*

2 small fennel bulbs (about 1½ pounds)

2 small red onions (about ½ pound)

¼ cup olive oil

Salt and freshly ground black pepper to taste

10 sun-dried tomatoes packed in olive oil,

   drained and cut into thin strips

1 tablespoon balsamic vinegar

¼ cup minced fresh basil leaves

1 pound pasta

Freshly grated Parmesan cheese to taste

1. Light the grill or make a charcoal fire. Bring 4 quarts of salted water to a boil in a large pot for cooking the pasta.

2. Remove and discard the green stems and the fronds from the fennel. Remove any blemished or tough layers from the fennel bulb but do not trim a thin slice from the base. (The base will help keep wedges intact.) Slice the bulb crosswise from top to bottom into ½-inch-thick wedges.

3. Peel the onions. Quarter the onions, making both cuts through the top and bottom ends on the onions. Brush the fennel wedges and red onion quarters with 2 tablespoons oil. Generously season the vegetables with salt and pepper.

4. Use a stiff wire brush to scrape the hot grill clean. Grill the fennel and onions, carefully turning them once, until the vegetables are marked by dark stripes and are tender, about 15 minutes.

5. Briefly cool the grilled vegetables. Cut the fennel and onions into thin strips. In a large bowl, toss the grilled vegetables with the sun-dried tomatoes as well as the remaining 2 tablespoons oil, the vinegar, and the basil. Taste for salt and pepper and adjust seasonings if necessary. (The vegetables can be covered and set aside for up to 1 hour, if desired.)

6. Cook and drain the pasta. Toss the hot pasta with the grilled vegetables. Mix well and transfer portions to warm pasta bowls. Serve immediately with grated cheese passed separately.

Braised Fennel with Raisins and Toasted Pine Nuts

• SERVES 4 •

TIME: 35 minutes

BEST PASTA CHOICE: Spaghetti or other long, very thin shape

The Arab influence on the cuisine of southern Italy, especially Sicily, is quite evident in this recipe with raisins, pine nuts, and cinnamon. To round out the meal, serve a salad of mixed greens with a lemon or other citrus dressing. A room-temperature marinated broccoli salad, preferably with a spicy lemon dressing, would also be a nice complement to this pasta.

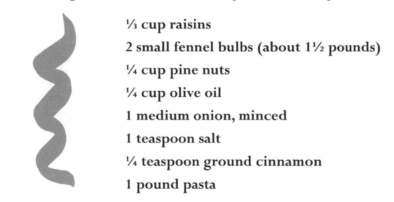

⅓ cup raisins

2 small fennel bulbs (about 1½ pounds)

¼ cup pine nuts

¼ cup olive oil

1 medium onion, minced

1 teaspoon salt

¼ teaspoon ground cinnamon

1 pound pasta

1. Bring 4 quarts of salted water to a boil in a large pot for cooking the pasta.

2. Place the raisins in a small bowl and cover them with boiling water. Soak for 5 minutes. Drain and set aside the raisins.

3. Remove the green stems and fronds from the fennel. Discard the stems. Chop the feathery fronds and reserve at least 1 tablespoon for garnish. Remove any blemished or tough layers from the fennel bulb and trim a thin slice from the base. Cut the bulb in half lengthwise through the base. Lay each half, cut side down, on a work surface and cut it into very thin slices. Set the fennel aside.

continued

4. Set a large sauté pan with a cover over medium heat. Add the pine nuts and toast, shaking the pan occasionally to turn the nuts, until golden brown (about 5 minutes). Do not let the nuts burn. Set the nuts aside.

5. Heat the oil in the empty pan. Add the onions and sauté until softened, about 4 minutes. Add the fennel, raisins, salt, cinnamon, and ½ cup cold water. Cover and cook over medium heat, stirring occasionally, until the fennel softens, about 20 minutes. Taste for salt and adjust seasonings if necessary.

6. While preparing the sauce, cook and drain the pasta, making sure that some water still clings to the noodles. Toss the hot pasta with the fennel sauce and the toasted pine nuts. Mix well and transfer portions to warm bowls. Garnish with chopped fennel fronds and serve immediately.

Braised Fennel and Bitter Greens with Balsamic Vinegar

● SERVES 4 ●

TIME: 30 minutes

BEST PASTA CHOICE: Whole-wheat spaghetti or other long, thin shape

The natural sweetness of fennel makes it a good partner for bitter greens like kale, mustard, turnip, or beet. My first choice is flowering purple or white kale, which lend their bright color as well as a rich, earthy flavor. Although I like to toss this sauce with whole-wheat pasta, it is equally good with regular spaghetti.

1 medium fennel bulb (about 1 pound)
¼ cup olive oil
1 medium onion, minced
¾ pound kale or other bitter greens
(see headnote above)

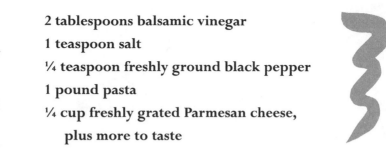

2 tablespoons balsamic vinegar

1 teaspoon salt

¼ teaspoon freshly ground black pepper

1 pound pasta

¼ cup freshly grated Parmesan cheese,
    plus more to taste

1. Bring 4 quarts of salted water to a boil in a large pot for cooking the pasta.

2. Remove the green stems and the fronds from fennel. Discard the stems. Chop the feathery fronds and reserve at least 1 tablespoon for garnish. Remove any blemished or tough layers from the fennel bulb and trim a thin slice from the base. Cut the bulb in half lengthwise through the base. Lay each half cut side down on a work surface and cut it into very thin slices. Set the fennel aside.

3. Heat the oil in a large sauté pan with a cover. Add the onion and sauté over medium heat until translucent, about 5 minutes. Stir in the fennel and cook until the strips begin to turn golden, about 10 minutes.

4. While the fennel is cooking, remove and discard the stems from the greens. Wash the leaves in several changes of cold water. Do not dry the leaves. Roughly chop the greens and add them to the pan along with ½ cup cold water. Cover and simmer over medium-low heat until the fennel is tender and the greens are fully cooked, 12 to 15 minutes.

5. Remove the cover from the pan, stir in the balsamic vinegar, salt, and pepper, and simmer for 1 minute. Taste for salt and pepper and adjust seasonings if necessary.

6. While preparing the sauce, cook and drain the pasta. Toss the hot pasta with the fennel sauce and ¼ cup grated Parmesan. Mix well and transfer portions to warm pasta bowls. Garnish with chopped fennel fronds. Serve immediately with more grated cheese passed separately.

Garlic, Onions, and Shallots

Garlic, onions, shallots, chives, and leeks are members of the botanical genus *Allium,* which is part of the lily family. For culinary purposes, it best to think of chives and scallions as seasonings that can be used like herbs to flavor other vegetables, meats, poultry, and fish. Leeks can be used in the same fashion or they can stand alone, acting as a vegetable. The same can be said of garlic, onions, and shallots. Since leeks are so perishable and unique, they deserve special consideration in their own chapter. The similarities among garlic, onions, and shallots are strong enough to group them together in one chapter.

Alliums have been much in the news for their supposed cancer-fighting properties. For this reason alone it is worth considering them as main ingredients in pasta sauces. While Americans may shy away from their potent flavors and associate this trio with "foreign" or ethnic cooking, all three have a long history in this country. In fact, George Washington once called onions "the most favored food that grows."

The history of garlic, onions, and scallions far predates our nation's first president. Alliums have been a part of the world's cuisines for as long as humans have been writing about food. From ancient China to Rome, garlic, onions, and shallots played a major role in the kitchen before the concept of kitchen even existed. The recipes in this chapter represent their diverse uses in pasta sauces. Their essential place in the Italian pantry is demonstrated by their presence, at least in some small quantity, in most recipes in this book.

• S E L E C T I O N •

Look for heads of garlic that are firm and free of blemishes. The skins should be dry and papery. Depending on the variety, the skins will be bright white or tinged with purple; either variety is excellent. Larger cloves tend to have more moisture in them and are easier to work since less peeling is involved. As garlic ages, green sprouts may emerge from the tips of cloves. Since these sprouts are bitter, cut them out before chopping peeled cloves.

Yellow globe onions are the most common variety in this country (they often come in red mesh plastic sacks) and should be used in recipes in this book unless a specific onion variety, like red onions, is mentioned. When shopping for all onions, look for bright, dry skins without soft spots or mold. The stem ends should be firm; softening means inner layers may be rotten.

Good shallots share the same characteristics with the added caveat to avoid shallots with green shoots protruding from the stem end. Shoots indicate that the shallots are past their prime. Also, try to buy shallots with thin red skins; they have the best flavor. Finally, smell garlic, onions, and shallots before buying them. If they have been properly cured and dried, there should not be a strong odor emanating from them.

• S T O R A G E •

Garlic and onions are "keepers" that can be stored for weeks if not months with little deterioration. Shallots have a slightly shorter shelf-life since they tend to sprout. At the first sign of sprouting, use the shallots. Since there is little moisture in any of these alliums, they can be kept in a cool pantry. Onions and shallots may also be kept in the refrigerator—chilling seems to tame some of their heat. A dry crisper drawer is best. In any case, make sure to keep refrigerated onions and shallots dry. Garlic is best kept at room temperature in an open basket that will allow air to circulate around the cloves and keep them from softening.

• P R E P A R A T I O N •

These vegetables require nothing more than peeling and chopping. It seems that everyone has a "special" method for accomplishing this seemingly simple task. Here are my suggestions. For garlic, use the side of a large chef's knife to gently crush the cloves. This effectively separates the skin from the pulp and makes scraping the skin away from cloves with your fingernails unnecessary. For onions and shallots, trim a thin slice from either end (called the poles on an onion) and make a very shallow incision from one pole to the other. Lift and peel the papery skin and the first layer of flesh, which is often a bit dried out, away from the inner flesh. Shallots can be minced like garlic. To chop an onion, make a cut through the equator of the onion. Slice the onion half in half again, making this second cut parallel to the first cut. Now make a series of cuts that go through the pole of the onion. (These cuts are perpendicular to the first and second cuts.) Holding the onion at the pole, start chopping from one side, making cuts that are perpendicular to the last series of cuts. Altering the size of these last cuts can change the size of the dice. Of course, any peeling and chopping method that works for you can be used.

• U S E   I N   S A U C E S •

While garlic, onions, and/or shallots play a supporting role in most of the recipes in this book, recipes in this chapter show how to use these alliums as the main attraction. For garlic, this can be as simple as sautéing a handful of minced cloves in oil, adding plenty of minced garlic to a raw sauce, or roasting whole cloves in the oven and adding them to a spicy tomato sauce. Onions work best as the main vegetable in a pasta sauce when they have been caramelized to heighten their sweetness. Sliced or chopped onions can be slowly sautéed in oil until golden brown or whole pearl onions can be oven-roasted until caramelized. Shallots can be used in much the same way with one possible addition—pan-frying in a shallow pool of hot oil until crisp and golden brown.

• R E L A T E D   R E C I P E S •

Roasted Beets and Red Onion with Balsamic Vinegar and Rosemary (page 59)
Broccoli Rabe with Caramelized Onions (page 74)
Red Cabbage Smothered with Onions and Red Wine (page 81)
Grilled Fennel and Red Onions with Sun-Dried Tomatoes and Basil (page 137)
Wilted Chicory with Caramelized Onions and Raisins (page 175)
Salsa Cruda with Zucchini, Tomatoes, Red Onion, and Lemon (page 311)

Oven-Roasted Garlic with Tomatoes and Basil

• SERVES 4 •

TIME: 45 minutes

BEST PASTA CHOICE: Linguine or other long, thin shape

This sauce features perhaps the three most basic flavors in Italian cooking, garlic, tomatoes, and basil, but with a twist. Instead of using just a few raw cloves to flavor a basic tomato sauce, the garlic is first roasted to accentuate its sweetness. This cooking method also allows garlic lovers to add two dozen cloves—yes, twenty-four cloves. Choose medium-sized heads of garlic with large, plump cloves. Most cooks roast the whole head of garlic together. Separating the cloves before roasting cuts the cooking time in half.

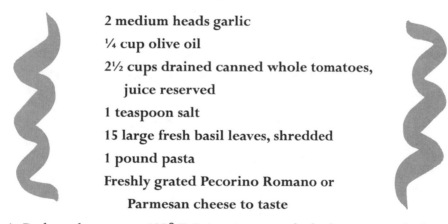

2 medium heads garlic

¼ cup olive oil

2½ cups drained canned whole tomatoes,
    juice reserved

1 teaspoon salt

15 large fresh basil leaves, shredded

1 pound pasta

Freshly grated Pecorino Romano or
    Parmesan cheese to taste

1. Preheat the oven to 400° F. Bring 4 quarts of salted water to a boil in a large pot for cooking the pasta.

2. Remove and discard the papery outer layer from the garlic and break the heads into individual unpeeled cloves. There should be about 24 large, plump cloves. Toss the unpeeled garlic with 1 tablespoon oil. Spread the garlic onto a small baking sheet in a single layer. Bake, turning occasionally, until the skins blister and the garlic becomes soft, about 25 minutes. Cool the garlic for several minutes. Lightly press each clove with the side of a large chef's

continued

knife to loosen the skin. Use your fingers to remove and discard the skin from each clove.

3. Meanwhile, coarsely chop the tomatoes and set them aside with ¾ cup of their packing liquid.

4. Heat the remaining 3 tablespoons oil in a large skillet. Add the tomatoes, their juice, and the salt. Simmer gently, occasionally using the back of a spoon to break apart the tomatoes, until the sauce thickens a bit, about 10 minutes.

5. Add the roasted garlic to the sauce and simmer until the sauce thickens to the proper consistency, about 5 minutes. Stir in the basil. Taste for salt and adjust seasonings if necessary.

6. While preparing the sauce, cook and drain the pasta. Toss the hot pasta with sauce. Mix well and transfer portions to warm pasta bowls. Serve immediately with grated cheese passed separately.

Salsa Verde with Garlic, Herbs, Green Olives, Capers, and Lemon

• SERVES 4 •

TIME: 20 minutes

BEST PASTA CHOICE: Linguine or other long, thin shape

Salsa verde is a piquant, raw green sauce usually served with boiled meats, grilled fish, or steamed vegetables. The combination of garlic, fresh parsley and basil, olives, capers, and lemon juice is equally fine as a simple pasta sauce that can be used much like basil pesto. Although most pestos are quite smooth and can be made in a food processor, salsa verde should be slightly chunky, with small pieces of the individual ingredients still visible. Mincing ingredients by hand (or very careful pulsing in a food processor) is therefore required.

2 medium cloves garlic, minced
⅓ cup minced fresh parsley leaves
2 tablespoons minced fresh basil leaves
2 tablespoons drained capers, minced
8 large green olives
2 tablespoons lemon juice
6 tablespoons olive oil
Salt to taste
1 pound pasta

1. Bring 4 quarts of salted water to a boil in a large pot for cooking the pasta.

2. Combine the minced garlic, parsley, basil, and capers in a medium bowl.

3. Pit and mince the olives. There should be about ¼ cup of minced olives. Stir the olives and lemon juice into the bowl with the other ingredients.

4. Slowly whisk the oil into the bowl with the minced ingredients. Taste the sauce and add salt. (If the capers and olives are very salty, you may need very little.)

5. While preparing the sauce, cook and drain the pasta, making sure that some liquid still clings to the noodles. Toss the hot pasta with the sauce. Mix well and transfer portions to warm pasta bowls. Serve immediately.

Garlic Sautéed in Olive Oil with Parsley and Lemon

• SERVES 4 •

TIME: 20 minutes

BEST PASTA CHOICE: Spaghetti or other long, very thin shape

This combination is a takeoff on the classic Italian sauce called *aglio e olio*, or garlic and oil. This variation, which adds a splash of lemon juice, is standard late-night fare in my house since I invariably have all of the ingredients on hand and since the sauce can be made in the time it takes water to boil. One caveat: Do not let the garlic burn or it will become bitter. Although parsley is my first choice (because of its mild, clean flavor), any fresh herb can be used to give the sauce some color. Also, feel free to use hot red pepper flakes instead of black pepper for more heat.

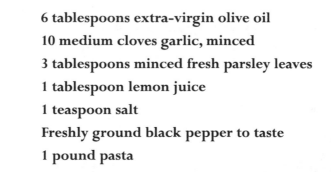

6 tablespoons extra-virgin olive oil

10 medium cloves garlic, minced

3 tablespoons minced fresh parsley leaves

1 tablespoon lemon juice

1 teaspoon salt

Freshly ground black pepper to taste

1 pound pasta

1. Bring 4 quarts of salted water to a boil in a large pot for cooking the pasta.

2. Heat the oil in a skillet large enough to hold the cooked pasta. Add the garlic and sauté over medium-low heat until richly colored but not burned, about 5 minutes. The garlic must be golden (or it will be raw-tasting) but should not be brown.

3. Stir the parsley, lemon juice, salt, and pepper into the oil. Cook for another 30 seconds or so. Remove the pan from the heat to prevent the garlic from overcooking.

4. While preparing the sauce, cook and drain the pasta, making sure that some liquid still clings to the noodles. Toss the hot pasta into the skillet with the sauce. Mix well and transfer portions to warm pasta bowls. Serve immediately.

Roasted Pearl Onions and Carrots with Thyme

● SERVES 4 ●

TIME: 55 minutes

BEST PASTA CHOICE: Penne or other short, tubular shape

Tiny pearl onions come in various hues—white, yellow, and purple—which can be used together in this sauce. The vegetables are roasted with carrots until nicely browned, and then tossed with pasta for a simple yet rich sauce. A final splash of olive oil moistens the pasta, while pungent thyme marries beautifully with the roasted vegetables. Although the total time for this dish is relatively long, it is remarkably easy to prepare and most of the time is spent waiting for the vegetables to cook in the oven. Serve with a steamed green vegetable or a brightly colored salad.

60 pearl onions (about 1 pound)
8 medium carrots (about 1 pound)
6 tablespoons olive oil
Salt and freshly ground black pepper to taste
1 pound pasta
1 tablespoon minced fresh thyme leaves

1. Preheat the oven to 400° F. Bring 4 quarts of salted water to a boil in a large pot for cooking the pasta.

2. Peel the papery outer skins from the pearl onions and set the onions aside. Peel the carrots and cut them into 2-inch lengths. Thin lengths from

continued

the root end can be halved; thicker pieces should be quartered or cut into eighths. The cut carrots should be between ¼ and ½ inch thick and 2 inches long.

3. Place the onions and carrots in a shallow baking pan large enough to hold them comfortably in a single layer. Toss the vegetables with 2 tablespoons oil and season generously with salt and pepper. Bake the onions and carrots, turning several times, until lightly browned and tender, about 35 minutes.

4. While the vegetables are roasting, cook and drain the pasta, making sure that some water still clings to the noodles. Toss the hot pasta with the roasted vegetables, the remaining 4 tablespoons oil, and the thyme. Transfer portions to warm pasta bowls and serve immediately.

Caramelized Onions with White Wine, Cream, and Fresh Herbs

● SERVES 4 ●

TIME: 50 minutes

BEST PASTA CHOICE: Fettuccine or other long, wide shape

Chopped onions are slow-cooked to bring out their sweetness, which is essential in this rich, luscious sauce. Once the onions are a deep golden color with crisp, brown edges, the pan is deglazed with some white wine that is neither overly dry nor overly sweet. Heavy cream is then added along with a handful of fresh herbs. Choose a mixture of mild and assertive herbs, including parsley, basil, sage, thyme, oregano, and marjoram. A final sprinkling of Parmesan cheese crowns this elegant pasta dish. Serve as a first course for a formal dinner or just with salad greens for a special weeknight dinner.

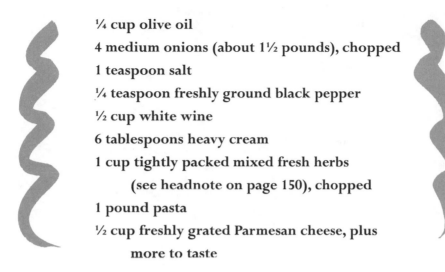

¼ **cup olive oil**

4 medium onions (about 1½ pounds), chopped

1 teaspoon salt

¼ **teaspoon freshly ground black pepper**

½ **cup white wine**

6 tablespoons heavy cream

1 cup tightly packed mixed fresh herbs
    (see headnote on page 150), chopped

1 pound pasta

½ **cup freshly grated Parmesan cheese, plus**
    more to taste

1. Bring 4 quarts of salted water to a boil in a large pot for cooking the pasta.

2. Heat the oil in a large skillet. Add the onions and sauté over medium-low heat, stirring occasionally, until golden brown, 35 to 40 minutes. If the onions start to burn, lower the heat. The onions should cook very slowly.

3. Season the caramelized onions with the salt and pepper. Raise the heat to medium and add the wine. Simmer, scraping the bottom of the pan to loosen any brown bits, until the aroma of the alcohol fades, about 3 minutes.

4. Add the cream and herbs to the pan. Bring the sauce to a boil and simmer until it has thickened slightly, about 1 minute. Taste for salt and pepper and adjust seasonings if necessary.

5. While preparing the sauce, cook and drain the pasta. Toss the hot pasta with the onion sauce and ½ cup grated Parmesan. Mix well and transfer portions to warm pasta bowls. Serve immediately with more grated cheese passed separately.

Caramelized Vidalia Onions with Black Olives and Rosemary

• SERVES 4 •

TIME: 35 minutes

BEST PASTA CHOICE: Fusilli or other short, curly shape

Sweet Vidalia onions are shipped from Georgia farms to supermarkets across the country in spring, a sure sign that warmer weather is here to stay. Other sweet varieties like Walla Wallas (from Washington) and Mauis (from Hawaii) are good candidates for caramelization—slow-cooking in oil that brings out the sweetness in onions. Kalamata olives (any brined black olives can be substituted) and rosemary give this sauce its Mediterranean character. The pasta calls out for grilled herb bread as an accompaniment. Round out the meal with asparagus that have been steamed, cooled to room temperature, and dressed with an assertive vinaigrette.

6 tablespoons olive oil

4 medium Vidalia or other sweet white onions
   (about 2 pounds), sliced crosswise
   into thin rings

15 large black olives such as Kalamatas
   (about 4 ounces), pitted and chopped

2 teaspoons minced fresh rosemary leaves

1 teaspoon salt

¼ teaspoon freshly ground black pepper

1 pound pasta

1. Bring 4 quarts of salted water to a boil in a large pot for cooking the pasta.

2. Heat the oil in a very large skillet. Add the onions and sauté over medium heat, stirring occasionally, until golden, 25 to 30 minutes. The onions should

be richly colored without any traces of burning or browning. If at any time the onions seem to be cooking too quickly, lower the heat.

3. Add the olives, rosemary, salt, and pepper to the skillet and continue cooking until the olives are warmed through, about 2 minutes. Taste for salt and pepper and adjust seasonings if necessary.

4. While preparing the sauce, cook and drain the pasta, making sure that plenty of water is still dripping from the noodles. Toss the hot pasta with the onion sauce. Mix well and transfer portions to warm pasta bowls. Serve immediately.

Crispy Fried Shallots with Chives and Parmesan

● SERVES 4 ●

TIME: 20 minutes

BEST PASTA CHOICE: Farfalle or other small shape with crevices

This sauce takes its cues from the crispy fried shallot and leek garnishes that have become so popular in restaurants in recent years. Here, thinly sliced shallots are pan-fried until crisp to highlight their sweetness and mellow their sometimes strong flavor. The shallot-flavored oil is used to coat the drained pasta, while chives and a sprinkling of Parmesan add some color and creaminess.

20 large shallots (about ¾ pound)
½ cup olive oil
2 tablespoons snipped fresh chives
1 teaspoon salt
¼ teaspoon freshly ground black pepper
1 pound pasta
Freshly grated Parmesan cheese to taste

continued

1. Bring 4 quarts of salted water to a boil in a large pot for cooking the pasta.

2. Peel the shallots and slice them lengthwise into very thin pieces.

3. Heat the oil in a medium skillet until quite hot but not yet smoking. Add the shallots and fry, turning them often, until nicely browned, about 6 minutes. Do not let the shallots burn. Lift the fried shallots from the oil with a slotted spoon and transfer them to a plate lined with paper towels.

4. Remove the skillet from the heat and cool the oil for several minutes. Stir the chives, salt, and pepper into the oil.

5. While preparing the shallots, cook and drain the pasta, making sure that some liquid still clings to the noodles. Toss the hot pasta with the seasoned oil and the fried shallots. Mix well and transfer portions to warm pasta bowls. Serve immediately with grated cheese passed separately.

Green Beans

Fresh green beans have enjoyed tremendous popularity both in America and Europe for more than a century. Although still referred to as string beans by many cooks, this term is now outdated since most green beans are bred to be stringless. While our grandmothers had to spend time removing the tough, fibrous string that ran the length of each bean, modern plant breeding has made this step unnecessary.

Today, most green beans sold in supermarkets are actually called "snap" or "pole" beans. The former term refers to the fact that fresh beans should snap and appear juicy when broken; the latter a reference to how bean plants run up poles in summer gardens. These green beans are light green in color and are about as thick as a regular school pencil.

In addition to the ubiquitous snap and pole beans, many markets stock very thin *haricots verts* (French for green beans), a darker green bean that is quite thin and delicate. The season for these beans usually lasts just a few weeks in the summer. The French prefer this variety, and it is grown in small quantities in this country. The term "Frenched" green beans refers to regular pole beans that have been split lengthwise to imitate the thinness of haricots verts. Unfortunately, "Frenched" pole beans cannot duplicate the rich, dark color and intense bean flavor of tender, young haricots verts.

• SELECTION •

Look for firm beans that will snap rather than bend. Avoid soggy beans or those with brown spots. Also, avoid extremely thick beans that are swollen by mealy, tasteless seeds. I prefer young, thin beans. They are usually more tender and have a sweeter, more intense flavor than thicker, older beans. In any case, choose beans of equal length and width so that the cooking time will be the same for the entire batch.

• S T O R A G E •

Green beans begin to lose their freshness and sweet flavor almost as soon as they are picked. Thicker, tougher beans won't be harmed by a few days in the refrigerator, but haricots verts and other thin, fresh beans should be used within a day or two of purchase.

• P R E P A R A T I O N •

While old-fashioned green beans had to be "stringed," modern varieties require only a simple trimming of the ends. This can be done with a small knife or with your hands—simply squeeze the thin ends between your thumb and forefinger to remove them. While thin haricots verts can be left as is in many sauces (they are usually only 3 inches long and quite thin), most green bean varieties should be cut into 1-inch lengths. This not only shortens cooking time but makes the beans easier to incorporate into pasta sauces.

• U S E   I N   S A U C E S •

Green beans take to a number of cooking methods. For the quickest results, beans can be either steamed or blanched just until tender and then tossed with other ingredients—anything from pesto to raw chopped tomatoes—to make a quick sauce. Haricots verts are best prepared in this manner. Older, thicker beans take well to braising in wine, tomato sauce, or other flavorful liquid. Cooked this way, beans will require a fair amount of time to soften. Unless otherwise indicated, cooking times in recipes are for regular green beans. Haricots verts will be tender in less time, as will especially fresh beans, so taste beans as they cook and do not let them become mushy.

• R E L A T E D   R E C I P E S •

Salsa Primavera with Tomatoes, Mushrooms, and Mixed Vegetables (page 298)

Steamed Green Beans with Basil and Gorgonzola

● SERVES 4 ●

TIME: 20 minutes

BEST PASTA CHOICE: Penne or other short, tubular shape

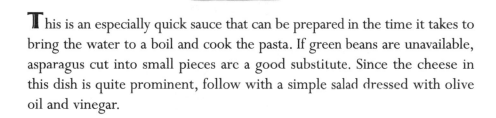

This is an especially quick sauce that can be prepared in the time it takes to bring the water to a boil and cook the pasta. If green beans are unavailable, asparagus cut into small pieces arc a good substitute. Since the cheese in this dish is quite prominent, follow with a simple salad dressed with olive oil and vinegar.

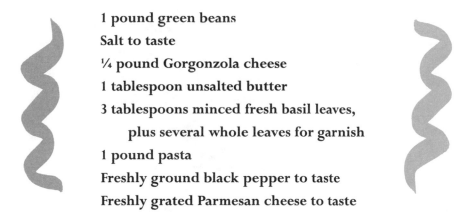

1 pound green beans

Salt to taste

¼ pound Gorgonzola cheese

1 tablespoon unsalted butter

3 tablespoons minced fresh basil leaves,
    plus several whole leaves for garnish

1 pound pasta

Freshly ground black pepper to taste

Freshly grated Parmesan cheese to taste

1. Bring 4 quarts of salted water to a boil in a large pot for cooking the pasta.

2. Bring several quarts of water to a boil in a medium saucepan. Snap the ends from the beans and cut them into ½-inch pieces. Add the beans and salt to taste to the boiling water. Cook until the beans are tender but not mushy, 2 to 3 minutes. Drain and set aside the beans.

3. Dice the Gorgonzola and butter and set them aside in a small bowl along with the minced basil.

continued

4. Cook and drain pasta. Return the pasta to the empty pot along with some of the cooking water still dripping from the noodles. Place the pot over low heat and stir in the reserved beans and the cheese mixture. Add salt (use sparingly if the cheese is salty) and pepper to taste along with a few gratings of fresh Parmesan. As soon as the Gorgonzola has melted, transfer portions to warm pasta bowls.

5. Garnish each bowl with one or two whole basil leaves. Serve immediately with more grated Parmesan passed separately.

Green Beans with Bell Peppers, White Wine, and Tarragon

• SERVES 4 •

TIME: 25 minutes

BEST PASTA CHOICE: Farfalle or other small shape with crevices

Green beans are simmered in white wine and then tossed with thin strips of bell pepper for this quick sauce. Choose colorful peppers—one red and one yellow would be my first choice. Other fresh herbs, especially basil or mint, can be substituted for the tarragon.

1 pound green beans

2 medium bell peppers (about ¾ pound)

¼ cup olive oil

1 medium onion, minced

1 teaspoon salt

½ **teaspoon freshly ground black pepper**
½ **cup dry white wine**
2 tablespoons minced fresh tarragon leaves
1 pound pasta
Freshly grated Parmesan cheese to taste

1. Bring 4 quarts of salted water to a boil in a large pot for cooking the pasta.

2. Snap the ends from the green beans and cut them into 1-inch lengths. Core, halve, and seed the peppers. Slice the peppers into 1 by ¼-inch strips. Set the vegetables aside.

3. Heat the oil in a large sauté pan with a cover. Add the onion and sauté over medium heat until golden, about 7 minutes.

4. Add the green beans and cook for 2 minutes. Season the beans with the salt and pepper. Add the wine and bring the liquid to a boil. Reduce the heat to medium-low, cover, and cook until beans are almost crisp-tender, about 7 minutes.

5. Uncover the pan, add the bell peppers and tarragon, and raise the heat to medium. Cook until the peppers and beans are tender, about 4 minutes. Taste for salt and pepper and adjust seasonings if necessary.

6. While preparing the sauce, cook and drain the pasta, making sure that some water still clings to the noodles. Toss the hot pasta with the vegetables. Mix well and transfer portions to warm pasta bowls. Serve immediately with grated cheese passed separately.

Braised Green Beans with Tomatoes and Goat Cheese

• SERVES 4 •

TIME: 45 minutes

BEST PASTA CHOICE: Fusilli or other short, curly shape

Slow-cooking in tomato sauce makes even the dullest supermarket beans sweet and tender. A swirl of goat cheese adds a pleasant tanginess and thickens the sauce, which otherwise would be too watery. Although it lacks the punch of good goat cheese, ricotta cheese may be used as a substitute. Serve plenty of bread to soak up every drop of the sauce.

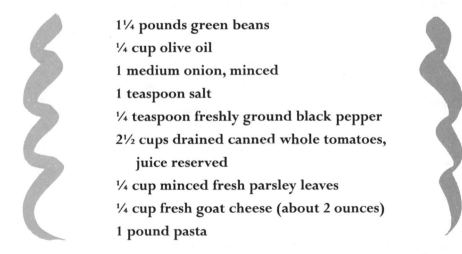

1¼ pounds green beans

¼ cup olive oil

1 medium onion, minced

1 teaspoon salt

¼ teaspoon freshly ground black pepper

2½ cups drained canned whole tomatoes, juice reserved

¼ cup minced fresh parsley leaves

¼ cup fresh goat cheese (about 2 ounces)

1 pound pasta

1. Bring 4 quarts of salted water to a boil in a large pot for cooking the pasta.

2. Snap the ends from the beans and cut them into 1-inch lengths. Set the beans aside.

3. Heat the oil in a large skillet. Add the onion and sauté over medium heat until translucent, about 5 minutes. Add the beans, salt, and pepper and cook until the beans lose their raw taste, about 5 minutes.

4. Coarsely chop the tomatoes. Add them to the pan along with 1 cup of their packing juice. Use the back of a spoon to break apart the tomatoes. Cover the pan and simmer gently, stirring occasionally, until the beans are quite tender and the sauce has thickened slightly, about 30 minutes.

5. Remove the pan from the heat and add the parsley and goat cheese. Stir until the cheese has melted into the sauce. Taste for salt and pepper and adjust seasonings if necessary.

6. While preparing the sauce, cook and drain the pasta. Toss the hot pasta with the green bean sauce. Mix well and transfer portions to warm pasta bowls. Serve immediately.

Steamed Green Beans with Roasted Potatoes and Pesto

• SERVES 4 •

TIME: 50 minutes

BEST PASTA CHOICE: Penne or other short, tubular shape

The city of Genoa is known the world over for pesto sauce. Green beans and potatoes are boiled, tossed with pesto, and served as a side dish in many local restaurants. For this pasta sauce, I have opted not to boil the beans and potatoes together—the beans often become limp when boiled and the potatoes can become watery. Instead the beans are steamed (which helps retain more nutrients than boiling) and the potatoes are roasted. In place of the traditional pine nuts, this rough pesto sauce is made with walnuts, which have a natural affinity for green beans. Note that the pesto (as well as the pasta sauce) does not contain cheese. Follow this pasta with a tomato salad.

continued

1 pound small red potatoes

½ cup olive oil

Salt and freshly ground black pepper to taste

2 cups loosely packed fresh basil leaves

¼ cup shelled walnut pieces

2 medium cloves garlic, peeled

1 pound green beans

1 pound pasta

1. Preheat the oven to 400° F. Bring 4 quarts of salted water to a boil in a large pot for cooking the pasta.

2. Scrub the potatoes under cold, running water but do not peel them. Cut the potatoes into ½-inch dice. Place the potatoes in a baking dish large enough to hold them in a single layer. Toss them with 2 tablespoons oil and season generously with salt and pepper. Roast until the potatoes are crisp and light brown in color, about 40 minutes.

3. Meanwhile, place the basil, walnuts, and garlic in the work bowl of a food processor. Process the ingredients into a rough puree, stopping once to scrape down the sides of the bowl. With the motor running, slowly pour the remaining 6 tablespoons oil through the feed tube and process until smooth. Scrape the sauce into a large bowl. Season generously with salt and pepper.

4. Snap the ends from the beans and cut them into 1-inch lengths. Steam the beans until tender, 4 to 8 minutes depending on their freshness and size. Toss the steamed beans with the pesto. Taste for salt and pepper and adjust seasonings if necessary. Set the beans aside.

5. While the potatoes are finishing up, cook and drain the pasta, making sure that some water still clings to the noodles. Toss the hot pasta with the green beans and the roasted potatoes. Mix well and transfer portions to warm pasta bowls. Serve immediately.

Haricots Verts with Raw Tomatoes and Mint

● SERVES 4 ●

TIME: 20 minutes

BEST PASTA CHOICE: Linguine or other long, thin shape

B lanched French green beans (haricots verts) are tossed with raw tomatoes for a quick summer sauce that is quite low in fat. Although thick green beans can be used in this dish, delicate haricots verts should be your first choice. (If thicker beans are used, cut them into 1-inch lengths before cooking.) Mint and lemon are refreshing accents to the sauce, but other fresh herbs like basil or tarragon would be equally appropriate.

¾ pound haricots verts

Salt to taste, plus 1 teaspoon

4 medium ripe tomatoes (about 1½ pounds)

3 tablespoons olive oil

1½ tablespoons lemon juice

2 tablespoons minced fresh mint leaves

1 pound pasta

1. Bring 4 quarts of salted water to a boil in a large pot for cooking the pasta.

2. Bring several quarts of water to a boil in a medium saucepan. Snap the ends from the beans. Add the beans and salt to taste to the boiling water. Cook until the beans are just tender, about 2 minutes. Drain the beans and cool them slightly.

3. Core and cut the tomatoes into ½-inch cubes. Place the tomatoes in a large bowl. Add the oil, lemon juice, mint, and 1 teaspoon salt and toss gently. Add the beans and mix gently. Taste for salt and adjust seasonings if necessary. *continued*

4. While preparing the sauce, cook and drain the pasta. Toss the hot pasta with the green bean sauce. Mix well and transfer portions to pasta bowls. Serve immediately.

Steamed Green Beans with Double Mushroom Sauce

• SERVES 4 •

TIME: 30 minutes

BEST PASTA CHOICE: Penne or other short, tubular shape

Green beans acquire a wonderful woodsy quality when added to a sauce with porcini and cultivated white mushrooms. This preparation is best for less-than-perfect beans, especially at the end of the season when the weather is becoming cool and thoughts turn to heavier sauces.

1 ounce dried porcini mushrooms

1 pound green beans

½ pound fresh white mushrooms

2 tablespoons olive oil

2 tablespoons unsalted butter

2 medium cloves garlic, minced

1 teaspoon salt

½ teaspoon freshly ground black pepper

2 tablespoons minced fresh parsley leaves

1 pound pasta

⅓ cup freshly grated Parmesan cheese,
    plus more to taste

1. Bring 4 quarts of salted water to a boil in a large pot for cooking the pasta.

2. Place the porcini in a small bowl and cover them with 1 cup boiling water. Soak for 20 minutes. Carefully lift the mushrooms from the liquid and pick through them to remove any foreign matter. Roughly chop the mushrooms and set them aside. Strain the soaking liquid through a colander lined with paper towels. Set the chopped mushrooms and strained liquid aside separately.

3. Snap the ends from the beans and cut them into 1-inch lengths. Steam the beans until crisp-tender, about 4 minutes. Set the steamed beans aside.

4. Wipe the fresh mushrooms with a paper towel to loosen and remove any dirt. Trim and discard a thin slice from the stem end of each mushroom. Thinly slice the mushrooms and set them aside.

5. Heat the oil and butter in a large skillet. Add the garlic and sauté over medium heat until golden, about 2 minutes. Add the sliced fresh mushrooms and cook, stirring occasionally, until golden brown, about 5 minutes. Add the chopped porcini, salt, and pepper and continue cooking for 3 minutes more.

6. Add the green beans and ½ cup of the reserved porcini soaking liquid to the pan. Simmer for several minutes or until the beans are completely tender. Stir in the parsley. Taste for salt and pepper and adjust seasonings if necessary.

7. While preparing the sauce, cook and drain the pasta. Toss the hot pasta with the green bean sauce and ⅓ cup Parmesan. Add as much of the remaining porcini soaking liquid as needed to moisten the pasta. Transfer portions to warm pasta bowls. Serve immediately with more grated cheese passed separately.

Buttered Haricots Verts with Pine Nuts and Parmesan

● SERVES 4 ●

TIME: 20 minutes

BEST PASTA CHOICE: Penne or other short, tubular shape

Tender, sweet haricots verts are the only kind of green beans suitable for this simple preparation. This sauce depends on butter, which brings out the sweetness in the beans in a way that olive oil cannot. Toasted pine nuts and a sprinkling of cheese reinforce the rich quality of this extravagant but easy-to-prepare sauce.

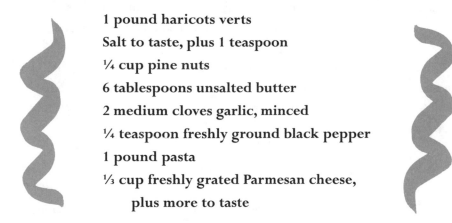

1 pound haricots verts

Salt to taste, plus 1 teaspoon

¼ cup pine nuts

6 tablespoons unsalted butter

2 medium cloves garlic, minced

¼ teaspoon freshly ground black pepper

1 pound pasta

⅓ cup freshly grated Parmesan cheese,
    plus more to taste

1. Bring 4 quarts of salted water to a boil in a large pot for cooking the pasta.

2. Bring several quarts of water to a boil in a medium saucepan. Snap the ends from the beans. Add the beans and salt to taste to the boiling water. Cook until the beans are just tender, about 2 minutes. Drain and set aside the beans.

3. Set a large skillet over medium heat. Add the pine nuts and toast, shaking the pan occasionally to turn them, until golden brown (about 5 minutes). Do not let the nuts burn. Set the nuts aside.

4. Add the butter to the empty skillet. When the butter foams, add the garlic and sauté over medium heat until golden, about 2 minutes. Stir in the beans, nuts, 1 teaspoon salt, and pepper and heat through for several minutes or until the beans are completely tender.

5. While preparing the sauce, cook and drain the pasta, reserving ¼ cup of the cooking liquid. Toss the hot pasta with the green beans, ⅓ cup grated cheese, and the reserved cooking water. Mix well and transfer portions to warm pasta bowls. Serve immediately with more grated cheese passed separately.

Greens

Vegetables in this section have two things in common—all are leafy and all are green. Leafy greens include everything from Swiss chard and escarole to collards and turnip greens. Miscellaneous leafy greens, many of which can be used interchangeably in the following recipes, are the focus here. Greens that are especially important in the Italian kitchen, like broccoli rabe and spinach, merit their own entries. However, they too can be used in many of the following recipes.

Greens divide themselves into two broad categories, which my friend and colleague Pam Anderson describes as tender and tough. Tender greens contain a high moisture content and generally possess a mild earthy or mineral flavor. Because of their high moisture content, these greens can be wilted in a covered pan with just the water that clings to the washed leaves. On the other hand, tough greens are much drier, often have a more assertive or bitter flavor, and must be blanched before further cooking or eating.

The tender greens category includes spinach as well as beet greens, Swiss chard, and such lettuce-like greens as escarole and chicory. Beet greens are the red-veined leafy tops of beets and are usually sold still attached to the roots. For more information on these greens, see the entry on beets on page 55. Swiss chard is a relative of the beet. In fact, it is a cold-weather variety that does not produce a large bulb. There are two varieties of Swiss chard; one has white stalks and veins, the other red stalks and veins. Red Swiss chard is almost identical to beet greens, only larger. All three greens—beet greens, red chard, and white chard—can be used interchangeably or as a substitute for spinach.

The lettuce-like tender greens such as escarole are different in appearance from chard and spinach but can be prepared in the same fashion. These lighter greens grow in heads, not on stalks or stems. However, since they are moisture-rich they do not require precooking in boiling water. Although Americans may find it odd to treat something that looks like lettuce as a vegetable, Italians are particularly fond of escarole in soups, pastas, and rice dishes. Supermarket-issue iceberg lettuce may not be suitable for cooking, but these hearty lettuces have enough character and flavor to stand up to garlic, onions, and other assertive ingredients.

Tough greens, such as kale, mustard greens, collards, turnip greens, and dandelion greens, usually require a two-step cooking process whether they are to be eaten as a side dish or incorporated into a pasta sauce. Tough stems and veins are first removed and the leaves are blanched until tender. Cooking in boiling water also tames the bitter flavor in these greens. The greens are drained, chopped if desired, and then added to pasta sauces. This final step is often as simple as sautéing partially cooked greens in olive oil and garlic and then tossing them with pasta.

Kale is a member of the cabbage family and comes in flowering and non-flowering varieties. Nonflowering kale has thick, lightly ruffled leaves that are uniformly dark green. The leaves on flowering varieties are generally more frilly and are tinged with either purple or white. Purple kale is my first choice, if only for its dramatic color, but all three can be used interchangeably.

Mustard greens, turnip greens, and collards have smaller leaves that grow on thick, woody stems, which must be discarded before cooking. All three are fall-to-spring vegetables that require cooler temperatures for proper growth. Dandelion greens, larger versions of the leaves that surround the yellow flowers that dot summer lawns, are a bit milder in flavor and softer in texture than these other tough greens. While kale or collards might need 5 or 7 minutes in boiling water to soften, dandelion greens are ready in 2 minutes.

• S E L E C T I O N •

Color is a good way to choose your greens. Look for greens that are bright green, not dull or yellow. Greens should not be limp or show signs of decay.

Look for young greens with thin stems (there will be less waste) with the roots still attached—a good indication of freshness. Like spinach, kale sometimes comes packaged in cellophane. The stems have been mostly removed and the leaves are washed and torn, making this product a nice convenience since stemming and washing is invariably tedious.

• STORAGE •

Store greens in a plastic bag in the refrigerator to prolong freshness for several days. It's fine if the leaves are slightly damp, but they should not be soaking wet. Do not wash greens until you are ready to cook them.

• PREPARATION •

Stemming and washing greens can be a tiresome chore, but this is absolutely necessary. Tender greens like Swiss chard and escarole have tough stems that can be snapped off by hand at the point where the leaf starts and discarded. Tougher greens like collards require more work. The stems can be trimmed and discarded but the leaves themselves are usually divided by a tough central vein, which is in fact a continuation of the stem. Once the stem has been removed, I usually tear off the leafy part on either side of the central vein and drop the leaves into a bowl of cold water. The bare vein can then be discarded.

Since greens grow close to the earth, they are usually covered with soil. Kale packed in plastic bags may be relatively clean, but should still be subjected to at least one soaking. Dirtier greens may need the process of covering leaves with cold water, swishing the greens in the water with your hands, and draining repeated several times or until no grit appears on the bottom of the bowl. Washed greens should be left damp; the liquid that clings to them is essential if the leaves are going to be wilted in a covered pan and cannot hurt greens that will be blanched.

Large leaves can be rolled into long cigar shapes and sliced crosswise into thin strips or torn by hand into bite-sized pieces. Cooking will cause tender greens like Swiss chard and escarole to shrink much more than tougher greens like kale, so slice or tear leaves with that in mind.

• USE IN SAUCES •

G reens like Swiss chard, escarole, chicory, beet greens, and spinach are tender and have enough moisture in their leaves to be cooked in a deep covered pan on the stove. I usually add the damp leaves to oil that has been flavored with garlic or maybe hot red pepper flakes. Extra moisture, provided by wine or the juice from canned tomatoes, will speed the cooking process. Tougher greens like kale, collards, turnip greens, mustard greens, and dandelion greens must first be blanched in boiling water. I often drain tough greens just before they are tender and finish cooking them in a skillet filled with oil and seasonings. Blanching also helps tame the flavor of assertive greens and makes them better suited to use in pasta sauces.

• RELATED RECIPES •

Boiled Beets and Wilted Beet Greens with Garlic and Lemon (page 58)
Braised Fennel and Bitter Greens with Balsamic Vinegar (page 140)
Sautéed Red Peppers with Escarole and Garlic (page 235)

See also the recipes in the Broccoli Rabe and Spinach chapters.

Red Swiss Chard with Wild Mushrooms and Sherry

● SERVES 4 ●

TIME: 30 minutes

BEST PASTA CHOICE: Penne or other short, tubular shape

Tender red Swiss chard leaves make a sauce that looks as good as it tastes. Choose a firm, wild-mushroom variety like cremini or shiitake for this sauce. This dish can be made with beet greens (their red veins make them the perfect substitute) or with white Swiss chard or even spinach.

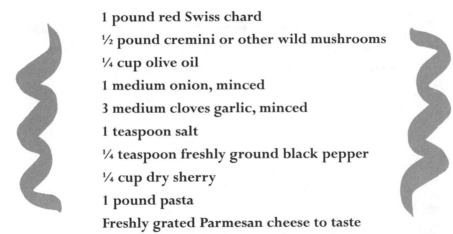

1 pound red Swiss chard

½ pound cremini or other wild mushrooms

¼ cup olive oil

1 medium onion, minced

3 medium cloves garlic, minced

1 teaspoon salt

¼ teaspoon freshly ground black pepper

¼ cup dry sherry

1 pound pasta

Freshly grated Parmesan cheese to taste

1. Bring 4 quarts of salted water to a boil in a large pot for cooking the pasta.

2. Trim and discard the tough stems from the Swiss chard. Wash the chard in a large bowl of cold water, changing the water several times until no sand appears on the bottom of the bowl. Slice the chard leaves crosswise into ½-inch-wide strips and set them aside.

3. Wipe the mushrooms with a paper towel to loosen and remove any dirt. Trim and discard a thin slice from the stem end of each mushroom. Thinly slice the mushrooms and set them aside.

4. Heat the oil in a deep pot or Dutch oven with a cover. Add the onion and sauté over medium heat until translucent, about 5 minutes. Add the garlic and cook until lightly colored, about 1 minute.

5. Add the mushrooms to the pan and cook, stirring occasionally, until they have wilted a bit and turned golden brown, about 6 minutes. Season the mushrooms with salt and pepper. Add the sherry and cook just until the aroma of the alcohol fades, about 2 minutes.

6. Add the Swiss chard to the pot and stir to coat the leaves with the oil. Cover and cook, stirring occasionally, until the Swiss chard has wilted, about 6 minutes. Taste for salt and pepper and adjust seasonings if necessary.

7. While preparing the sauce, cook and drain the pasta. Toss the hot pasta with the Swiss chard sauce. Mix well and transfer portions to warm pasta bowls. Serve immediately with grated cheese passed separately.

Wilted Swiss Chard with Garlic and Ricotta Salata Cheese

• SERVES 4 •

TIME: 20 minutes

BEST PASTA CHOICE: Linguine or other long, thin shape

Ricotta salata is a pressed and lightly salted sheep's milk cheese. This bright white cheese is fairly moist with a texture that is akin to feta cheese and just dry enough to stand up to the grater. Pecorino Romano, Italy's most famous sheep's milk cheese, is much drier but can be used in its place. The flavor will be slightly different.

continued

2 pounds Swiss chard
¼ cup olive oil
3 medium cloves garlic, peeled
½ teaspoon hot red pepper flakes or to taste
1 teaspoon salt
1 pound pasta
⅓ cup grated ricotta salata or
    Pecorino Romano cheese

1. Bring 4 quarts of salted water to a boil in a large pot for cooking the pasta.

2. Trim and discard the tough stems from the Swiss chard. Wash the chard in a large bowl of cold water, changing the water several times or until no sand appears on the bottom of the bowl. Slice the chard leaves crosswise into ½-inch-wide strips and set them aside.

3. Heat the oil in a deep pot or Dutch oven with a cover. Add the garlic and sauté over medium heat, turning the cloves occasionally, until golden brown, about 5 minutes. Use a slotted spoon to remove and discard the garlic.

4. Add the hot red pepper flakes to the pot and cook for 30 seconds to release their flavor. Add the damp Swiss chard and salt. Stir several times to coat the leaves with the oil. Cover and cook, stirring occasionally, until the chard has completely wilted, about 5 minutes. Taste for salt and hot pepper and adjust seasonings if necessary.

5. While preparing the sauce, cook and drain the pasta, reserving ⅓ cup of the cooking liquid. Toss the hot pasta with the Swiss chard sauce, the reserved cooking liquid, and the grated cheese. Mix well until the cheese has softened, about 30 seconds. Transfer portions to warm pasta bowls and serve immediately.

Wilted Chicory with Caramelized Onions and Raisins

• SERVES 4 •

TIME: 40 minutes

BEST PASTA CHOICE: Linguine or other long, thin shape

This dish is inspired by the cooking of southern Italy where wild bitter greens like chicory are often paired with sweet elements like caramelized onions and raisins to make gutsy pasta sauces. While other bitter greens like collards and mustard greens must be parboiled before use in pasta dishes, chicory has enough natural moisture to wilt in a covered pan without any precooking.

3 large onions (about 1½ pounds)

¼ cup olive oil

2 teaspoons sugar

1 large head chicory (about 1 pound)

⅓ cup dry sherry or dry white wine

½ cup raisins

1 teaspoon salt

½ teaspoon freshly ground black pepper

1 pound pasta

Freshly grated Parmesan cheese to taste

1. Bring 4 quarts of salted water to a boil in a large pot for cooking the pasta.

2. Peel and cut the onions in half through the top and bottom ends. Lay the halves flat side down on a work surface and slice into thin half circles. Heat the oil in a deep pot or Dutch oven with a cover. Add the onions and cook,

continued

stirring occasionally, over medium heat until golden, about 20 minutes. Stir in the sugar and continue cooking until the onions are a rich brown color, about 5 minutes more. If at any time the onions start to burn, lower the heat.

3. While the onions are cooking, discard any wilted or bruised chicory leaves. Trim and discard the tough stems from the chicory. Wash the leaves in a large bowl of cold water, changing the water several times until no sand appears on the bottom of the bowl. Coarsely chop the damp chicory and set it aside.

4. Add the sherry, raisins, salt, and pepper to the pan with the caramelized onions. Simmer until the aroma of the alcohol fades, 1 to 2 minutes.

5. Add the chopped chicory to the pan and stir several times to coat the leaves with the liquid in the pan. Cover and cook, stirring occasionally, until the chicory has completely wilted, about 8 minutes. Taste for salt and pepper and adjust seasonings if necessary.

6. While preparing the sauce, cook and drain the pasta, making sure that some water still clings to the noodles. Toss the hot pasta with the chicory sauce. Mix well and transfer portions to warm pasta bowls. Serve immediately with grated cheese passed separately.

Sautéed Escarole with Black Olives and Oregano

● SERVES 4 ●

TIME: 25 minutes

BEST PASTA CHOICE: Penne or other short, tubular shape

Mildly bitter escarole is an excellent foil for briny black olives and oregano. Other tender greens such as Swiss chard, spinach, or chicory could also be used in this sauce. Also feel free to use whatever fresh herb is on hand, especially thyme or marjoram.

1 large head escarole (about 1¼ pounds)
¼ cup olive oil
1 medium onion, minced
4 medium cloves garlic, minced
12 large black olives such as Kalamatas
(about 3 ounces), pitted and chopped
2 tablespoons minced fresh oregano leaves
1 teaspoon salt
¼ teaspoon freshly ground black pepper
1 pound pasta

1. Bring 4 quarts of salted water to a boil in a large pot for cooking the pasta.

2. Discard any dry or tough outer leaves from the escarole. Trim and discard the core and any tough stems. Wash the leaves in a large bowl of cold water, changing the water several times until no sand appears on the bottom of the bowl. Tear the damp leaves into bite-sized pieces and set them aside.

3. Heat the oil in a deep pot or Dutch oven with a cover. Add the onion and sauté over medium heat until translucent, about 5 minutes. Add the garlic and cook until lightly colored, about 1 minute.

4. Add the damp escarole, olives, oregano, salt, and pepper to the pan. Stir to coat the escarole with the oil. Cover and cook, stirring occasionally, until the escarole has completely wilted, about 10 minutes.

5. Remove the cover from the pan and simmer for several more minutes or until the escarole is no longer soupy but not yet dry. Taste for salt and pepper and adjust seasonings if necessary.

6. While preparing the sauce, cook and drain the pasta. Toss the hot pasta with the escarole sauce. Mix well and transfer portions to warm pasta bowls. Serve immediately.

Wilted Escarole and White Beans with Garlic

● SERVES 4 ●

TIME: 70 minutes (plus time for soaking the beans)

BEST PASTA CHOICE: Shells or other open shape

Although Americans may think of escarole as a salad green, Italians use this mildly bitter green in soups, pasta sauces, and vegetable side dishes. Here, escarole is matched with tiny navy beans for a substantial sauce flavored with plenty of garlic. Other tender greens such as chicory, Swiss chard, or spinach could be used in this sauce, if desired. The beans, which should be soaked for at least 8 hours or overnight, can be prepared up to 3 days in advance and refrigerated in their cooking liquid until needed. If you have the beans on hand, this sauce can be ready in 20 minutes.

⅔ cup dried navy beans

1 bay leaf

2 medium cloves garlic, peeled, plus
**   4 medium cloves, minced**

Salt to taste, plus 1 teaspoon

1 large head escarole (about 1¼ pounds)

¼ cup olive oil

1 medium onion, minced

¼ teaspoon freshly ground black pepper

1 pound pasta

Freshly grated Parmesan cheese to taste

1. Place the beans in a medium bowl and cover them with several inches of cold water. Soak the beans for at least 8 hours or overnight. Drain the beans. Place the beans in a medium saucepan and add cold water to cover. Add the bay leaf and the 2 whole garlic cloves. Bring the water to a boil. Simmer

gently until the beans are tender, about 45 minutes. Add salt to taste and let the beans stand off the heat for 10 minutes. Drain the beans, reserving ⅓ cup of the cooking liquid but discarding the bay leaf and garlic. Set the beans and their cooking liquid aside together.

2. Bring 4 quarts of salted water to a boil in a large pot for cooking the pasta.

3. While the beans are cooking, discard any dry or tough outer leaves from the escarole. Trim and discard the core and any tough stems. Wash the leaves in a large bowl of cold water, changing the water several times until no sand appears on the bottom of the bowl. Tear the damp leaves into bite-sized pieces and set them aside.

4. Heat the oil in a deep pot or Dutch oven with a cover. Add the onion and sauté over medium heat until translucent, about 5 minutes. Add the garlic and cook until lightly colored, about 1 minute.

5. Add the damp escarole, 1 teaspoon salt, and the pepper to the pan. Stir to coat the escarole with the oil. Cover and cook, stirring occasionally, until the escarole is partially wilted, about 5 minutes.

6. Add the beans and their reserved cooking liquid to the pan. Simmer, uncovered, until the escarole has wilted completely and the sauce is no longer soupy, about 5 minutes. Taste for salt and pepper and adjust seasonings if necessary.

7. While preparing the sauce, cook and drain the pasta. Toss the hot pasta with the escarole and bean sauce. Mix well and transfer portions to warm pasta bowls. Serve immediately with grated cheese passed separately.

Blanched Kale with Garlic-Roasted Potatoes

● SERVES 4 ●

TIME: 50 minutes

BEST PASTA CHOICE: Spaghetti or other long, thin shape

Roasted new potatoes laced with garlic and rosemary are the perfect foil for blanched kale tossed with olive oil and lemon juice. This hearty sauce is excellent over whole-wheat noodles or regular spaghetti. Either regular green kale or flowering versions with white or purple veins can be used in this recipe. Turnip greens, mustard greens, or dandelions could also be used.

1 pound new potatoes

6 tablespoons olive oil

4 medium cloves garlic, minced

1 teaspoon minced fresh rosemary leaves

1 teaspoon salt

1 pound kale

2 tablespoons lemon juice

Freshly ground black pepper to taste

1 pound pasta

Freshly grated Parmesan cheese to taste

1. Preheat the oven to 400° F. Bring 4 quarts of salted water to a boil in a large pot for cooking the pasta.

2. Scrub the potatoes under cold running water but do not peel them. Cut the potatoes into ½-inch cubes. Place the potatoes in a baking dish large enough to hold them in a single layer. In a small bowl, combine 2 tablespoons oil with the garlic, rosemary, and 1 teaspoon salt. Brush the oil mixture over the potatoes. Bake until the potatoes are crisp and golden brown, about 40 minutes.

3. While the potatoes are roasting, bring several quarts of water to a boil in a medium pot. Trim and discard the tough kale stems just below the base of the leaves. Working with one leaf at a time, tear the tender, dark green leafy portion on one side of the tough center vein away. Remove the leafy portion from the other side of the vein. Discard the vein and wash the leaves in a large bowl of cold water, changing the water several times until no sand appears on the bottom of the bowl. Slice the damp leaves crosswise into ½-inch-wide strips. Add the kale and salt to taste to the boiling water. Cook until the kale is tender but not mushy, about 4 minutes. Drain the kale and toss it in a large bowl with 2 tablespoons oil, the lemon juice, and salt and pepper to taste.

4. When the potatoes are golden brown, add them and any garlic and herbs that can be scraped from the baking dish to the bowl with the kale. Mix well. Taste for salt and pepper and adjust seasonings if necessary.

5. While preparing the sauce, cook and drain the pasta, making sure that some liquid still clings to the noodles. Toss the hot pasta with the vegetables and the remaining 2 tablespoons oil. Mix well and transfer portions to warm pasta bowls. Serve immediately with grated cheese passed separately.

Spicy Collard Greens with Garlic and Chile Flakes

● SERVES 4 ●

TIME: 35 minutes

BEST PASTA CHOICE: Fusilli or other short, curly shape

Blanching the collard greens until they are tender gives them a silky texture and helps tame their pungent, earthy flavor. The cooked greens are then briefly sautéed in olive oil that has been infused with the flavors of garlic and hot red pepper flakes. This treatment can also be used with turnip or mustard greens.

continued

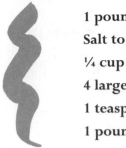

1 pound collard greens
Salt to taste, plus 1 teaspoon
¼ cup olive oil
4 large cloves garlic, minced
1 teaspoon hot red pepper flakes or to taste
1 pound pasta

1. Bring 4 quarts of salted water to a boil in a large pot for cooking the pasta.

2. Bring several quarts of water to a boil in a medium saucepan. Trim and discard the stems and tough veins from the collard greens. Chop the collards into large, bite-sized pieces. Wash the collards in a large bowl of cold water, changing the water several times until no sand appears on the bottom of the bowl. Add the collards and salt to taste to the boiling water. Cook until the collards are almost tender, about 7 minutes. Drain the collards and set them aside.

3. Heat the oil in a large sauté pan. Add the garlic and hot red pepper flakes and sauté over medium heat until the garlic is golden, about 2 minutes.

4. Add the cooked collards and 1 teaspoon salt to the pan. Stir the collards several times to coat them with the oil. Cook until the collards are tender, about 3 minutes. Taste for salt and hot pepper and adjust seasonings if necessary.

5. While preparing the sauce, cook and drain the pasta, making sure that some liquid still clings to the noodles. Toss the hot pasta with the collard greens sauce. Mix well and transfer portions to warm pasta bowls. Serve immediately.

Dandelion Greens with Lemon Oil and Toasted Pine Nuts

● SERVES 4 ●

TIME: 25 minutes

BEST PASTA CHOICE: Linguine or other long, thin shape

Dandelion greens are a treat for savvy shoppers who know how to cook them. Their delicately bitter flavor stands up to olive oil that has been infused with the oils from a lemon peel. Sautéed garlic and toasted pine nuts round out the flavors in this silky sauce. Swiss chard or spinach could be substituted for the dandelion greens, if desired.

1¼ pounds dandelion greens

Salt to taste, plus 1 teaspoon

2 tablespoons pine nuts

¼ cup olive oil

1 teaspoon grated lemon zest

4 medium cloves garlic, minced

¼ teaspoon freshly ground black pepper

1 pound pasta

1. Bring 4 quarts of salted water to a boil in a large pot for cooking the pasta.

2. Bring several quarts of water to a boil in a medium saucepan. Trim and discard the stems from the dandelion greens. Wash the dandelion greens in a large bowl of cold water, changing the water several times until no sand appears on the bottom of the bowl. Slice the damp leaves crosswise into ½-inch-wide strips. Add the greens and salt to taste to the boiling water. Cook until the greens are almost tender, about 2 minutes. Drain the greens and set them aside.

continued

3. Set a large sauté pan over medium heat. Add the pine nuts and toast, shaking the pan occasionally to turn them, until golden (about 5 minutes). Do not let the nuts burn. Set the toasted nuts aside.

4. Heat the oil in the empty pan. Add the lemon zest and cook over medium heat for 30 seconds to release the oils from the zest. Add the garlic and sauté until golden, about 2 minutes.

5. Add the cooked greens, 1 teaspoon salt, and the pepper to the pan. Stir the greens several times to coat them with the oil. Cook until the greens are tender, about 3 minutes. Taste for salt and pepper and adjust seasonings if necessary.

6. While preparing the sauce, cook and drain the pasta, making sure that some liquid still clings to the noodles. Toss the hot pasta with the dandelion greens sauce and the toasted nuts. Mix well and transfer portions to warm pasta bowls. Serve immediately.

Leeks

Leeks are a member of the allium family of bulb vegetables, which also includes onions, garlic, scallions, and chives. Leeks are sweeter and milder than any of their culinary relatives, which allows them to act as the main ingredient, rather than just a flavoring agent, in many dishes.

In Italy and France, leeks are stewed, poached, baked, sautéed, or braised and served as a cold salad, appetizer, or vegetable side dish. Most American cooks are probably less familiar with the virtues of leeks, although soup lovers will surely recognize them as an ingredient in soup stocks. Leeks can also take the main role in pureed country soups, sometimes sharing top billing with potatoes. Finally, leeks have an affinity for creamy fresh cheeses like chèvre and ricotta and often appear in savory cheese tarts and quiches. The recipes in this chapter demonstrate that leeks are equally appropriate as a mainstay in a variety of pasta sauces.

· SELECTION ·

Look for firm, crisp leeks with no shriveling or decay in the leafy green tops or outer layers. Leeks can vary in size greatly with the smallest stalks not much wider than a scallion. I find that leeks of average width, about one inch in diameter, are the easiest to work with and are usually the best tasting. Very large leeks with a diameter of more than 2 inches tend to have very dry outer layers, which must be discarded, reducing the yield substantially. Waste is quite high even in the best small samples. After trimming and discarding the dark green top, the root end, and any tough outer layers, the usable portion is usually about half the original weight.

• S T O R A G E •

Leeks can be refrigerated for several days without any deterioration in flavor. Eventually the outer leaves will become dry and have to be discarded, but the inner layers should remain crisp and fresh for up to 1 week.

• P R E P A R A T I O N •

Leeks are notoriously dirty and must be cleaned with care to prevent grit from ruining the final dish. Start by trimming and discarding the dark green leafy top. (This part of the leek is too dry and tough to eat.) Next, trim a thin slice from the bottom of the leek to remove the white roots. If the leeks must stay together when cooked (for instance, leeks are halved but not cut into rings when grilled), remove only the thinnest slice possible in order to keep layers from falling apart. Peel away any tough or dry outer layers from the remaining white and light green portions and then slice the leek in half lengthwise.

Trimmed leeks that are only a bit sandy can be washed under running water. Simply spread apart, but don't separate, the layers to flush dirt from the inner parts of the leek. If the leeks seem particularly muddy, soak them in a large bowl of cold water, changing the water as necessary until no sand is visible at the bottom.

• U S E   I N   S A U C E S •

In most pasta sauce recipes, cleaned and trimmed leek halves are cut crosswise into thin strips that can be quickly sautéed in oil or butter. There are a number of variations on this basic cooking method. To make leeks especially moist and tender, cover the pan and cook over low heat, as if braising. Like all members of the allium family, leeks become very sweet when caramelized. This can be done on the stove—simply sauté leeks until golden brown—or on the grill. Cleaned leek halves can be brushed with oil and grilled as is without slicing. Once nicely charred, cool the leeks slightly and then slice them crosswise into thin strips and add the grilled rings to a pasta sauce.

• R E L A T E D   R E C I P E S •

Broccoli Rabe and Leeks Braised in White Wine and Tomatoes (page 73)

Leeks Sautéed in White Wine with Parmesan and Parsley

• SERVES 4 •

TIME: 25 minutes

BEST PASTA CHOICE: Penne or other short, tubular shape

Leeks sautéed in white wine make a quick, light sauce perfect for the warm days of spring. The cheese and the parsley round out the flavors in this delicate sauce. Serve with steamed asparagus or as the first course for a more elaborate meal.

4 medium leeks (about 2 pounds)

¼ cup olive oil

½ cup dry white wine

1 teaspoon salt

½ teaspoon freshly ground black pepper

2 tablespoons minced fresh parsley leaves

1 pound pasta

⅓ cup freshly grated Parmesan cheese

1. Bring 4 quarts of salted water to a boil in a large pot for cooking the pasta.

2. Trim and discard the dark green tops and tough outer leaves from the leeks. Trim a thin slice from the root end and cut each leek in half lengthwise. Wash the leeks under cold, running water, gently spreading apart but not separating the inner layers to remove all traces of soil. If the leeks are particularly sandy, soak them in several changes of clean water. Lay the leeks cut side down on a work surface and cut them crosswise into very thin strips.

continued

3. Heat the oil in a large skillet. Add the leeks and sauté over medium heat until completely wilted, about 10 minutes. If the leeks start to brown, reduce the heat.

4. Add the wine, salt, and pepper to the pan and simmer over low heat until the aroma of the wine fades and the sauce thickens a bit, about 5 minutes. Stir in the parsley. Taste for salt and pepper and adjust seasonings if necessary.

5. While preparing the sauce, cook and drain the pasta, making sure that some water still clings to the noodles. Toss the hot pasta with the leek sauce and the grated cheese. Mix well and transfer portions to warm pasta bowls. Serve immediately.

Grilled Leeks and Red Potatoes with Ricotta and Mixed Herbs

● SERVES 4 ●

TIME: 45 minutes

BEST PASTA CHOICE: Penne or other short, tubular shape

Leeks, potatoes, and cheese are a classic combination, especially in savory tarts. Here, the leeks and potatoes are parboiled, grilled, and then combined with ricotta cheese and a mixture of fresh herbs. Any combination of available herbs can be used, although it is best to add larger amounts of relatively mild herbs like parsley, basil, and chives and smaller amounts of more pungent herbs like thyme, marjoram, and oregano.

4 medium leeks (about 2 pounds)
4 medium red potatoes (about 1 pound)
3 tablespoons olive oil
Salt and freshly ground black pepper to taste

1 cup ricotta cheese

⅓ cup minced fresh herbs

   (see headnote on page 188)

1 pound pasta

1. Light the grill or make a charcoal fire. Bring 4 quarts of salted water to a boil in a large pot for cooking the pasta. Bring several quarts of water to a boil in another pot for parboiling the vegetables.

2. Trim and discard the dark green tops and tough outer leaves from the leeks. Trim a thin slice from the root end, but do not cut so much that the leek layers come apart. Cut each leek in half lengthwise. Wash the leeks under cold, running water, gently spreading apart but not separating the inner layers to remove all traces of soil. If the leeks are particularly sandy, soak them in several changes of clean water. Scrub the potatoes under cold, running water but do not peel them. Cut the potatoes crosswise into ½-inch-thick circles.

3. Add the leeks and potatoes to the boiling water. Cook until the leeks are tender and the potatoes can be pierced with a metal skewer but are still firm, about 4 minutes. Drain the vegetables and brush them lightly with 2 tablespoons oil. Season generously with salt and pepper. (The vegetables can be prepared to this point and set aside for up to 1 hour, if desired.)

4. Use a stiff wire brush to scrape the hot grill clean. Grill the leeks and potatoes, turning them once, until both sides of the vegetables are marked by dark stripes, about 4 minutes per side for the leeks and 7 minutes per side for the potatoes. Remove the vegetables from the grill and cool them briefly. Cut the leeks crosswise into thin strips. Cut the potatoes into ½-inch cubes. Toss the grilled vegetables with the remaining tablespoon of oil and set them aside.

5. Mix the ricotta, minced herbs, and salt and pepper to taste in a bowl large enough to hold the cooked pasta.

6. Cook and drain the pasta, reserving ¼ cup of the cooking water. Stir the hot cooking liquid into the ricotta mixture. Add the hot pasta and grilled vegetables to the bowl with the thinned ricotta mixture. Mix well and transfer portions to warm pasta bowls. Serve immediately.

Leeks Sautéed in Brown Butter with Almonds and Sherry

• SERVES 4 •

TIME: 30 minutes

BEST PASTA CHOICE: Linguine or other long, thin shape

Chopped almonds are sautéed in butter, which is then used as a cooking medium for shredded leeks. Some mild vegetable oil is added to the browned butter to prevent it from burning while the leeks cook down. The dish is finished with a splash of dry sherry. This pasta sauce is quite rich and would make a good first course for a formal meal.

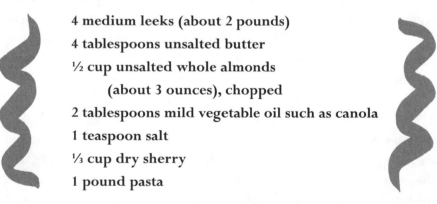

4 medium leeks (about 2 pounds)

4 tablespoons unsalted butter

½ cup unsalted whole almonds
  (about 3 ounces), chopped

2 tablespoons mild vegetable oil such as canola

1 teaspoon salt

⅓ cup dry sherry

1 pound pasta

1. Bring 4 quarts of salted water to a boil in a large pot for cooking the pasta.

2. Trim and discard the dark green tops and tough outer leaves from the leeks. Trim a thin slice from the root end and cut each leek in half lengthwise. Wash the leeks under cold, running water, gently spreading apart but not separating the inner layers to remove all traces of soil. If the leeks are particularly sandy, soak them in several changes of clean water. Lay the leeks flat side down on a work surface and cut them crosswise into very thin rings. Set the leeks aside.

3. Melt the butter in a large skillet. Add the chopped nuts and cook, stirring occasionally, over medium heat until the nuts have softened and the butter is light brown in color, about 5 minutes. Use a slotted spoon to transfer the nuts to a small bowl.

4. Add the oil to the pan and then the leeks and salt. Sauté the leeks over medium heat, stirring occasionally, until tender and completely wilted, about 10 minutes.

5. Add the sherry to the pan and simmer until the aroma of the alcohol has faded and the liquid has partially evaporated, about 2 minutes. Taste for salt and adjust seasonings if necessary.

6. While preparing the sauce, cook and drain the pasta, making sure that some water still clings to the noodles. Toss the hot pasta with the leek sauce and the reserved almonds. Mix well and transfer portions to warm pasta bowls. Serve immediately.

Braised Leeks with Yellow Bell Peppers and Fresh Tomatoes

● SERVES 4 ●

TIME: 25 minutes

BEST PASTA CHOICE: Linguine or other long, thin shape

Leeks are cooked in a covered saucepan with olive oil and some water. Once the leeks are tender, thin strips of yellow (or orange) bell peppers are added to the pan along with thyme. Diced fresh tomatoes add color and help moisten the pasta.

continued

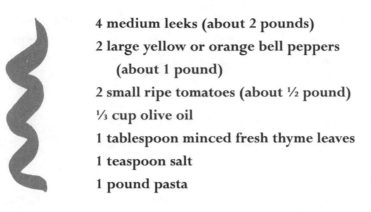

4 medium leeks (about 2 pounds)

2 large yellow or orange bell peppers (about 1 pound)

2 small ripe tomatoes (about ½ pound)

⅓ cup olive oil

1 tablespoon minced fresh thyme leaves

1 teaspoon salt

1 pound pasta

1. Bring 4 quarts of salted water to a boil in a large pot for cooking the pasta.

2. Trim and discard the dark green tops and tough outer leaves from the leeks. Trim a thin slice from the root end and cut each leek in half lengthwise. Wash the leeks under cold, running water, gently spreading apart but not separating the inner layers to remove all traces of soil. If the leeks are particularly sandy, soak them in several changes of clean water. Lay the leeks cut side down on a work surface and cut them crosswise into very thin strips. Set the leeks aside.

3. Core, halve, seed, and thinly slice the peppers. Core and cut the tomatoes into ½-inch cubes. Set the vegetables aside separately.

4. Heat the oil in a large sauté pan with a cover. Add the leeks and ¼ cup water. Cover and cook over medium heat until the leeks are tender, about 8 minutes.

5. Uncover the pan, stir in the peppers, thyme, and salt. Sauté until the peppers are tender but not mushy, about 2 minutes. Add the diced tomatoes and cook until they are heated through, about 2 minutes more. Taste for salt and adjust seasonings if necessary.

6. While preparing the sauce, cook and drain the pasta, making sure that some water still clings to the noodles. Toss the hot pasta with the leek sauce. Mix well and transfer portions to warm pasta bowls. Serve immediately.

Caramelized Leeks with Tomatoes and Tarragon

● SERVES 4 ●

TIME: 35 minutes

BEST PASTA CHOICE: Fettuccine or other long, wide shape

When sautéed, leeks eventually soften completely and begin to brown. In this recipe, the leeks are cooked to this stage and then used as the base for a quick tomato sauce. A small amount of fresh tarragon adds a pleasant anise flavor, which contrasts nicely with the sweetness of the caramelized leeks.

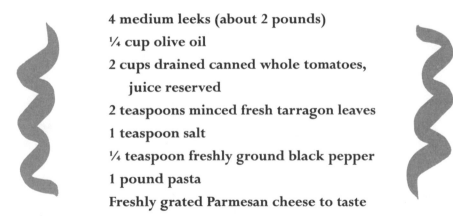

4 medium leeks (about 2 pounds)
¼ cup olive oil
2 cups drained canned whole tomatoes,
    juice reserved
2 teaspoons minced fresh tarragon leaves
1 teaspoon salt
¼ teaspoon freshly ground black pepper
1 pound pasta
Freshly grated Parmesan cheese to taste

1. Bring 4 quarts of salted water to a boil in a large pot for cooking the pasta.

2. Trim and discard the dark green tops and tough outer leaves from the leeks. Trim a thin slice from the root end and cut each leek in half lengthwise. Wash the leeks under cold, running water, gently spreading apart but not separating the inner layers to remove all traces of soil. If the leeks are particularly sandy, soak them in several changes of clean water. Lay the leeks cut side down on a work surface and cut them crosswise into very thin strips.   *continued*

3. Heat the oil in a large skillet. Add the leeks and sauté over medium-high heat just until they begin to brown, about 12 minutes.

4. Coarsely chop the tomatoes and add them to the pan along with ⅔ cup of their packing juice, the tarragon, salt, and pepper. Use the back of a spoon to break apart the tomatoes. When the liquid in the pan comes to a boil, reduce the heat to low and simmer gently until the sauce thickens, about 10 minutes. Taste for salt and pepper and adjust seasonings if necessary.

5. While preparing the sauce, cook and drain the pasta. Toss the hot pasta with the leek and tomato sauce. Mix well and transfer portions to warm pasta bowls. Serve immediately with grated cheese passed separately.

Mushrooms

Since mushrooms do not have leaves or roots and do not produce seeds, they technically are not vegetables but are a type of fungus. However, their flavor and myriad uses in the kitchen put them clearly in the vegetable kingdom, at least as an honorary member worthy of special mention.

Mushroom varieties have traditionally been broken down into two basic categories, cultivated and wild. Recent improvements in cultivation technology have blurred this distinction in many cases, but most markets continue to observe this demarcation in terms of pricing ("wild" mushrooms, even if they are cultivated, are always more expensive) and packaging (fresh mushrooms are generally sold in shrink-wrapped plastic cartons; wild mushrooms are sold loose).

Until as recently as the eighteenth century, all mushrooms were wild. They were harvested seasonally, usually in the fall or spring when the weather was neither too hot nor too cold, and enjoyed as a local staple. Until the past decade or so, cultivated white button mushrooms, the most common variety, were the only mushrooms regularly available to American supermarket shoppers.

Most cultivated white mushrooms were, and still are, grown in cellars, caves, and dark greenhouses in Pennsylvania. However, recent advances have allowed mushroom entrepreneurs (they really aren't farmers) to grow many wild varieties indoors. The result is that mushrooms that were once considered exotic or were infrequently available are now sold in supermarkets twelve months of the year. Researchers have yet to unlock the secrets to cultivating some wild mushrooms, such as morels, which remain extremely expensive and in limited supply during their short spring season. For this reason, I have focused on cultivated varieties in this chapter.

Shiitake mushrooms, an Asian variety with a distinctive umbrella shape and medium brown color, are among my favorite cultivated "wild" varieties. I also regularly purchase cremini, an Italian variety that is light brown in color. Cremini are the same size and shape as button mushrooms but are usually a bit firmer and contain less moisture. I use them whenever I can in recipes that call for fresh white mushrooms since they are prepared in the same manner but have a heartier flavor. Portobellos are oversized creminis that have an especially strong, earthy flavor that reminds many meat eaters of beef. I find the flavor of portobellos to be unique, although the rich texture does remind me of a tender steak.

In addition to these varieties, I make frequent use of porcini mushrooms, the king of Italian mushrooms. Although Italians are able to purchase fresh porcini, they are rarely available to Americans. Luckily, porcini are sold dried. Just an ounce of dried porcini is enough to flavor a pot of tomato sauce. They can be used as a seasoning—in effect, fortifying the flavor of relatively bland white mushrooms—or on their own with the potent liquid that results from the reconstituting process.

• SELECTION •

Fresh mushrooms should be firm, never soft, and dry, not sticky or tacky. White mushrooms should have closed caps with the gills on the underside of the cap not visible. As white mushrooms age, the cap slowly separates from the stem, making the gills visible. Of course, if the gills are just barely coming into view, the mushrooms will be fine for a day or two. However, white mushrooms with gills plainly in view are best avoided.

All other mushrooms will have open, visible gills, no matter how fresh they are. In these cases, it is best to stick with the first traits outlined: firmness and dryness. Look for shiitakes with meaty, domed caps that are not flat or leathery. Cremini should look and feel like white mushrooms, only with exposed gills on the underside. Portobellos should have thick caps and the gills should not show any signs of softness or decay. Also, since many of these "wild" varieties are sold loose, try smelling them before you buy. A strong hint of the woods is always a good indication of freshness.

Dried porcini mushrooms are often sold in shrink-wrapped packages to protect their flavor. Look for packages with large mushroom pieces that are either tan or brown in color but not black. Choose packages with very little black dust or crumbled mushrooms on the bottom. If the porcini are sold loose, smell them. The aroma should be strong and earthy, not stale or musty. Choose the thickest pieces that you can.

• S T O R A G E •

Mushrooms can be refrigerated in a paper bag for several days without much harm. Never wash mushrooms before refrigerating as this will hasten their demise. Also, do not store mushrooms in plastic bags, which trap moisture and can cause the mushrooms to become prematurely soggy. Dried porcini mushrooms can be stored in an airtight container in the pantry for six months or longer.

• P R E P A R A T I O N •

Embedded soil is the cook's biggest challenge when it comes to preparing mushrooms. While it certainly would be easier to soak mushrooms in cold water, soaking will dilute the flavor of fresh mushrooms and cause the texture to become soggy. Therefore, your best option is to wipe mushrooms clean, one at a time, with a paper towel that can be slightly damp if desired. If mushrooms are particularly dirty, place them in a colander and rinse them quickly under cold, running water. Wipe them immediately to remove loosened dirt and excess moisture.

Once the mushrooms are clean, a thin slice should be trimmed from the stem end of each mushroom or, in some cases, the whole stem should be trimmed and discarded. If the stem is woody, there is no point in trying to cook it. This is the case with shiitakes, which have limp, tasteless stems, as well as portobellos, which have extremely thick and tough stems. The stems on cultivated white mushrooms and cremini, however, can be quite delicious and need only be trimmed to remove the dried-out ends. Once the stem issue has been resolved, slice or dice fresh mushrooms as indicated in recipes.

Dried porcini mushrooms, of course, require a different preparation method. In order to soften these mushrooms, cover them with hot (but not boiling) water and let them soak for 20 to 30 minutes. Dried porcini are often quite sandy so soaking helps to clean as well as soften them. Once the porcini are reconstituted, carefully lift them from the soaking liquid and chop. (Note that if the porcini are still sandy when you remove them from the soaking liquid, it is a good idea to place the mushrooms in a colander and briefly run them under cold water.) The porcini-soaking liquid, with its rich, woodsy flavor, is just as essential to many recipes as the mushrooms themselves. Strain the liquid through a sieve or colander lined with paper towels to trap and remove all dirt and sand. Any liquid not used immediately should be reserved for use in stocks or soups. If you have a piece of cheesecloth on hand, use it to strain the soaked porcini mushrooms since it will trap even less liquid than paper towels.

• USE IN SAUCES •

I usually choose a cooking method based on the variety of fresh mushrooms that I have purchased. I find that white mushrooms, creminis, and shiitakes take best to sautéing. This method concentrates their flavor and improves their texture by causing the evaporation of some of their moisture.

Oversized portobellos can withstand the heat of the grill and so this is how I usually cook them. Grilling also seems to intensify their flavor. A quick brush with oil will keep portobellos from drying out as will cooking them with the gill sides up. Once the caps are marked with dark streaks, I remove the portobellos from the grill and slice or dice them. Make sure to save any accumulated juices from the mushrooms while slicing and add them back to the pasta sauce.

With their two separate components (the mushrooms themselves and the soaking liquid), dried porcini are suitable for slow-cooked sauces. The rehydrated mushrooms and their liquid may be added to sautéed fresh white mushrooms to boost the flavor of this bland cultivated variety or they can stand on their own. The porcini soaking liquid is fairly intense and is best mellowed by the addition of another liquid, preferably tomatoes or cream.

• R E L A T E D   R E C I P E S •

Sautéed White Mushrooms with Carrots and Oregano

• SERVES 4 •

TIME: 30 minutes

BEST PASTA CHOICE: Penne or other short, tubular shape

Relatively bland cultivated mushrooms, the kind that come in shrink-wrapped packages, are easily invigorated by strongly flavored ingredients. Here, the sweetness of caramelized carrots and onions as well as syrupy balsamic vinegar do the job. Fresh oregano—thyme, marjoram, and rosemary can be used instead—adds an herbaceous punch. Of course, if you have access to wild mushrooms use them; the sauce will be even more flavorful.

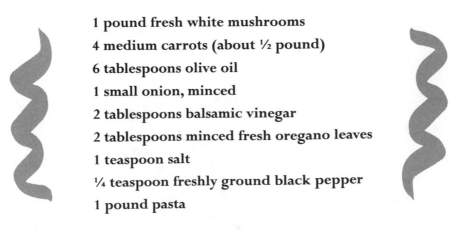

1 pound fresh white mushrooms

4 medium carrots (about ½ pound)

6 tablespoons olive oil

1 small onion, minced

2 tablespoons balsamic vinegar

2 tablespoons minced fresh oregano leaves

1 teaspoon salt

¼ teaspoon freshly ground black pepper

1 pound pasta

1. Bring 4 quarts of salted water to a boil in a large pot for cooking the pasta.

2. Wipe the mushrooms with a paper towel to loosen and remove any dirt. Trim and discard a thin slice from the stem end of each mushroom. Thinly slice the mushrooms and set them aside. Peel and trim the ends from the

carrots. Cut the carrots into ¼-inch dice. Set the carrots aside separately from the mushrooms.

3. Heat the oil in a large sauté pan. Add the carrots and onion and sauté over medium heat until the vegetables start to brown around the edges, about 12 to 15 minutes.

4. Add the mushrooms to the pan and cook, stirring occasionally, until golden and considerably shrunken, about 8 minutes.

5. Add the vinegar, oregano, salt, and pepper to the pan and cook until the liquid in the pan thickens and becomes syrupy, about 1 minute. Taste for salt and pepper and adjust seasonings if necessary.

6. While preparing the sauce, cook and drain the pasta, making sure that some liquid still clings to the noodles. Toss the hot pasta with the mushroom sauce. Mix well and transfer portions to warm pasta bowls. Serve immediately.

Sautéed White Mushrooms Scented with Orange and Marjoram

● SERVES 4 ●

TIME: 25 minutes

BEST PASTA CHOICE: Linguine or other long, thin shape

Freshly squeezed orange juice and grated orange zest enliven this simple sauce. My first choice for the herb in this sauce is marjoram because of its mild but aromatic qualities. Other fresh herbs—especially chives, thyme, or cilantro—would also be appropriate.

continued

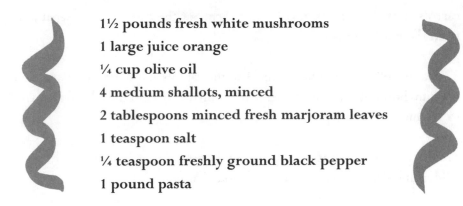

1½ pounds fresh white mushrooms

1 large juice orange

¼ cup olive oil

4 medium shallots, minced

2 tablespoons minced fresh marjoram leaves

1 teaspoon salt

¼ teaspoon freshly ground black pepper

1 pound pasta

1. Bring 4 quarts of salted water to a boil in a large pot for cooking the pasta.

2. Wipe the mushrooms with a paper towel to loosen and remove any dirt. Trim and discard a thin slice from the stem end of each mushroom. Thinly slice the mushrooms and set them aside.

3. Remove the colored peel but not the white pith from the orange with a grater. Set 2 teaspoons grated zest aside. Squeeze ¼ cup juice from the orange and set it aside separately.

4. Heat the oil in a large sauté pan. Add the shallots and sauté over medium heat until the shallots have softened slightly, about 4 minutes. Add the mushrooms and orange zest to the pan and cook, stirring occasionally, until the mushrooms are golden and considerably shrunken, about 8 minutes.

5. Stir in the orange juice, marjoram, salt, and pepper. Cook, stirring occasionally, until the sauce has thickened, about 2 minutes. Taste for salt and pepper and adjust seasonings if necessary.

6. While preparing the sauce, cook and drain the pasta, making sure that some liquid still clings to the noodles. Toss the hot pasta with the mushroom sauce. Mix well and transfer portions to warm pasta bowls. Serve immediately.

Grilled Portobello Mushrooms with Raw Tomato Sauce

• SERVES 4 •

TIME: 25 minutes

BEST PASTA CHOICE: Linguine or other long, thin shape

Meaty portobellos—their meatiness means that a small amount of this pricey mushroom goes a long way—stand up beautifully to the intense heat of the grill. In order to protect the delicate, gill-like undersides, grill the mushrooms with the caps facing the coals. The grilled mushrooms are sliced and then tossed with chopped raw tomatoes, olive oil, and red wine vinegar. Choose a variety of fresh herbs that will marry well with the mushrooms. Good options include parsley, oregano, thyme, marjoram, chives, and mint.

**2 large portobello mushrooms
     (about ½ pound)
¼ cup extra-virgin olive oil
2 large ripe tomatoes (about 1 pound)
¼ cup minced fresh herbs (see headnote above)
1 teaspoon salt
½ teaspoon freshly ground black pepper
1 tablespoon red wine vinegar
1 pound pasta**

1. Light the grill or make a charcoal fire. Bring 4 quarts of salted water to a boil in a large pot for cooking the pasta.

2. Trim and discard the stems from the mushrooms. Wipe the caps with a paper towel to loosen and remove any dirt. Generously brush both sides of the caps with 2 tablespoons oil.

continued

3. Use a stiff wire brush to scrape the hot grill clean. Grill the mushrooms over a medium fire, with the gill-like undersides facing up, until the caps are streaked with dark lines and tender, about 8 minutes. Cool the mushrooms slightly and cut them into ¼-inch-thick strips. Reserve the mushrooms and any juices they give off in a small bowl.

4. Meanwhile, core and cut the tomatoes into ½-inch cubes. Toss the tomatoes in a large bowl with the herbs, salt, and pepper. Drizzle the remaining 2 tablespoons oil and the vinegar over the tomatoes. Gently mix in the mushrooms and any accumulated juices. Taste for salt and pepper and adjust seasonings if necessary.

5. While preparing the sauce, cook and drain the pasta. Toss the hot pasta with the mushroom-tomato mixture. Mix well and transfer portions to warm pasta bowls. Serve immediately.

Grilled Portobello Mushrooms with Rosemary Puree

• SERVES 4 •

TIME: 25 minutes

BEST PASTA CHOICE: Spaghetti or other long, very thin shape

A pungent rosemary puree is the perfect foil for grilled portobello mushrooms. Since fresh rosemary is so strong, parsley is also added to the puree. The parsley flavor fades into the background, while keeping the rosemary from overwhelming the sauce.

**3 large portobello mushrooms
(about ¾ pound)**

½ **cup olive oil**

2 **medium cloves garlic, peeled**

2 **tablespoons pine nuts**

¼ **cup tightly packed fresh rosemary leaves**

½ **cup tightly packed fresh parsley leaves**

1 **teaspoon salt**

¼ **teaspoon freshly ground black pepper**

⅓ **cup freshly grated Parmesan cheese**

1 **pound pasta**

1. Light the grill or make a charcoal fire. Bring 4 quarts of salted water to a boil in a large pot for cooking the pasta.

2. Trim and discard the stems from the mushrooms. Wipe the caps with a paper towel to loosen and remove any dirt. Generously brush both sides of the caps with 2 tablespoons oil.

3. Use a stiff wire brush to scrape the hot grill clean. Grill the mushrooms over a medium fire, with the gill-like undersides facing up, until the caps are streaked with dark lines and tender, about 8 minutes. Cool the mushrooms slightly and cut them into ½-inch cubes. Reserve the mushrooms and any juices they give off in a small bowl.

4. Place the garlic, pine nuts, rosemary, and parsley in the work bowl of a food processor. Process, scraping down the sides of the bowl as needed, until the mixture is finely ground. With the motor running, slowly pour the remaining 6 tablespoons oil through the feed tube and process until smooth.

5. Scrape the rosemary sauce into a large bowl. Stir in the salt, pepper, and cheese. Stir in the mushrooms and their juices. Taste for seasonings and adjust salt and pepper if necessary.

6. While preparing the sauce, cook and drain the pasta. Toss the hot pasta with the mushroom sauce. Mix well and transfer portions to warm bowls. Serve immediately.

Sautéed Shiitake Mushrooms with Plum Tomatoes and Basil

● SERVES 4 ●

TIME: 25 minutes

BEST PASTA CHOICE: Farfalle or short, tubular shape like penne

Fresh tomatoes and basil are the perfect counterpoints for woodsy shiitake mushrooms. Cultivated white button mushrooms can also be used successfully in this sauce. Other fresh herbs, including parsley, oregano, thyme, or chives, could be used instead of basil, if desired. Since plum tomatoes are not terribly juicy, make sure not to drain the pasta too thoroughly.

1 pound fresh shiitake or white mushrooms

¼ cup olive oil

1 medium onion, chopped

4 medium cloves garlic, minced

1 teaspoon salt

¼ teaspoon freshly ground black pepper

¾ pound ripe plum tomatoes

¼ cup minced fresh basil leaves

1 pound pasta

Freshly grated Parmesan cheese to taste

1. Bring 4 quarts of salted water to a boil in a large pot for cooking the pasta.

2. Remove and discard the stems from the mushrooms. Wipe the caps with a paper towel to loosen and remove any dirt. Thinly slice the caps and set them aside.

3. Heat the oil in a large sauté pan. Add the onion and sauté over medium heat until translucent, about 5 minutes. Add the garlic and cook until golden, about 2 minutes.

4. Add the mushrooms and sauté, stirring occasionally, until they have wilted a bit and turned golden brown, about 6 minutes. Season the mushrooms with salt and pepper.

5. Core and cut the tomatoes into ½-inch cubes. Stir the tomatoes into the pan. Cook until the tomatoes are soft but not yet mushy, about 3 minutes. Stir in the basil. Taste for salt and pepper and adjust seasonings if necessary.

6. While preparing the sauce, cook and drain the pasta, making sure that some liquid still clings to the noodles. Toss the hot pasta with mushroom sauce. Mix well and transfer portions to warm pasta bowls. Serve immediately with grated cheese passed separately.

Sautéed Shiitake Mushrooms with Garlic and Lemon

● SERVES 4 ●

TIME: 25 minutes

BEST PASTA CHOICE: Fettuccine or other long, wide shape

Any meaty, fresh mushrooms can be used in this simple sauce; cremini are an especially good choice. White button mushrooms, the most common supermarket variety, are much more watery and not as flavorful as shiitakes. They are not recommended in this dish where the mushrooms are relatively unadorned. Since a portion of the olive oil is drizzled directly onto the hot pasta, this is one dish where I suggest using only the highest-quality extra-virgin oil.

continued

1 pound shiitake or other fresh mushrooms
   (see headnote above)
2 small lemons
6 tablespoons extra-virgin olive oil
2 medium cloves garlic, minced
1 teaspoon salt
¼ teaspoon freshly ground black pepper
¼ cup minced fresh parsley leaves
1 pound pasta

1. Bring 4 quarts of salted water to a boil in a large pot for cooking the pasta.

2. Remove and discard the stems from the mushrooms. Wipe the caps with a paper towel to loosen and remove any dirt. Cut the caps into ½-inch pieces and set them aside.

3. Remove the colored peel but not the white pith from the lemons with a grater. Set 1½ teaspoons grated zest aside. Squeeze ¼ cup juice from the lemons and set it aside separately.

4. Heat 4 tablespoons oil in a large sauté pan. Add the garlic and sauté over medium heat until the garlic is golden, about 2 minutes.

5. Add the mushrooms and lemon zest and sauté, stirring occasionally, until the mushrooms have wilted a bit and turned golden brown, about 6 minutes. Remove the pan from the heat and stir in the lemon juice, salt, pepper, and parsley. Taste for salt and pepper and adjust seasonings if necessary.

6. While preparing the sauce, cook and drain the pasta, making sure that some water still clings to the noodles. Toss the hot pasta with the mushroom sauce. Mix well and transfer portions to warm pasta bowls. Drizzle remaining 2 tablespoons oil over the bowls of pasta and serve immediately.

Porcini Mushroom Sauce with Tomatoes

• SERVES 4 •

TIME: 40 minutes

BEST PASTA CHOICE: Rigatoni or other large, tubular shape

This recipe demonstrates the principle that a small quantity of a potent ingredient can go a long way. Here, regular white mushrooms receive a tremendous boost from just 1 ounce of dried porcini mushrooms and the soaking liquid used to rehydrate them.

1 ounce dried porcini mushrooms
1 pound fresh white mushrooms
¼ cup olive oil
1 medium onion, minced
4 medium cloves garlic, minced
2 cups drained canned whole tomatoes,
    juice discarded
1 teaspoon salt
¼ teaspoon freshly ground black pepper
2 tablespoons minced fresh parsley leaves
1 pound pasta
Freshly grated Parmesan cheese to taste

1. Bring 4 quarts of salted water to a boil in a large pot for cooking the pasta.

2. Place the porcini mushrooms in a small bowl and cover them with 1½ cups of hot water. Soak for 20 minutes. Carefully lift the mushrooms from the liquid and pick through them to remove any foreign debris. Chop the mushrooms. Strain the soaking liquid through a colander lined with paper towels. Reserve the porcini mushrooms and the strained soaking liquid separately.

continued

3. Wipe the fresh mushrooms with a paper towel to loosen and remove any dirt. Trim and discard a thin slice from the stem end of each mushroom. Thinly slice the mushrooms and set them aside.

4. Heat the oil in a large sauté pan. Add the onion and cook over medium heat until translucent, about 5 minutes. Stir in the garlic and continue cooking for another minute.

5. Add the sliced white mushrooms to the pan. Cook, stirring often, until they release their juices, about 6 minutes. Add the chopped porcini and their soaking liquid and simmer for another minute or two.

6. Coarsely chop the tomatoes. Add them to the pan along with the salt and pepper. Simmer, stirring occasionally, until the liquid in the pan thickens to a sauce consistency, about 15 minutes. Stir in the parsley. Taste for salt and pepper and adjust seasonings if necessary.

7. While preparing the sauce, cook and drain the pasta. Toss the hot pasta with the mushroom sauce. Mix well and transfer portions to warm pasta bowls. Serve immediately with grated cheese passed separately.

Porcini Mushrooms with Cream and Parmesan

● SERVES 4 ●

TIME: 40 minutes

BEST PASTA CHOICE: Fettuccine or other long, wide shape

This elegant sauce showcases the earthy flavor of dried porcini mushrooms in the simplest manner possible. The reconstituted mushrooms and their soaking liquid are cooked down into a sauce that concentrates their flavor. A small amount of cream is swirled in at the last minute to enrich the mushrooms. A generous dusting of Parmesan adds a nutty note.

2 ounces dried porcini mushrooms
3 tablespoons unsalted butter
1 medium onion, minced
1 teaspoon salt
¼ teaspoon freshly ground black pepper
¼ cup heavy cream
1 pound pasta
½ cup freshly grated Parmesan cheese, plus
more to taste

1. Bring 4 quarts of salted water to a boil in a large pot for cooking the pasta.

2. Place the porcini mushrooms in a small bowl and cover them with 2 cups of hot water. Soak for 20 minutes. Carefully lift the mushrooms from the liquid and pick through them to remove any foreign debris. Chop the mushrooms. Strain the soaking liquid through a colander lined with paper towels. Reserve the porcini mushrooms and the strained soaking liquid separately.

3. Melt the butter in a large skillet. When the butter foams, add the onions and sauté over medium heat until they are just beginning to brown around the edges, about 7 minutes.

4. Add the chopped porcini mushrooms, salt, and pepper to the pan and cook for 2 minutes. Add the porcini soaking liquid and simmer briskly until the liquid has reduced by half, about 10 minutes. The sauce should no longer be soupy, but don't reduce the sauce so much that the pan becomes dry.

5. Stir the cream into the pan and simmer just until the sauce thickens, about 2 minutes. Taste for salt and pepper and adjust seasonings if necessary.

6. While preparing the sauce, cook and drain the pasta. Toss the hot pasta with the mushroom sauce and ½ cup grated Parmesan. Mix well and transfer portions to warm pasta bowls. Serve immediately with more grated cheese passed separately.

Many Americans may not think of olives as a vegetable, but given the important role that olives play in Italian cooking it seems appropriate to mention them in this context. Many pasta sauces rely on a few chopped olives to add a briny, meaty note. In some cases, however, olives take center stage, in effect acting as a vegetable and not as a seasoning or condiment.

Olives can be broken into several categories based on size, color (either green, when not ripe, or black, when ripe, with plenty of shades for each), and processing. Most olives are packed in a solution of water, vinegar, and salt with perhaps some added herbs or seasonings. Brined olives can be eaten as is with an aperitif or pitted, chopped, and used in a pasta sauce. Black olives are sometimes cured in oil and dried. Because of their leathery texture and concentrated flavor, oil-cured olives are best for cooking. They are wonderful when added to a tomato sauce where their intensity can be diluted.

Although oil-cured and brined olives are not interchangeable, olives that fall within either broad category can be substituted for one another. It's more important to use the freshest, meatiest olives you can find, rather than doggedly searching for a particular variety.

• SELECTION •

The first rule of buying good olives is to avoid varieties in cans. Choose olives that are sold loose by weight in a delicatessen or those packed in brine and sold in bottles. If buying olives in a bottle, look for imported brands from Italy, Greece, or Spain for the highest quality. For the most part, the California olive industry produces inferior specimens. Brined olives should be plump and juicy. While extremely firm, underripe olives will be difficult to pit and should be avoided; excessive softness indicates that the olives have either been mishandled or are past their prime. Oil-cured black olives will be shriveled and leathery and should be soft.

• S T O R A G E •

Keep olives refrigerated in their brine until they are ready to be used. Olives packed in brine should last for several months, although check to see if there are signs of mold before using olives that have been in the refrigerator for some time. Oil-cured olives should be refrigerated as is and should stay mold-free for weeks if not longer. Unopened bottles of brined olives can be stored in the pantry and are a great emergency resource.

• P R E P A R A T I O N •

Removing the pit from an olive can be a chore. The best way to loosen the tender flesh is to exert some pressure on the olive with either your palm or, better yet, the side of a large chef's knife. Gentle but firm pressure with the side of a knife should loosen the flesh and make it easier to tear it from the pit with your fingers. In some cases, it may be necessary to use a small knife to slice the meat off a particularly large, hard green olive. Simply make four lengthwise cuts around the pit in a rectangular pattern. This should remove the meat from the four sides of the pit. Any meat remaining at the ends of the olive can now be trimmed.

• U S E   I N   S A U C E S •

Pitted olives lend themselves to several preparations. They can be pureed in a food processor to make a smooth tapenade. They also can be marinated in olive oil and used raw as a pasta sauce. Chopped olives can be added to a simmering tomato sauce as well. Since olives have such a strong flavor, a little will go a long way in most cases.

• RELATED RECIPES •

Artichoke Puree with Olives, Capers, and Oregano (page 33)
Arugula with Black Olive–Tomato Sauce (page 37)
Raw Arugula with Chick-Pea Salsa (page 42)
Blanched Broccoli with Spicy Black Olive Vinaigrette (page 67)
Cauliflower with Tomatoes, Green Olives, and Capers (page 96)
Stewed Eggplant with Tomatoes, Mushrooms, and Green Olives (page 117)
Salsa Verde with Garlic, Herbs, Green Olives, Capers, and Lemon (page 146)
Caramelized Vidalia Onions with Black Olives and Rosemary (page 152)
Sautéed Escarole with Black Olives and Oregano (page 176)
Spicy Tomato Sauce with Olives and Capers (page 290)
Raw Tomato Sauce with Black Olive Paste (page 294)

Marinated Black and Green Olives with Mixed Fresh Herbs

● SERVES 4 ●

TIME: 30 minutes

BEST PASTA CHOICE: Linguine or other long, thin shape

Chopped black and green olives are marinated in olive oil flavored with garlic, hot red pepper flakes, and fresh herbs. Parsley and basil are used in this recipe but other herbs are equally appropriate, including mint, oregano, and thyme. Although I prefer the contrasting flavors, textures, and colors of several kinds of olives, this sauce can be made with a single variety, if desired.

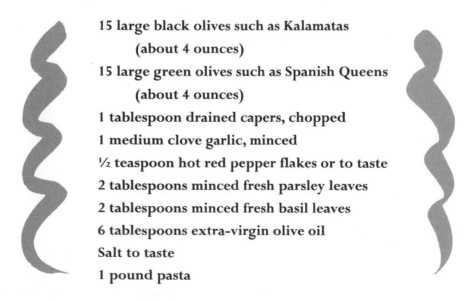

15 large black olives such as Kalamatas
    (about 4 ounces)
15 large green olives such as Spanish Queens
    (about 4 ounces)
1 tablespoon drained capers, chopped
1 medium clove garlic, minced
½ teaspoon hot red pepper flakes or to taste
2 tablespoons minced fresh parsley leaves
2 tablespoons minced fresh basil leaves
6 tablespoons extra-virgin olive oil
Salt to taste
1 pound pasta

1. Bring 4 quarts of salted water to a boil in a large pot for cooking the pasta.

2. Pit and finely chop the olives. There should be a generous cup of chopped olives. Place the olives in a bowl large enough to hold the cooked pasta.

continued

3. Add the capers, garlic, hot red pepper flakes, and fresh herbs to the bowl and mix well. Add the olive oil, mix well, and let stand for 20 minutes to allow the flavors to blend. (The bowl can be covered and set aside at room temperature for up to 8 hours, if desired.)

4. Just before serving, taste the sauce and add salt sparingly, especially if the olives and capers are salty. Taste for hot pepper and adjust seasonings if necessary.

5. Cook and drain the pasta, making sure that some liquid still clings to the noodles. Toss the hot pasta with the olive sauce. Mix well and transfer portions to warm pasta bowls. Serve immediately.

Black Olive Tapenade with Lemon and Fresh Herbs

• SERVES 4 •

TIME: 25 minutes

BEST PASTA CHOICE: Linguine or other long, thin shape

Pitted black olives, garlic, and lemon juice make a pungent puree that can be used as a spread on appetizer toasts or as a sauce for pasta. Since the olive paste will stain the pasta purplish-black, the sauce is spooned over the top of individual portions of linguine that have already been tossed with a mixture of fresh herbs and olive oil. If fresh mint is not available, use thyme, oregano, marjoram, or more parsley in its place. Instead of the usual grated cheese, this pasta is topped with long Parmesan curls.

24 large black olives such as Kalamatas
    (about 6 ounces)
2 medium cloves garlic, peeled
2 tablespoons lemon juice
½ cup olive oil
Salt and freshly ground black pepper to taste
¼ cup minced fresh parsley leaves
¼ cup minced fresh basil leaves
2 tablespoons minced fresh mint leaves
Long hunk of Parmesan cheese,
    about 6 inches in length
1 pound pasta

1. Bring 4 quarts of salted water to a boil in a large pot for cooking the pasta.

2. Pit the olives and place them in the work bowl of a food processor. Add the garlic and lemon juice and process, scraping down the sides of the bowl as needed, until they form a coarse puree. With the motor running, slowly pour 4 tablespoons oil through the feed tube and process until smooth. Scrape the black olive tapenade into a small bowl and season with salt and pepper to taste.

3. Combine the remaining 4 tablespoons oil with the herbs in a bowl large enough to hold the cooked pasta. Add salt and pepper to taste and set the bowl aside.

4. Use a vegetable peeler to remove about one dozen long, very thin cheese curls from the piece of Parmesan. Set the curls aside.

5. While preparing the sauce, cook and drain the pasta, making sure that some liquid still clings to the noodles. Toss the hot pasta with the herbs and oil. Mix well and transfer portions to warm pasta bowls. Spread some of the black olive tapenade over the top of each serving and garnish with several Parmesan curls. Serve immediately.

Green Olive Tapenade with Spinach, Shallot, and Orange Zest

● SERVES 4 ●

TIME: 20 minutes

BEST PASTA CHOICE: Spaghetti or other long, very thin shape

The combination of ingredients in this sauce may at first seem odd but the strong flavors actually complement each other nicely. Pitted greens olives are pureed with spinach (which mellows the olive flavor and gives the sauce a bright green color), a shallot (which provides some heat), and grated orange zest (which adds a citrusy, acid component). Lemon zest can be substituted for the orange zest.

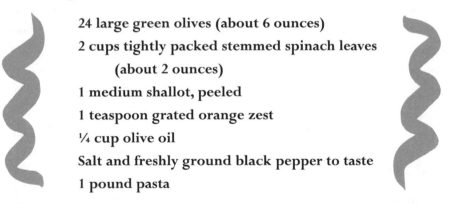

24 large green olives (about 6 ounces)
2 cups tightly packed stemmed spinach leaves
(about 2 ounces)
1 medium shallot, peeled
1 teaspoon grated orange zest
¼ cup olive oil
Salt and freshly ground black pepper to taste
1 pound pasta

1. Bring 4 quarts of salted water to a boil in a large pot for cooking the pasta.

2. Pit the olives and place them in the work bowl of a food processor.

3. Wash the spinach leaves in a large bowl of cold water, changing the water several times or until no grit appears on the bottom of the bowl. Shake the leaves partially dry. Add the damp leaves to the work bowl with the olives.

4. Add the shallot and orange zest to the work bowl and process, scraping down the sides of the bowl as needed, until the mixture forms a coarse puree. With the motor running, slowly pour the oil through the feed tube and process until smooth. Scrape the tapenade into a small bowl. Season the mixture with salt and pepper.

5. While preparing the sauce, cook and drain the pasta, making sure that some liquid still clings to the noodles. Toss the hot pasta with the tapenade. Mix well and transfer portions to warm pasta bowls. Serve immediately.

Peas

Technically a legume, fresh garden peas are a culinary treat with an all-too-brief season. While snow peas or sugar snap peas are available year-round and make excellent side dishes and can be used in Asian cooking, Italian pasta sauces rely on tender shell peas that are removed from their pods. Unfortunately, these peas are generally only available for a matter of weeks in May, June, or July.

Also known as garden peas, English peas, petite peas, and petit pois, these seasonal items are best enjoyed by gardeners and patrons of farmers' markets. Shell peas that end up in supermarkets are often old and house mealy, flavorless peas. However, at the height of the season, some local peas may make their way to supermarkets so it's worth keeping on eye on the produce aisle during the late spring and early summer months.

Part of the reason why peas are so perishable lies in their history. Heirloom varieties that date back before the rise of the Roman Empire were hard and tough and generally stored in dried form and reconstituted much like navy beans or black-eyed peas are today. Not until the advent of a variety with more moisture and hence a softer texture in the seventeenth century were peas regularly consumed fresh. Even today, the moisture and flavor in fresh peas dissipates soon after harvesting, which accounts for their short season and high price tag.

Given the limited availability of quality fresh peas, many cooks turn to frozen. Although peas take better to commercial freezing than most vegetables, frozen peas are my second choice for the recipes that follow. However, all recipes list the amount of shelled peas needed for the sauce (as well as the weight of the fresh peas in pods), so feel free to try frozen peas noting that cooking times will be shorter. There is no need to thaw frozen peas before use in pasta sauces. Simply blanch them until tender (about 30 seconds), drain, and use in the recipes below. In all cases, avoid soft, drab green canned peas.

• SELECTION •

Look for firm, plump pods that are bright green in color. If pods appear limp or soft, the peas are past their prime. Fresh pods will snap not bend under pressure. Also, feel the pods. If the peas were picked too early and were not fully formed, the pod will feel relatively flat and empty. Look for swollen pods that contain mature peas, although varieties with oversized peas are not necessarily desirable since their flavor and texture are often second-rate.

• STORAGE •

The delicate flavor of fresh peas starts to deteriorate as soon as the pods are removed from the vine. Keeping the peas in their pods slows the process so make sure to refrigerate peas in their pods and shell them just before cooking. While peas in pods can certainly be held in a plastic bag in the refrigerator for several days, try to use peas as soon as possible to capture their full flavor and best texture.

• PREPARATION •

Peas require no preparation other than shelling. Most varieties have tiny strings that can be pulled the length of the pod to help open it. As you work, you will invariably encounter some shrunken or partially formed peas. Discard any peas that do not look fully formed or fresh.

• USE IN SAUCES •

Most recipes for peas, both for pasta sauces and other dishes, call for blanching the peas until tender, no more than 2 to 5 minutes, depending on the size and freshness of the peas. Especially fresh, tender peas can be braised in a tomato sauce, for instance. However, most of the peas sold in supermarkets will not soften properly unless cooked in boiling water.

• RELATED RECIPES •

Asparagus and Fresh Peas in Orange-Saffron Sauce (page 48)
Salsa Primavera with Tomatoes, Mushrooms, and Mixed Vegetables (page 298)

Blanched Peas with Wild Mushrooms and Ricotta Cheese

● SERVES 4 ●

TIME: 35 minutes

BEST PASTA CHOICE: Penne or other short, tubular shape

Fresh peas are quickly blanched and then added to sautéed wild mushrooms. This mixture is combined with ricotta cheese and a hint of Parmesan to make a creamy sauce. Meaty wild mushrooms like cremini or shiitake are wonderful in this sauce, although regular white cultivated mushrooms can be used, if desired.

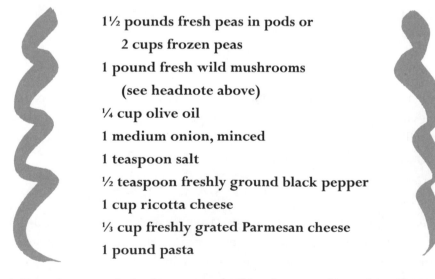

1½ pounds fresh peas in pods or
   2 cups frozen peas
1 pound fresh wild mushrooms
   (see headnote above)
¼ cup olive oil
1 medium onion, minced
1 teaspoon salt
½ teaspoon freshly ground black pepper
1 cup ricotta cheese
⅓ cup freshly grated Parmesan cheese
1 pound pasta

1. Bring 4 quarts of salted water to a boil in a large pot for cooking the pasta.

2. Bring 1 quart of water to a boil in a small saucepan. Shell fresh peas, if using. There should be about 2 cups of shelled fresh or frozen peas. Add the peas to the boiling water and cook until tender, 3 to 4 minutes for fresh or 30 seconds for frozen. Drain the peas and set them aside.

3. Wipe the mushrooms with a paper towel to loosen and remove any dirt. Trim and discard a thin slice from the stem end of each mushroom. Thinly slice the mushrooms and set them aside.

4. Heat the oil in a large sauté pan. Add the onion and sauté over medium heat until translucent, about 5 minutes. Add the mushrooms and raise the heat to medium-high. Cook, stirring often, until the mushrooms have wilted a bit and shed some of their moisture, about 6 minutes. Stir in the salt and the pepper and continue cooking until the mushrooms are completely cooked, another minute or so. Stir in the peas and heat through for another minute.

5. Combine the ricotta and Parmesan cheese together in a large bowl. Stir in the mushroom-pea mixture. Taste for salt and pepper and adjust seasonings if necessary.

6. While preparing the sauce, cook and drain the pasta, making sure that some water still clings to the noodles. Toss the hot pasta with the sauce. Mix well and transfer portions to warm pasta bowls. Serve immediately.

Blanched Peas with Quick Scallion Broth and Parmesan

● SERVES 4 ●

TIME: 30 minutes

BEST PASTA CHOICE: Small shells or other small open shape

Sliced scallions are cooked in oil until they caramelize and then covered with a small amount of water and steamed until tender. This brothy sauce is the perfect foil for fresh peas. A healthy dose of Parmesan brings the two elements together and binds the sauce to the cooked pasta. *continued*

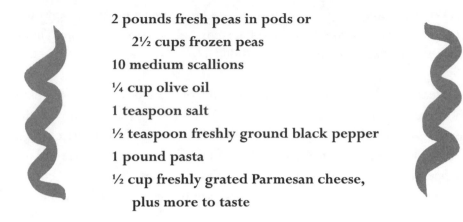

2 pounds fresh peas in pods or
    2½ cups frozen peas
10 medium scallions
¼ cup olive oil
1 teaspoon salt
½ teaspoon freshly ground black pepper
1 pound pasta
½ cup freshly grated Parmesan cheese,
    plus more to taste

1. Bring 4 quarts of salted water to a boil in a large pot for cooking the pasta.

2. Bring 1 quart of water to a boil in a small saucepan. Shell fresh peas, if using. There should be about 2½ cups of shelled fresh or frozen peas. Add the peas to the boiling water and cook until almost tender, 2 to 3 minutes for fresh or 20 seconds for frozen. Drain the peas and set them aside.

3. Slice the white and crisp green parts of the scallions into very thin rings. There should be about 1½ cups of sliced scallions.

4. Heat the oil in a large sauté pan with a cover. Add the scallions and cook over medium heat until they start to brown, about 7 minutes. Add the salt, pepper, and 1 cup cold water to the pan. Cover and simmer until the scallions are tender and the broth is green, about 5 minutes.

5. Add the peas to the scallion broth and cook uncovered until the peas are completely tender, about 1 minute. Taste for salt and pepper and adjust seasonings if necessary.

6. While preparing the sauce, cook and drain the pasta. Toss the hot pasta with the peas and scallions and ½ cup grated Parmesan. Mix well and transfer portions to warm pasta bowls. Serve immediately with more grated cheese passed separately.

Flash-Braised Peas with Tomatoes and Mint

• SERVES 4 •

TIME: 30 minutes

BEST PASTA CHOICE: Orecchiette or small shells

Tender frozen peas simultaneously defrost and cook in a sauce made with ripe summer tomatoes. The mint provides an herbaceous contrast that could also come from basil, if desired. This sauce is a bit soupy so serve this pasta with plenty of bread. Since the peas are not blanched, this sauce is not the best choice for fresh peas that may not soften properly with this quick-cooking method.

4 medium ripe tomatoes (about 2 pounds)
¼ cup olive oil
1 small onion, minced
1 teaspoon salt
¼ teaspoon freshly ground black pepper
2 cups frozen peas
¼ cup shredded fresh mint leaves
1 pound pasta
Freshly grated Parmesan cheese to taste

1. Bring 4 quarts of salted water to a boil in a large pot for cooking the pasta. Add the tomatoes and turn them several times to resubmerge the parts of the tomatoes that bob to the surface. Keep the tomatoes in the water for 20 seconds. Use a slotted spoon to transfer the tomatoes to a work surface. Cool them slightly and peel the skins with your fingers. Core and cut the tomatoes into ½-inch dice. Set the chopped, peeled tomatoes aside. Reserve the water in the pot for cooking the pasta.

continued

2. Heat the oil in a large skillet. Add the onion and sauté over medium heat until translucent, about 5 minutes. Add the tomatoes, salt, and pepper and simmer until a rough sauce forms, about 5 minutes.

3. Stir the peas and mint into the pan and cook just until the peas defrost and become tender, 2 to 3 minutes. Taste for salt and pepper and adjust seasonings if necessary.

4. While preparing the sauce, cook and drain the pasta. Toss the hot pasta with the sauce. Mix well and transfer portions to warm pasta bowls. Serve immediately with grated cheese passed separately.

Blanched Peas with Yellow Bell Peppers and Tomatoes

● SERVES 4 ●

TIME: 30 minutes

BEST PASTA CHOICE: Small shells or other small open shape

Green peas, yellow peppers, and red ripe tomatoes combine for a colorful early summer sauce. The anise flavor of the tarragon complements the gentle sweetness of the ingredients. Other fresh herbs, especially basil or mint, could be used instead. This sauce can also be made with fresh fava beans.

1½ pounds fresh peas in pods or
2 cups frozen peas
1 large yellow bell pepper (about ½ pound)
2 large ripe tomatoes (about 1 pound)
¼ cup olive oil

4 medium shallots, minced

1½ tablespoons minced fresh tarragon leaves

1 teaspoon salt

¼ teaspoon freshly ground black pepper

1 pound pasta

Freshly grated Parmesan cheese to taste

1. Bring 4 quarts of salted water to a boil in a large pot for cooking the pasta.

2. Bring 1 quart of water to a boil in a small saucepan. Shell fresh peas, if using. There should be about 2 cups of shelled fresh or frozen peas. Add the peas to the boiling water and cook until almost tender, 2 to 3 minutes for fresh or 30 seconds for frozen. Drain the peas and set them aside.

3. Core, halve, seed, and chop the pepper into ½-inch squares and set them aside. Core and cut the tomatoes into ½-inch cubes and set them aside.

4. Heat the oil in a large skillet. Add the shallots and sauté over medium heat until soft, about 3 minutes. Stir in the bell pepper and cook, stirring occasionally, until tender, about 6 minutes.

5. Add the tomatoes, tarragon, salt, and pepper and cook until the tomatoes are heated through but still retain their shape, about 2 minutes. Stir in the peas and cook just until the peas are tender, about 1 minute. Taste for salt and pepper and adjust seasonings if necessary.

6. While preparing the sauce, cook and drain the pasta. Toss the hot pasta with the sauce. Mix well and transfer portions to warm pasta bowls. Serve immediately with grated cheese passed separately.

Blanched Peas with Watercress, Basil Oil, and Parmesan Curls

• SERVES 4 •

TIME: 25 minutes

BEST PASTA CHOICE: Orecchiette or small shells

Watercress has a gentle but peppery bite that complements the sweet flavor of garden-fresh peas. A rough basil oil can be made by chopping several basil leaves into good-quality olive oil in a food processor. If you have a commercial basil oil in the pantry, replace the olive oil with an equal amount of basil oil and omit the fresh basil. The Parmesan curls can be cut from the wedge of cheese in advance or while working directly over the bowls of pasta. Simply glide a vegetable peeler along the surface of the cheese, moving down the length of the wedge to remove a paper-thin curl that is several inches long. This sauce can also be made with fava beans.

**1½ pounds fresh peas in pods or
    2 cups frozen peas
1 large bunch watercress or arugula
    (about ½ pound)
12 large fresh basil leaves
6 tablespoons olive oil
1 teaspoon salt
Long hunk of Parmesan cheese,
    about 6 inches in length
1 pound pasta**

1. Bring 4 quarts of salted water to a boil in a large pot for cooking the pasta.

2. Bring 1 quart of water to a boil in a small pan. Shell fresh peas, if using. There should be about 2 cups of shelled fresh or frozen peas. Add the peas to the boiling water and cook until tender, 3 to 4 minutes for fresh or 30 seconds for frozen. Drain the peas and set them aside in a bowl large enough to hold the cooked pasta.

3. Discard any limp stalks or leaves from the watercress. Trim the stalks about ½ inch below the leaves. Discard the tough stalks. Wash and pat dry the leaves and the small portion of tender stalk attached to them. Add the raw watercress to the bowl with the peas.

4. Place the basil, oil, and salt in the work bowl of a food processor. Process, scraping down the sides of the bowl several times, until the basil is evenly chopped in the oil. Scrape the oil into the bowl with the peas and toss gently to coat the vegetables. Taste for salt and adjust seasonings if necessary.

5. Use a vegetable peeler to remove about one dozen long, very thin cheese curls from the piece of Parmesan. Set the curls aside.

6. While preparing the sauce, cook and drain the pasta, making sure that some water still clings to the noodles. Toss the hot pasta with the vegetables. Mix well until the watercress has wilted, about 30 seconds. Transfer portions to warm pasta bowls. Garnish each bowl of pasta with several Parmesan curls and serve immediately.

Peppers

Sweet peppers, including the versatile bell-shaped pepper, are mainstays in the Italian kitchen. Green peppers, once the only variety sold in many American supermarkets, are actually unripe and have a strong, sometimes bitter flavor. Because they ship well, green peppers are usually the cheapest peppers in the store. However, their strong flavor must be tamed by cooking, so they are not appropriate in raw sauces.

In contrast, ripe red, yellow, and orange peppers are naturally sweet and may be eaten raw or cooked. Purple-skinned peppers shield green flesh and share more traits with green peppers than with other brightly colored varieties. In fact, when purple peppers are cooked to counteract some of their natural bitterness, their skins turn green and I find little difference between them and their much cheaper green cousins.

All peppers, whether sweet like a bell or spicy like a jalapeño, are members of the *Capsicum* family, which was first introduced to Europe by Christopher Columbus. A note of explanation with regards to the confusing names for chile peppers, bell peppers, and the common spice we call black pepper, which is not a member of the *Capsicum* family. Columbus's original mission was partly inspired by Europe's taste for black pepper and the desire to find a quicker transport route to bring back this and other spices from Asia. When Columbus landed in the Americas, he thought spicy New World chile peppers were related to black peppercorns. He named these fresh peppers as well as their mild cousins (bell peppers) after black pepper, although there is no botanical connection between black peppercorns and any fresh pepper.

• S E L E C T I O N •

Look for firm peppers with taut skins and no signs of wilting or decay. The stems should be green and firm as well. Soft peppers or those with shriveled skins should be avoided. Bell peppers can range in size from 3 to 8 ounces. For this reason, I have given the total weight of peppers needed for each recipe. Whichever size you choose, select peppers that feel heavy for their size—an indication that the flesh is particularly meaty. Only the meatiest, thickest peppers can withstand the intense heat of roasting, so shop accordingly.

• S T O R A G E •

Place unwashed peppers in a plastic bag and refrigerate them. If peppers are fresh when purchased, they should hold up well for several days. If peppers begin to soften or skins start to shrivel, use them immediately or roast them and cover with olive oil. Roasted pepper halves (remove seeds and membranes but do not slice until ready to use them) can be refrigerated in oil for 1 week.

• P R E P A R A T I O N •

Bell peppers are cleaned in order to separate the sweet, flavorful flesh from the bitter or dull core, seeds, and membranes. Use a small, sharp knife to cut closely around the core. Pull out the core and then slice the pepper in half through the open end. To remove the seeds and the tasteless white membranes in one motion, flatten the pepper half with the side of a heavy knife and then slide the blade across the inner surface of the pepper to dislodge the seeds and cut away the top layer of flesh and the membranes. Cleaned pepper halves can then be cut into small squares or thin strips as directed in individual recipes.

While many recipes call for peppers with the skin on, in some cases you will want to remove the outer layer of skin. This is best accomplished by a process called "roasting." Under the intense heat of a broiler or gas flame, the skin will shrivel and pucker, making for easy removal. After coring and seeding, what is left is a silky, rich flesh with a concentrated pepper flavor. (Roasting causes some of the water to evaporate, leaving behind the flavorful oils and juices in the pepper.) Roasted peppers packed in oil are available in every supermarket. While they might do in a pinch, I find that their texture is too soft and their flavor too dull, especially when compared to peppers roasted at home. There are two easy methods for roasting peppers that I recommend. Choose one or the other based on your type of stove or personal convenience.

To roast peppers under the broiler in an electric or gas oven: Adjust the oven rack to the top position and heat the broiler. Place the peppers on the rack so that they are an inch or two from the heating element. Broil, turning carefully several times with tongs and taking care not to puncture the peppers, until the skins are lightly charred but not ashen on all sides, about 15 minutes. Place the charred peppers in a small paper bag, roll the bag closed, and set the peppers aside to steam for about 5 minutes or until the skins pucker. When cool enough to handle, peel the peppers with your fingers (although rinsing makes this job easier, it also washes away some flavor), then core and seed them.

To roast peppers over a gas flame: Hold one pepper at a time with a pair of tongs (a fork will puncture the skin and permit the loss of flavorful juices) over a gas flame on top of the stove, turning the pepper often, until lightly charred on all sides, no more than a couple of minutes. Transfer the charred pepper to a small paper bag, roll the bag closed, and set it aside while repeating the process with other peppers. Add each charred pepper to the bag and steam for 5 minutes more after the addition of the last pepper. When cool enough to handle, peel the peppers with your fingers, then core and seed them.

To grill peppers, simply core, halve, and seed them as usual. Cut the halves into several wedges and brush both sides lightly with olive oil. Grill, turning once, until both sides are marked with dark stripes, about 10 minutes. Grilled peppers can then be sliced and added to pasta sauces.

• USE IN SAUCES •

Bell peppers can be incorporated into pasta sauces in a number of ways. Raw sweet peppers (red, yellow, or orange, but not green) can be cleaned, diced, and used as is. All varieties take well to cooking on the stove—either sautéing quickly in hot oil or slow-cooking in a covered pan to intensify and concentrate flavors. In either case, peppers should be cooked until soft (to highlight their silky qualities) but not mushy (they should retain their shape in the sauce).

Peppers may also be roasted and then added at the last moment to a pasta sauce, merely to heat them through since they are already cooked. Roasted peppers can also be pureed to form the basis for a vibrant sauce. Peppers can be mixed and matched to contrast colors and flavors or used solo with other ingredients. The flavor of grilled peppers is so unique it can be used as is, with perhaps some herbs and vinegar, to sauce cooked pasta.

• R E L A T E D   R E C I P E S •

Artichokes, Mushrooms, and Roasted Red Peppers with Parmesan (page 30)
Roasted Eggplant and Red Bell Pepper Puree (page 106)
Sautéed Endive with Red Bell Peppers, Shallots, and White Wine (page 124)
Green Beans with Bell Peppers, White Wine, and Tarragon (page 158)
Braised Leeks with Yellow Bell Peppers and Fresh Tomatoes (page 191)
Blanched Peas with Yellow Bell Peppers and Tomatoes (page 226)

Spicy Mixed Peppers with Basil and Parmesan

● SERVES 4 ●

TIME: 35 minutes

BEST PASTA CHOICE: Fettuccine or other long, wide shape

An array of colored peppers are cooked in olive oil and their own juices in a covered pan to make this simple sauce. Make sure to include several red peppers as well as a selection of yellow, orange, and green varieties. To ensure the quickest possible cooking time, cut the peppers into very thin matchstick strips.

5 medium bell peppers (about 2 pounds)
⅓ cup olive oil
4 medium cloves garlic, minced
½ teaspoon hot red pepper flakes or to taste
1 teaspoon salt
¼ cup minced fresh basil leaves
1 pound pasta
Freshly grated Parmesan cheese to taste

1. Bring 4 quarts of salted water to a boil in a large pot for cooking the pasta.

2. Core and halve the peppers. Scrape out and discard the seeds and white membranes. Cut the peppers into very thin slices. Cut the slices in half lengthwise.

3. Heat the oil in a large skillet. Add the garlic and hot red pepper flakes and sauté over medium heat until the garlic is lightly colored, about 1 minute.

4. Add the peppers and salt to the skillet and toss to coat peppers with the oil. Reduce the heat to medium-low and cover the pan. Cook, stirring occasionally, until the peppers have softened considerably but are not

mushy, 15 to 20 minutes. Stir in the basil. Taste for salt and adjust seasonings if necessary.

5. While preparing the sauce, cook and drain the pasta, making sure that some water still clings to the noodles. Toss the hot pasta with the pepper sauce. Mix well and transfer portions to warm pasta bowls. Serve immediately with grated cheese passed separately.

Sautéed Red Peppers with Escarole and Garlic

● SERVES 4 ●

TIME: 30 minutes

BEST PASTA CHOICE: Ziti or other short, tubular shape

Sweet red peppers cooked in garlicky olive oil are a good partner for slightly bitter escarole. While Americans may think of this green in terms of salad, Italians often serve braised escarole as a vegetable side dish. Although I like the buttery, relatively mild flavor of escarole in this sauce, other greens (everything from spinach to arugula) can be substituted. Yellow and/or orange bell peppers can be used if desired.

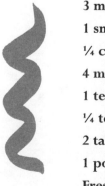

3 medium red bell peppers (about 1¼ pounds)
1 small head escarole (about ¾ pound)
¼ cup olive oil
4 medium cloves garlic, minced
1 teaspoon salt
¼ teaspoon freshly ground black pepper
2 tablespoons balsamic vinegar
1 pound pasta
Freshly grated Parmesan cheese to taste

continued

1. Bring 4 quarts of salted water to a boil in a large pot for cooking the pasta.

2. Core and halve the peppers. Scrape out and discard the seeds and white membranes. Cut the peppers into ½-inch squares and set them aside.

3. Discard any dry or tough outer leaves from the escarole. Trim and discard the core and any tough stems. Wash the leaves in a large bowl of cold water, changing the water several times until no grit appears on the bottom of the bowl. Cut the damp escarole leaves crosswise into thin strips and set them aside.

4. Heat the oil in a large sauté pan with a cover. Add the garlic and sauté over medium heat until lightly colored, about 1 minute. Add the peppers and cook until they begin to soften, about 5 minutes.

5. Add the damp escarole, salt, and pepper to the pan. Stir several times to coat greens with the oil. Cover the pan and reduce the heat to medium-low. Cook, stirring several times, until the escarole is tender, about 5 minutes.

6. Add the balsamic vinegar to the pan and cook uncovered for 1 minute. Taste for salt and pepper and adjust seasonings if necessary.

7. While preparing the sauce, cook and drain the pasta, making sure that some water still clings to the noodles. Toss the hot pasta with the sauce. Mix well and transfer portions to warm pasta bowls. Serve immediately with grated cheese passed separately.

Roasted Peppers with Tomatoes and Capers

• SERVES 4 •

TIME: 40 minutes

BEST PASTA CHOICE: Fusilli or other short, curly shape

Roasted peppers are peeled, seeded, and cut into thin strips and then added at the last minute to a simple tomato sauce. Choose yellow and green peppers, which will stand out against the red tomato background. The capers, which are added along with peppers, add a pleasant saltiness and another dash of contrasting color. The strong flavors in this sauce stand up well to a sprinkling of Pecorino Romano, although Parmesan is equally appropriate.

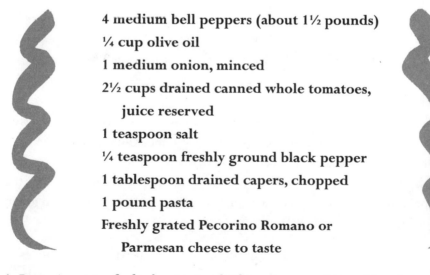

4 medium bell peppers (about 1½ pounds)
¼ cup olive oil
1 medium onion, minced
2½ cups drained canned whole tomatoes,
juice reserved
1 teaspoon salt
¼ teaspoon freshly ground black pepper
1 tablespoon drained capers, chopped
1 pound pasta
Freshly grated Pecorino Romano or
Parmesan cheese to taste

1. Bring 4 quarts of salted water to a boil in a large pot for cooking the pasta.

2. Roast the peppers (see page 232 for specific instructions). When cool enough to handle, peel the peppers with your fingers. Core, halve, seed, and cut the peppers into thin strips. Set the roasted pepper strips aside.

continued

3. Heat the oil in a large skillet. Add the onion and sauté over medium heat until translucent, about 5 minutes.

4. Coarsely chop the tomatoes and add them to the pan along with ½ cup of their packing juice, salt, and pepper. Simmer gently, stirring occasionally, until the sauce thickens, about 15 minutes.

5. Add the peppers and capers to the sauce and heat through for several minutes. Taste for salt and pepper and adjust seasonings if necessary.

6. While preparing the sauce, cook and drain the pasta. Toss the hot pasta with the pepper sauce. Mix well and transfer portions to warm pasta bowls. Serve immediately with grated cheese passed separately.

Roasted Red Pepper Sauce

● SERVES 4 ●

TIME: 35 minutes

BEST PASTA CHOICE: Spaghetti or other long, very thin shape

This vibrant puree has the consistency of pesto sauce, only with roasted red peppers taking the place of basil. The same technique can also be used with yellow and orange peppers. Although any fresh herb can provide a splash of color to the pureed sauce, I recommend parsley here so that the pepper flavor can really shine through. Serve this pasta with a steamed green vegetable and/or a leafy salad.

2 large bell peppers (about 1 pound)
1 tablespoon pine nuts
1 small clove garlic, peeled
2 tablespoons olive oil
¼ cup freshly grated Parmesan cheese
1 tablespoon minced fresh parsley leaves

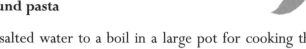

1 teaspoon salt

¼ teaspoon freshly ground black pepper

1 pound pasta

1. Bring 4 quarts of salted water to a boil in a large pot for cooking the pasta.

2. Roast the peppers (see page 232 for specific instructions). When cool enough to handle, peel them with your fingers. Core, halve, and seed the peppers.

3. Place the peppers, pine nuts, and garlic in the work bowl of a food processor and process, scraping down the sides of the bowl as needed, until smooth. With the motor running, slowly pour the oil through the feed tube and process until smooth.

4. Scrape the red pepper puree into a bowl. Stir in the cheese, parsley, salt, and pepper. Taste for salt and pepper and adjust seasonings if necessary. (A small quantity of sauce has to cover a pound of pasta so it should be very well seasoned.)

5. While preparing the sauce, cook and drain the pasta, making sure that some water still clings to the noodles. Toss the hot pasta with all but a few tablespoons of the red pepper puree. Mix well and transfer portions to warm pasta bowls. Dollop a small amount of the reserved pepper puree onto each portion and serve immediately.

Raw Peppers with Garden Vegetables and Fresh Mozzarella

• SERVES 4 •

TIME: 25 minutes

BEST PASTA CHOICE: Penne or other short, tubular shape

This uncooked summer sauce relies on diced garden vegetables—tomatoes, cucumber, and red onion led by bell peppers of various hues. Yellow, red, and orange peppers are my first choices in this sauce since their flavor is sweet even when raw; avoid green peppers, which tend to be bitter unless cooked. After all the vegetables have been prepared, they are combined with basil (any fresh herb on hand can be used), a little olive oil, lemon juice, and diced fresh mozzarella. The whole mixture is then tossed with hot pasta for a light, brightly flavored dish that won't heat up the kitchen. This dish is packed with vegetables so a simple salad of leafy greens and bread will round out the meal.

4 medium bell peppers (about 1½ pounds)

2 large ripe tomatoes (about 1 pound)

1 large cucumber (about ¾ pound)

1 small red onion

12 fresh basil leaves, shredded

½ pound fresh mozzarella packed in water, drained

¼ cup olive oil

3 tablespoons lemon juice

1 teaspoon salt

½ teaspoon freshly ground black pepper

1 pound pasta

1. Bring 4 quarts of salted water to a boil in a large pot for cooking the pasta.

2. Core and halve the peppers. Scrape out and discard the seeds and white membranes. Cut the peppers into ½-inch squares and place them in a large bowl.

3. Core and cut the tomatoes into ½-inch cubes and add them to the bowl with the peppers. Peel and cut the cucumber in half lengthwise. Use a small spoon to scoop out and discard the seeds. Cut the seeded cucumber into ½-inch cubes and add it to the bowl. Peel and cut the onion into ¼-inch dice and add them to the bowl. Add the basil to the bowl. Cut the mozzarella into ¼-inch chunks and add them to the bowl.

4. Drizzle the oil and lemon juice over the ingredients in the bowl. Sprinkle with salt and pepper and mix gently. Taste for salt and pepper and adjust seasonings if necessary.

5. While preparing the sauce, cook and drain the pasta. Toss the hot pasta with the sauce. Mix well until chopped vegetables and cheese are warmed through. Transfer portions to pasta bowls and serve immediately.

Grilled Peppers with Red Wine Vinegar and Tarragon

● SERVES 4 ●

TIME: 25 minutes

BEST PASTA CHOICE: Fettuccine or other long, wide shape

An array of colored peppers (use red, yellow, and orange varieties in this recipe) are grilled and then tossed with red wine vinegar and tarragon to make simple sauce for pasta. If you have an herb-flavored red wine vinegar in the pantry, this is the place to use it. Other fresh herbs, especially basil or

continued

mint, can be substituted for the tarragon. Although I like the flavor that grilling imparts, the peppers can be broiled until lightly browned on both sides.

5 medium bell peppers (about 2 pounds)

6 tablespoons olive oil

Salt and freshly ground black pepper to taste

2 tablespoons red wine vinegar

1 tablespoon minced fresh tarragon leaves

1 pound pasta

1. Light the grill or make a charcoal fire. Bring 4 quarts of salted water to a boil in a large pot for cooking the pasta.

2. Core and halve the peppers. Scrape out and discard the seeds and white membranes. Cut each half into two or three wedges. Brush the peppers with 2 tablespoons oil and season generously with salt and pepper.

3. Use a stiff wire brush to scrape the hot grill clean. Grill the peppers, turning them once, until both sides are marked with dark stripes, about 10 minutes.

4. Slice the grilled peppers into very thin strips. Place the peppers and any juices they give off while slicing in a large bowl. Add the remaining 4 table-spoons oil, vinegar, and tarragon and toss gently. Taste for salt and pepper and adjust seasonings if necessary.

5. While preparing the sauce, cook and drain the pasta, making sure that some liquid still clings to the noodles. Toss the hot pasta with the pepper sauce. Mix well and transfer portions to warm pasta bowls. Serve immediately.

Potatoes

As with other members of the nightshade family, which include tomatoes and eggplant, potatoes were not grown in Italy until after the return of Columbus from the New World. Surrounded by mystery and superstition regarding their effects on human health, nightshades were not immediately accepted into the European larder. However, after a struggle for recognition that lasted well into the eighteenth century, potatoes eventually took their place at the Italian table.

Although potatoes are commonly roasted with garlic and rosemary and served as a side dish or mashed and formed into dumplings called gnocchi, their use in pasta sauces in Italy is rather limited. However, there are a number of regional recipes, mainly from the north, that call for potatoes. Given Americans' passion for potatoes, I have included several of these fairly obscure recipes as well as a few new creations of my own.

There are two points to keep in mind when making pasta sauces with potatoes. First, since potatoes will keep longer than most other vegetables, you almost always have some on hand. Even if your refrigerator is empty, there probably are a few potatoes somewhere in your pantry that can be used to form the basis of a great pasta sauce. Second, sauces with potatoes will have the greatest appeal to carbohydrate lovers. If for some strange reason you have an aversion to carbs, the following recipes may seem too hearty. But that is after all the point of pairing pasta and potatoes.

• S E L E C T I O N •

Look for potatoes without sprouts or signs of decay. The skins should be smooth and not cut or bruised. Avoid potatoes with a greenish hue, which may indicate they are bitter. In general, potatoes should feel heavy for their size. When cut, the flesh should be creamy white not dull or gray. Of course, the flesh on a Yukon Gold or purple potato will not be white.

• S T O R A G E •

Potatoes can be stored in a cool, dry pantry or cellar for weeks if not months. In fact, potatoes that are harvested over a period of a few short weeks are stored and then distributed slowly over the course of many months, sometimes almost a year. New potatoes should be used relatively quickly, certainly within a few weeks. Baking and russet potatoes will last much longer. Storing potatoes in the refrigerator is not advised since it will make them soft and may cause them to sprout.

• P R E P A R A T I O N •

Potatoes are easy to ready for cooking. Simply scrub them under cold, running water to remove any caked-on dirt. If necessary, soak potatoes briefly to help loosen mud on the skin. Potatoes that will be boiled should be left whole. If the potatoes are going to be roasted, cut them into small cubes no larger than ½-inch to speed their cooking.

• U S E   I N   S A U C E S •

I find that crisp, golden brown potatoes are a particularly good foil for tender pasta. Roasting cubed new potatoes is one way to achieve this effect. The other way is to boil a whole potato, cut it into cubes, and then either broil or pan-fry these small "croutons." Either way, the result is especially crisp potatoes that are a good vehicle for olive oil, garlic, and a handful of fresh herbs. Of course, since potatoes do not have much moisture, it is imperative that you pair them with ingredients, like tomatoes, that have plenty of liquid, or use some of the pasta cooking water to create a sauce.

• R E L A T E D   R E C I P E S •

Steamed Green Beans with Roasted Potatoes and Pesto (page 161)
Blanched Kale with Garlic-Roasted Potatoes (page 180)
Grilled Leeks and Red Potatoes with Ricotta and Mixed Herbs (page 188)

Crunchy Potato Croutons with Tomatoes and Parsley Pesto

● SERVES 4 ●

TIME: 30 minutes

BEST PASTA CHOICE: Linguine or other long, thin shape

This summer sauce relies on uncooked ripe tomatoes, a rough parsley pesto, and crunchy potato croutons, which are made by broiling small pieces of boiled potatoes until golden brown. Any fresh herb on hand, including basil or cilantro, can be used to make the pesto.

2 medium baking potatoes (about 1¼ pounds)
Salt to taste
5 tablespoons olive oil
Freshly ground black pepper to taste
½ cup tightly packed fresh Italian parsley leaves
2 medium cloves garlic, peeled
3 medium ripe tomatoes (about 1¼ pounds)
1 pound pasta

1. Bring 4 quarts of salted water to a boil in a large pot for cooking the pasta.

2. Bring several quarts of water to a boil in a medium saucepan. Scrub the potatoes under cold, running water but do not peel them. Add the potatoes and salt to taste to the boiling water. Cook until a metal skewer slides easily into the center of the potatoes, 15 to 20 minutes. The potatoes should be soft but not mushy or falling apart. Drain the potatoes. When cool enough to handle, peel the potatoes and cut them into ¼-inch cubes. Toss the potatoes with 2 tablespoons oil and salt and pepper to taste and set them aside.

continued

3. Mince the parsley leaves with the garlic and combine with the remaining 3 tablespoons oil. Add salt and pepper to taste. (This may be done in a small food processor if desired.) Some oil can separate from the pesto, which does not need to be perfectly smooth.

4. Core and cut the tomatoes in half. Working over the sink, squeeze out as many of the seeds as possible. Cut the tomatoes into ½-inch cubes and toss them with the parsley pesto in a large bowl. Taste for salt and pepper and adjust seasonings if necessary.

5. Preheat the broiler and spread the potato cubes in a single layer onto a lightly greased baking sheet. Broil, turning several times, until the potato croutons are golden brown and crisp, 5 to 7 minutes.

6. While the potatoes are broiling, cook and drain pasta. Toss the hot pasta with the tomato and parsley pesto mixture and most of the potato croutons. Mix well and transfer portions to warm pasta bowls. Garnish the bowls of pasta with the remaining croutons and serve immediately.

Pan-Fried Potatoes with Fresh Herbs and Ricotta Cheese

• SERVES 4 •

TIME: 45 minutes

BEST PASTA CHOICE: Penne or other short, tubular shape

Potatoes are first boiled until almost tender, then cubed and pan-fried in olive oil until crisp and golden. A sprinkling of fresh herbs—use whatever is on hand, including chives, oregano, thyme, or rosemary—is added during the final phase of cooking. The whole mixture is tossed with ricotta cheese and grated Parmesan and then thinned with some pasta cooking water for a rich, complex sauce that should satisfy any carbohydrate craving.

2 medium baking potatoes (about 1¼ pounds)

Salt to taste, plus 1 teaspoon

¼ cup olive oil

4 medium cloves garlic, minced

3 tablespoons minced fresh chives or
other fresh herb

¼ teaspoon freshly ground black pepper

1 cup ricotta cheese

¼ cup freshly grated Parmesan cheese

1 pound pasta

1. Bring 4 quarts of salted water to a boil in a large pot for cooking the pasta.

2. Bring several quarts of water to a boil in a medium saucepan. Scrub the potatoes under cold, running water but do not peel them. Add the potatoes and salt to taste to the boiling water. Cook until a metal skewer slides easily into the center of the potatoes, 15 to 20 minutes. The potatoes should be soft but not mushy or falling apart. Drain the potatoes. When cool enough to handle, cut the potatoes into ½-inch cubes.

3. Heat the oil in a large nonstick skillet. Add the potatoes and garlic and fry, using a spatula to turn the potatoes often, over medium-high heat until the potatoes are golden brown and fully cooked, about 15 minutes. Add the chives, 1 teaspoon salt, and the pepper and cook for another minute or so, tossing the potatoes to season them evenly.

4. While preparing the potatoes, combine the ricotta and Parmesan cheeses in a bowl large enough to hold the cooked pasta. Add the hot potatoes to the bowl and toss well. Taste for salt and pepper and adjust seasonings if necessary.

5. While preparing the sauce, cook and drain the pasta, reserving ½ cup of the cooking liquid. Thin the potato-cheese mixture with ¼ cup cooking liquid. Toss the hot pasta with the thinned sauce. Mix well, adding more cooking liquid as needed to coat the pasta with the sauce. Transfer portions to warm pasta bowls and serve immediately.

Roasted New Potatoes with Herbs, Garlic, and Balsamic Vinegar

● SERVES 4 ●

TIME: 55 minutes

BEST PASTA CHOICE: Farfalle or other small shape with crevices

Small new potatoes are roasted with plenty of fresh herbs, garlic, and olive oil for this sauce and then tossed with balsamic vinegar and butterfly-shaped pasta. Choose the smallest possible new potatoes, ideally no larger than a whole walnut. Briefly soaking the potatoes in cold water helps them to maintain moisture as they roast. Although rosemary and sage are my first choices for this sauce, other fresh herbs such as thyme, oregano, marjoram, or even fresh bay leaves could be used. The chives are tossed with the cooked pasta to give the dish some color. Minced parsley may be used as a substitute for the chives, if desired.

1 pound tiny new potatoes

5 tablespoons olive oil

4 medium cloves garlic, minced

1 tablespoon chopped fresh rosemary

6 large fresh sage leaves, chopped

1 teaspoon salt

¼ teaspoon freshly ground black pepper

1 tablespoon balsamic vinegar

1 pound pasta

2 tablespoons snipped fresh chives

1. Preheat the oven to 450° F. Bring 4 quarts of salted water to a boil in a large pot for cooking the pasta.

2. Scrub the potatoes under cold, running water but do not peel them. Cut the potatoes into ½-inch cubes. Place the potatoes in a large bowl and cover them with cold water. Set the potatoes aside for 10 minutes.

3. Combine 3 tablespoons oil with the garlic, rosemary, sage, salt, and pepper in a small bowl. Drain the potatoes and place them in a single layer in a large baking dish. Drizzle the oil mixture over them and mix well until the potatoes are evenly seasoned.

4. Roast the potatoes, turning them occasionally to promote even cooking, until golden brown, about 40 minutes. Scrape the potatoes plus any oil in the baking dish into a bowl large enough to hold the cooked pasta. Toss the potatoes with the remaining 2 tablespoons oil and the balsamic vinegar. Taste for salt and pepper and adjust seasonings if necessary.

5. While the potatoes are roasting, cook and drain the pasta, making sure that some liquid still clings to the noodles. Toss the hot pasta with the potatoes and chives. Mix well and transfer portions to warm pasta bowls. Serve immediately.

Radicchio

This once-obscure Italian vegetable has become very popular in this country during the past decade. When partnered with endive and arugula, radicchio makes the quintessential "Italian" tricolor salad. In Italy, radicchio is eaten raw in salads but is also treated (and cooked) as a vegetable and can appear in rice dishes, pasta sauces, or alone as a side dish. Radicchio can be sautéed, roasted, or even grilled. No matter the method, radicchio darkens, softens, and becomes less bitter as it cooks.

Although radicchio looks like a miniature member of the cabbage family, it is actually a red chicory. Its pleasantly bitter flavor and crisp, lettuce-like texture make this connection clear. Radicchio starts out its growth cycle with green leaves that eventually become edged and streaked with crimson or magenta. There are several varieties of radicchio grown in Italy, some with elongated leaves (much like endive) and others with rounded heads. The latter variety is most common in American markets, although all are interchangeable in recipes.

• SELECTION •

Look for compact heads with outer leaves that seem moist and crisp, not dried out or limp. Avoid heads with brown spots either on the leaves or at the base. (Given the high cost of radicchio, you want to peel away and discard as few leaves as possible.) There is little difference between small and large heads in cooking, so choose either.

• S T O R A G E •

Radicchio will stay fresh for several days if refrigerated in a plastic bag. As time passes, outer leaves may dry out and more leaves will need to be discarded. However, inner leaves will remain crisp and fresh for some time. Do not wash radicchio until just before use.

• P R E P A R A T I O N •

Because radicchio generally needs little washing, prep time is quite short. Simply use a small, sharp knife to cut around the core and remove it. Then slice the radicchio (with the leaves still attached to each other) crosswise into thin strips. Quickly wash the shredded radicchio and dry well. There are cases when you want some added moisture on the radicchio. This is best done by not fully drying the washed leaves.

• U S E   I N   S A U C E S •

Like leafy greens or cabbage, radicchio must cook down before it is used to sauce pasta. A great quantity of radicchio will shrink considerably so don't be worried by the abundance of ingredients in the pan at the start. Speaking of pans, radicchio needs to be cooked in a deep sauté pan or other deep pot. Shredded radicchio can be completely wilted in an open pan or partially wilted and then braised in a tomato sauce. If radicchio is cooked long enough, the leaves will actually brown and caramelize. In any event, the longer radicchio cooks the more mellow its flavor becomes.

• R E L A T E D   R E C I P E S •

Braised Endive with Pink Tomato Sauce and Basil (page 122)

Pan-Wilted Radicchio with Cream and Parmesan

• SERVES 4 •

TIME: 35 minutes

BEST PASTA CHOICE: Farfalle or short, tubular shape like penne

Thin strips of bright red radicchio lose their color as they slowly cook in a base of garlic, onions, and olive oil. As their color fades so does their bitterness. By the time the radicchio begins to brown, the leaves have a pleasant combination of sweet and bitter flavors. A few tablespoons of cream and a liberal dusting of Parmesan add a creamy, nutty note.

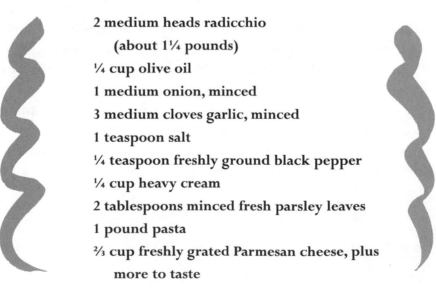

**2 medium heads radicchio
    (about 1¼ pounds)
¼ cup olive oil
1 medium onion, minced
3 medium cloves garlic, minced
1 teaspoon salt
¼ teaspoon freshly ground black pepper
¼ cup heavy cream
2 tablespoons minced fresh parsley leaves
1 pound pasta
⅔ cup freshly grated Parmesan cheese, plus
    more to taste**

1. Bring 4 quarts of salted water to a boil in a large pot for cooking the pasta.

2. Remove the core and tough outer leaves from the radicchio. Slice the heads crosswise into thin ¼-inch strips. Place the radicchio in a large bowl and cover it with cold water. Drain the radicchio well and set it aside.

3. Heat the oil in a large sauté pan. Add the onion and sauté over medium heat until a rich golden color, about 8 minutes. Add the garlic and cook until lightly colored, about 1 minute.

4. Raise the heat to medium-high and add the damp radicchio, salt, and pepper to the pan. Stir several times to coat the radicchio with the oil. Cook, stirring occasionally, until the radicchio has wilted completely and is beginning to brown, about 20 minutes.

5. Stir the cream and parsley into the pan. Simmer gently until the sauce thickens, about 1 minute. Taste for salt and pepper and adjust seasonings if necessary.

6. While preparing the sauce, cook and drain the pasta, making sure that some liquid still clings to the noodles. Toss the hot pasta with the radicchio sauce and ⅔ cup Parmesan. Mix well and transfer portions to warm pasta bowls. Serve immediately with more grated cheese passed separately.

Braised Radicchio with Spicy Tomato Sauce and Basil

● SERVES 4 ●

TIME: 30 minutes

BEST PASTA CHOICE: Penne or other short, tubular shape

In this recipe, thin strips of radicchio are partially cooked in a hot pan and then braised in a tomato sauce flavored with hot red pepper flakes. The acidic/sweet tomatoes and hot pepper flakes work nicely with the bitterness of the radicchio. Shredded basil is added just before serving to give the sauce some color. This sauce can also be prepared with endive instead of radicchio.

continued

**2 medium heads radicchio
(about 1¼ pounds)
¼ cup olive oil
4 medium cloves garlic, minced
2 cups drained canned whole tomatoes,
juice reserved
1 teaspoon salt
½ teaspoon hot red pepper flakes
or to taste
¼ cup shredded fresh basil leaves
1 pound pasta
Freshly grated Parmesan cheese to taste**

1. Bring 4 quarts of salted water to a boil in a large pot for cooking the pasta.

2. Remove the core and tough outer leaves from the radicchio. Slice the heads crosswise into thin ¼-inch strips, wash and dry them, and set aside.

3. Heat the oil in a large sauté pan. Add the garlic and sauté over medium heat until lightly colored, about 1 minute.

4. Raise the heat to medium-high and add the radicchio to the pan. Stir several times to coat the radicchio with the oil. Cook, stirring occasionally, until the radicchio has wilted, about 6 minutes.

5. Coarsely chop the tomatoes and add them to the pan along with 1 cup of their packing liquid, the salt, and the hot red pepper flakes. Simmer, stirring occasionally, until the sauce thickens, about 15 minutes. Stir in the basil. Taste for salt and hot pepper and adjust seasonings if necessary.

6. While preparing the sauce, cook and drain the pasta. Toss the hot pasta with the radicchio sauce. Mix well and transfer portions to warm pasta bowls. Serve immediately with grated cheese passed separately.

Caramelized Radicchio with Balsamic Vinegar

● SERVES 4 ●

TIME: 30 minutes

BEST PASTA CHOICE: Fettuccine or other long, wide shape

Cooking radicchio over high heat causes the vegetable to lose its natural moisture and caramelize. Deglazing the pan with balsamic vinegar heightens the sweetness created by prolonged cooking. The result is a sauce with a round, sweet flavor tinged with just a hint of softened bitterness. Since the radicchio becomes quite dark as it cooks, it can be difficult to tell when it has begun to brown. Once the radicchio starts to stick to the pan, you know it has cooked long enough and it is time to add the vinegar. Endive can be treated in the same fashion but will not become quite as dark as radicchio.

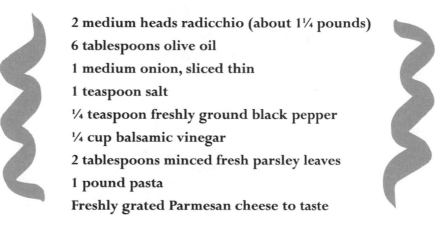

2 medium heads radicchio (about 1¼ pounds)
6 tablespoons olive oil
1 medium onion, sliced thin
1 teaspoon salt
¼ teaspoon freshly ground black pepper
¼ cup balsamic vinegar
2 tablespoons minced fresh parsley leaves
1 pound pasta
Freshly grated Parmesan cheese to taste

1. Bring 4 quarts of salted water to a boil in a large pot for cooking the pasta.

2. Remove the core and tough outer leaves from the radicchio. Slice the heads crosswise into thin ¼-inch strips, wash and dry them, and set aside.

3. Heat the oil in a large sauté pan. Add the onion and sauté over medium heat until a rich golden color, about 8 minutes. *continued*

4. Raise the heat to medium-high and add the radicchio, salt, and pepper to the pan. Stir several times to coat the radicchio with the oil. Cook, stirring occasionally, until the radicchio has wilted completely and is beginning to caramelize, about 15 minutes.

5. Add the vinegar and parsley to the pan, stirring constantly for 30 seconds to loosen any browned bits that are stuck to the bottom of the pan. Taste for salt and pepper and adjust seasonings if necessary.

6. While preparing the sauce, cook and drain the pasta, making sure that some liquid still clings to the noodles. Toss the hot pasta with the radicchio sauce. Mix well and transfer portions to warm pasta bowls. Serve immediately with grated cheese passed separately.

Perhaps spinach has been popular for so long because it is so easy to prepare. While sturdy greens like kale or collards require long, slow cooking, spinach can be steamed in its own juices in a matter of minutes. In addition, spinach has a milder flavor, only faintly reminiscent of the earth, making it a good choice in any number of sauces. And, like most other greens, spinach is rich in minerals and vitamins.

Spinach appears in three guises in most supermarkets. Frozen spinach may be the most convenient but it is also the least flavorful and not recommended in these sauces or other recipes. Fresh spinach is often partially stemmed and packed in clear cellophane packages, usually weighing about 10 ounces. This variety often has curly, somewhat tough leaves and is usually a bit dry. It is a second choice in recipes that call for fresh spinach.

By far the best kind of spinach is the flat-leaf variety with long stems attached that is usually sold in bundles. This product is the tenderest and most flavorful, probably because it has a much shorter shelf-life than prestemmed and packaged curly spinach. Because fresh spinach in bundles usually has a higher proportion of stems (which will be discarded in most recipes), 1 pound of the flat-leaf variety yields the same amount of leaves as a 10-ounce bag.

• SELECTION •

When shopping for either flat or curly spinach look for tender leaves without brown or yellow patches or wilting. Leaves should be crisp but not dry and should not show any signs of decay.

• S T O R A G E •

Spinach can usually be refrigerated for a couple of days without much harm. Leave spinach in the cellophane package if purchased that way. Wrap the ends of bundled spinach stems in a damp paper towel and place the whole bunch in a plastic bag. Keep the towel damp in order to supply the stems (and the leaves) with some moisture.

• P R E P A R A T I O N •

All spinach (whether in bags or bundles) must be stemmed and washed thoroughly. Although packaged spinach does contain more leaves, it still has to be stemmed and does not save that much work. Packages may claim that spinach has been washed, but after some gritty sauces I advise that you view these claims with a grain of sand. Stemming and washing can be accomplished in a large bowl of cold water. Simply pinch the stems where they meet the leaves to remove them. (This can be done with several stems at once.) Swirl the leaves in several changes of cold water until no grit or sand falls to the bottom of the bowl. Some recipes call for relatively dry spinach (in that case, shake dry and roughly towel-dry the leaves), while others rely on the water that clings to just-washed leaves to act as a cooking medium. In either case, refer to specific recipes for more instructions.

• U S E   I N   S A U C E S •

My favorite cooking method for spinach is a combination of wilting and sautéing. Washed spinach leaves can be thrown into a covered pot and cooked in their own juices, oil, or tomato sauce. The combination of steam and direct heat wilts the spinach in about 5 minutes. The idea is not to cook spinach until it is limp, but rather to cook it until the leaves have softened just enough to be easily twirled with pasta on a fork. Spinach can also be blanched briefly in boiling water, then drained and chopped for later use in sauces. Blanching retains the bright green color slightly better than wilting in a covered pot but cannot infuse the spinach with the flavor of garlicky olive oil or a rich tomato sauce.

• R E L A T E D   R E C I P E S •

Red Swiss Chard with Wild Mushrooms and Sherry (page 172)
Sautéed Escarole with Black Olives and Oregano (page 176)
Wilted Escarole and White Beans with Garlic (page 178)
Dandelion Greens with Lemon Oil and Toasted Pine Nuts (page 183)
Green Olive Tapenade with Spinach, Shallot, and Orange Zest (page 218)
Sautéed Red Peppers with Escarole and Garlic (page 235)

Spinach and Mushrooms with Garlic and White Wine

• SERVES 4 •

TIME: 25 minutes

BEST PASTA CHOICE: Penne or other short, tubular shape

Spinach and mushrooms are natural partners—one leafy and herbaceous, the other tender and woodsy. Plenty of minced garlic and a generous splash of white wine round out the flavors in this sauce. Of course, more flavorful fresh mushroom varieties, like cremini, are best but regular white buttons will make a fine sauce.

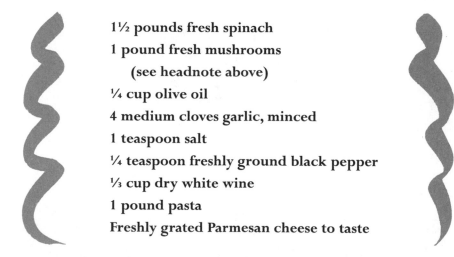

1½ pounds fresh spinach

1 pound fresh mushrooms
   (see headnote above)

¼ cup olive oil

4 medium cloves garlic, minced

1 teaspoon salt

¼ teaspoon freshly ground black pepper

⅓ cup dry white wine

1 pound pasta

Freshly grated Parmesan cheese to taste

1. Bring 4 quarts of salted water to a boil in a large pot for cooking the pasta.

2. Stem the spinach and wash the leaves in a large bowl of cold water, changing the water several times until no sand appears on the bottom of the bowl. Shake the excess water from the spinach and roughly dry the leaves with paper towels. (Leaves can be damp but not waterlogged.) Set the spinach aside.

3. Wipe the mushrooms with a paper towel to loosen and remove any dirt. Trim and discard a thin slice from the stem end of each mushroom. Thinly slice the mushrooms and set them aside.

4. Heat the oil in a deep pot or Dutch oven with a cover. Add the garlic and sauté over medium heat until lightly colored, about 1 minute. Add the mushrooms and cook until they have begun to give off their juices, about 4 minutes. Add the salt and pepper and then the white wine. Simmer until the aroma of the alcohol fades, about 2 minutes.

5. Add the spinach to the pot, stir to coat the leaves with the mushrooms and their juices, and cover. Cook, removing the cover once to stir, until the spinach has wilted, about 5 minutes. Taste for salt and pepper and adjust seasonings if necessary.

6. While preparing the sauce, cook and drain the pasta. Toss the hot pasta with the spinach sauce. Mix well and transfer portions to warm pasta bowls. Serve immediately with grated cheese passed separately.

Wilted Spinach with Golden Raisins and Pine Nuts

● SERVES 4 ●

TIME: 25 minutes

BEST PASTA CHOICE: Linguine or other long, thin shape

This quick sauce takes its cues from a popular Italian side dish of garlicky spinach paired with nuts and raisins. Here, the combination is the basis for a rich, silky pasta sauce. To make sure that the noodles are not too dry, toss 2 tablespoons of olive oil with the drained pasta and cooked spinach. Since this oil is added just before serving, its flavor is quite prominent and only the finest extra-virgin olive oil should be used.

continued

¼ **cup pine nuts**

1½ **pounds fresh spinach**

4 **tablespoons extra-virgin olive oil**

3 **medium cloves garlic, minced**

½ **cup golden raisins**

Salt and freshly ground black pepper to taste

1 **pound pasta**

1. Preheat the oven to 325° F. Bring 4 quarts of salted water to a boil in a large pot for cooking the pasta.

2. Spread the nuts in a single layer on a small baking sheet and toast, shaking the pan occasionally to turn them, until golden, about 5 minutes. Do not let the nuts burn. Set the toasted nuts aside.

3. Stem the spinach and wash the leaves in a large bowl of cold water, changing the water several times until no sand appears on the bottom of the bowl. Set the damp spinach aside.

4. Heat 2 tablespoons oil in a deep pot or Dutch oven with a cover. Add the garlic and sauté over medium heat until golden, about 2 minutes. Stir in the raisins and toss until well coated with the oil.

5. Add the damp spinach to the pot. Toss several times to coat the leaves with the oil. Cover and cook, removing the lid once to stir, until the spinach has wilted, about 5 minutes. Season generously with salt and pepper to taste.

6. While preparing the spinach, cook and drain the pasta, making sure that some water still clings to the noodles. Toss the hot pasta with the spinach, the toasted pine nuts, and the remaining 2 tablespoons oil. Mix well and transfer portions to warm pasta bowls. Serve immediately.

Spinach in Tomato Sauce with Shallots and Carrots

● SERVES 4 ●

TIME: 30 minutes

BEST PASTA CHOICE: Fusilli or other short, curly shape

This sweet garden-fresh tomato sauce stands up nicely to the slight bitterness in spinach leaves. A dusting of Parmesan cheese rounds out the flavors. Serve with plenty of crusty bread to soak up all of the sauce.

1 pound fresh spinach

¼ cup olive oil

3 medium shallots, minced

2 small carrots (about ¼ pound), peeled and diced small

2 cups drained canned whole tomatoes, juice reserved

1 teaspoon salt

¼ cup minced fresh basil leaves

1 pound pasta

Freshly grated Parmesan cheese to taste

1. Bring 4 quarts of salted water to a boil in a large pot for cooking the pasta.

2. Stem the spinach and wash the leaves in a large bowl of cold water, changing the water several times until no sand appears on the bottom of the bowl. Shake the excess water from the spinach and roughly dry the leaves with paper towels. (Leaves can be damp but not waterlogged.) Set the spinach aside.

3. Heat the oil in a deep pot or Dutch oven with a cover. Add the shallots and carrots and sauté over medium heat until the vegetables soften but do not brown, about 8 minutes.

continued

4. While the shallots and carrots are cooking, coarsely chop the tomatoes. Add chopped tomatoes to the pot along with ½ cup of their packing juice, the salt, and the basil. Use the back of a spoon to break apart the tomatoes. Simmer gently, continuing to crush the tomatoes as necessary, until the sauce thickens, about 10 minutes.

5. Add the spinach to the pot, tossing several times to coat leaves with tomato sauce. Cover and continue cooking, removing the lid once to stir, until the spinach has wilted, about 5 minutes. Taste for salt and adjust seasonings if necessary.

6. While preparing the sauce, cook and drain the pasta. Toss the hot pasta with the spinach sauce. Mix well and transfer portions to warm pasta bowls. Serve immediately with grated cheese passed separately.

Creamed Spinach with Gorgonzola

● SERVES 4 ●

TIME: 25 minutes

BEST PASTA CHOICE: Spaghetti or other long, very thin shape

This sauce is an Italian version of creamed spinach minus the cream and most of the fat. Just a few ounces of Gorgonzola add plenty of richness to the spinach, which is boiled, drained, chopped, and then tossed in garlicky olive oil. Gorgonzola is an Italian blue cheese that is salty, sharp, and sweet all at once. Other blue cheeses can be substituted but none quite compare to Gorgonzola.

1½ pounds fresh spinach
Salt to taste, plus 1 teaspoon salt
¼ cup olive oil

4 medium cloves garlic, minced

1 pound pasta

4 ounces Gorgonzola cheese, crumbled

1. Bring 4 quarts of salted water to a boil in a large pot for cooking the pasta.

2. Bring several quarts of water to a boil in another pot. Stem the spinach and wash the leaves in a large bowl of cold water, changing the water several times until no sand appears on the bottom of the bowl. Add the spinach and salt to taste to the boiling water. Cook until the spinach is tender, about 2 minutes. Drain and briefly cool the spinach. Finely chop the cooled spinach, pressing out most of the liquid. Set the spinach aside.

3. Heat the oil in a large skillet. Add the garlic and sauté over medium heat until golden, about 2 minutes. Add the spinach and 1 teaspoon salt and cook until heated through, about 2 minutes.

4. While preparing the sauce, cook and drain the pasta, making sure that some water still clings to the noodles. Immediately transfer the hot pasta back to the pot it was cooked in and toss with the crumbled cheese and the spinach sauce. Mix well until the cheese melts. (If necessary place the pot over low heat and keep tossing to melt the cheese.) Transfer portions to warm pasta bowls and serve immediately.

Wilted Spinach with Tomatoes and Slivered Garlic

● SERVES 4 ●

TIME: 25 minutes

BEST PASTA CHOICE: Fusilli or other short, curly shape

Damp spinach leaves wilt in a simple fresh tomato sauce made with golden garlic slivers and hot red pepper flakes. A dusting of Parmesan at the table finishes this dish. I don't bother to peel the tomato skins for this rustic sauce, but you may do so if you choose.

1½ pounds fresh spinach

2 medium tomatoes (about ¾ pound)

¼ cup olive oil

6 large cloves garlic, slivered

1 teaspoon salt

½ teaspoon hot red pepper flakes or to taste

1 pound pasta

Freshly grated Parmesan cheese to taste

1. Bring 4 quarts of salted water to a boil in a large pot for cooking the pasta.

2. Stem the spinach and wash the leaves in a large bowl of cold water, changing the water several times until no sand appears on the bottom of the bowl. Shake the excess water from the spinach and roughly dry the leaves with paper towels. (Leaves should be damp but not waterlogged.) Roughly chop the spinach and set it aside.

3. Core and cut the tomatoes into ½-inch cubes and set them aside.

4. Heat the oil in a deep pot or Dutch oven with a cover. Add the garlic slivers and sauté over medium heat until deeply colored but not browned or burned, about 5 minutes. Add the tomatoes, salt, and hot red pepper flakes and continue cooking for another 30 seconds.

5. Add the damp spinach to the pot and cover. Cook, stirring occasionally, until the spinach has wilted, about 5 minutes. Taste for salt and hot pepper and adjust seasonings if necessary.

6. While preparing the sauce, cook and drain the pasta. Toss the hot pasta with the spinach sauce. Mix well and transfer portions to warm pasta bowls. Serve immediately with grated cheese passed separately.

Sautéed Spinach and Chick-Peas with Lemon and Thyme

● SERVES 4 ●

TIME: 25 minutes, plus time for preparing the chick-peas
BEST PASTA CHOICE: Farfalle or other small shape with crevices

In this recipe, the spinach is cooked alone then drained of excess moisture. In order to preserve the brilliant green color of the cooked spinach, the lemon juice is not added to the sauce but rather tossed with the hot pasta. While I prefer to cook my own chick-peas after soaking overnight, canned versions make an acceptable substitute in this dish. One 19-ounce can of chick-peas is enough for this recipe. Run the drained chick-peas under cold water to remove all traces of their viscous packing liquid before using them in any recipe.

continued

⅔ cup dried chick-peas

1 bay leaf

1 medium clove garlic, peeled, plus

   3 medium cloves, minced

1½ pounds fresh spinach

¼ cup olive oil

2 teaspoons minced fresh thyme leaves

1 teaspoon salt

1 pound pasta

3 tablespoons lemon juice

1. Place the chick-peas in a medium bowl and cover them with at least 2 inches of water. Soak overnight and drain. Place the chick-peas, bay leaf, and whole garlic clove in a medium pot and cover them with several inches of water. Bring the water to a boil and simmer gently uncovered until the chick-peas are tender, 35 to 40 minutes. Drain the chick-peas and discard the bay leaf and garlic. Place the chick-peas in a medium bowl and set it aside. (The chick-peas can be covered and refrigerated for up to 2 days.)

2. Bring 4 quarts of salted water to a boil in a large pot for cooking the pasta.

3. Stem the spinach and wash the leaves in a large bowl of cold water, changing the water several times until no sand appears on the bottom of the bowl. Place the spinach with some water still clinging to the leaves in a deep pot or Dutch oven. Cover and set the pot over medium heat. Cook, stirring occasionally, until the spinach has wilted, about 5 minutes. Drain and set aside the spinach.

4. Heat the oil in a large skillet. Add the minced garlic and thyme and sauté over medium heat for 2 minutes. Add the chick-peas and cook until warmed through, about 1 minute. Add the spinach and salt and heat through, tossing several times, for about 2 minutes. Taste for salt and adjust seasonings if necessary.

5. While preparing the sauce, cook and drain the pasta. Toss the hot pasta with the lemon juice and the spinach sauce. Mix well and transfer portions to warm pasta bowls. Serve immediately

Spicy Wilted Spinach with Toasted Bread Crumbs

● SERVES 4 ●

TIME: 25 minutes

BEST PASTA CHOICE: Linguine or other long, thin shape

Spinach is wilted in hot olive oil that has been infused with the flavors of garlic and hot red pepper. The spinach is then tossed with cooked pasta and a toasted bread crumb mixture that contains Parmesan cheese and fresh parsley. A little of the pasta cooking water is used to moisten this dish. While commercial bread crumbs will work fine in this recipe, crumbs that you make yourself from stale Italian, French, or sourdough bread are preferable.

¼ **cup plain white bread crumbs,**
   preferably homemade
¼ **cup freshly grated Parmesan cheese**
2 **tablespoons minced fresh parsley leaves**
5 **tablespoons olive oil**
1½ **pounds fresh spinach**
4 **medium cloves garlic, minced**
1 **teaspoon hot red pepper flakes or to taste**
1 **teaspoon salt**
1 **pound pasta**

1. Bring 4 quarts of salted water to a boil in a large pot for cooking the pasta.

2. Set a small skillet over medium heat. Add the bread crumbs and toast, shaking the pan occasionally to turn the crumbs, until golden brown. Do not let the bread crumbs burn. Combine the toasted bread crumbs with the cheese and parsley in a small bowl. Drizzle with 1 tablespoon oil, mix gently, and set aside.

continued

3. Stem the spinach and wash the leaves in a large bowl of cold water, changing the water several times until no sand appears on the bottom of the bowl. Shake the excess water from the spinach and roughly dry the leaves with paper towels. (Leaves should be damp but not waterlogged.) Roughly chop the spinach and set it aside.

4. Heat the remaining 4 tablespoons oil in a deep pot or Dutch oven with a cover. Add the garlic and hot red pepper flakes and sauté over medium heat until the garlic is deeply colored but not browned or burned, about 3 minutes.

5. Add the damp spinach and salt to the pot. Toss several times to coat the leaves with the oil, then cover the pot. Cook, removing the lid once to stir, until the spinach has wilted, about 5 minutes. Taste for salt and hot pepper and adjust seasonings if necessary.

6. While preparing the spinach, cook and drain the pasta, reserving ½ cup of the cooking liquid. Toss the hot pasta with the spinach, the toasted bread crumbs, and several tablespoons of the reserved cooking liquid. Mix well, adding more cooking liquid as needed to moisten the pasta. Transfer portions to warm pasta bowls and serve immediately.

Squash

When the Pilgrims arrived in this country, they were thankful for this native vegetable with a skin thick enough to protect the delicately flavored flesh through even the longest, coldest winter. There are at least a dozen varieties of winter squash available in supermarkets in this country. While most varieties can be used interchangeably in recipes (their flavors and textures are slightly different, but performance is generally similar), I have limited my discussion here to two particularly versatile squash that are widely available for much of the fall and winter, and sometimes even into spring.

My favorite variety is butternut squash, which has a deep orange color, firm texture, and sweet, nutty flavor. Italians use butternut squash as a filling for ravioli or tortellini. By adding a little more moisture, the same mixture can be used to sauce pasta. Butternut squash is also firm enough to withstand sautéing and can be used to make quick pan sauces for pasta.

The other variety that I find useful when making pasta sauces is spaghetti squash. This squash gets its name from the long, stringy fibers that result when the flesh is baked and then teased with a fork. Spaghetti squash is relatively bland and has more moisture that butternut squash. For this reason, I like to jazz it up with a spicy tomato sauce and then toss the whole mixture with real spaghetti.

Thin-skinned yellow summer squash are really more akin to zucchini, in terms of both flavor and uses, and are mentioned in that chapter. For starters, winter squash have much less moisture than their summer cousins.

In addition, their tough skins and large seeds are inedible. Summer squash are entirely edible, skins and seeds included. Lastly, summer squash are quite perishable, while winter squash, which are related to gourds, will keep for months.

• S E L E C T I O N •

Choose hard squash with very few blemishes and no signs of mold. A winter squash should feel heavy for its size. Lightness may indicate that the squash has lost too much moisture and is old. The skin on a butternut squash should be smooth and a deep tan color. The skin on a spaghetti squash should also be smooth, but pale yellow. The stem on either variety will still be attached if the squash is relatively fresh.

• S T O R A G E •

Winter squash have traditionally been stored for months in a cool pantry or cellar. Most varieties will do fine for weeks at room temperature. If you have leftover cut squash, wrap it tightly in plastic and store it in the refrigerator for up to 3 days.

• P R E P A R A T I O N •

Most squash varieties have numerous seeds and stringy fibers at their core. The easiest way to remove them is to cut the squash in half lengthwise and then scrape out the seeds and stringy fibers with a metal spoon. Recipes that call for squash cubes will require peeling of the tough outer skin as well. A sturdy vegetable peeler should be able to handle the job on a butternut squash, although you may need to use a small knife if the skin is particularly tough or thick.

• U S E   I N   S A U C E S •

Butternut squash can be baked and then pureed to form the basis of a creamy sauce. Butternut squash can also be peeled, cut into small cubes, and steamed. The squash cooks much faster when steamed as opposed to baked, but can become a bit watery and will lose some of its sweetness. While there are times when I want to tone down the sweetness of squash for use in savory pasta sauces, the wateriness is still a problem. Therefore, I usually sauté pieces of steamed squash in oil or butter for several minutes to concentrate their flavor and cook off some of their moisture.

The tiny threads that result when baked spaghetti squash is teased with a fork can be used as the vegetable base for a quick pasta sauce. I usually pair strands of spaghetti squash with tomato sauce, which adds plenty of moisture, although a splash of olive oil will also do the job.

• R E L A T E D   R E C I P E S •

See the zucchini chapter on page 301 for recipes using yellow summer squash and zucchini.

Sautéed Butternut Squash with Garlic and Sage

• SERVES 4 •

TIME: 30 minutes

BEST PASTA CHOICE: Penne or other short, tubular shape

Peeled cubes of butternut squash are steamed until tender and then sautéed in a mixture of olive oil and butter that has been infused with garlic. This is one of those rare occasions where I find the garlic too overpowering to leave in the sauce. My solution is to sauté thin garlic slivers in the oil and butter until they are golden brown and have released their flavor, and then discard them. A fragrant garlic aroma is imparted to the sauce without the sharpness that garlic sometimes causes. Although the recipe calls for one small butternut squash, only half is used for this sauce.

1 small butternut squash (about 2½ pounds)

2 tablespoons olive oil

3 tablespoons unsalted butter

4 medium cloves garlic, slivered

12 large fresh sage leaves, shredded, plus
     several whole leaves for garnish

1 teaspoon salt

¼ teaspoon freshly ground black pepper

1 pound pasta

Freshly grated Parmesan cheese to taste

1. Bring 4 quarts of salted water to a boil in a large pot for cooking the pasta.

2. Cut the squash in half lengthwise and use a spoon to scrape out and discard the seeds and stringy fibers. Discard one half or reserve for another use if you like. Use a vegetable peeler or small knife to remove the skin from the other half. Cut the peeled squash into ½-inch cubes. There should be

about 3 cups of cubed squash. Steam the squash until tender but not mushy, 10 to 12 minutes.

3. Heat the oil and 2 tablespoons of the butter in a large skillet. Add the garlic and sauté over medium heat until golden brown, about 4 minutes. The garlic should be richly colored but not dark brown or burned. Use a slotted spoon to lift the garlic slivers from the oil. Discard the garlic.

4. Add the steamed squash, shredded sage leaves, salt, and pepper to the pan. Toss to coat the squash with the oil and butter. Cook, stirring occasionally, until the squash is heated through, about 3 minutes. The squash should be cooked long enough so that it is just beginning to lose its shape. However, do not cook it so long that the squash becomes a mushy puree. Taste for salt and pepper and adjust seasonings if necessary.

5. While preparing the sauce, cook and drain the pasta, making sure that some water still clings to the noodles. Toss the hot pasta with the squash sauce and the remaining tablespoon of butter. Mix well and transfer portions to warm pasta bowls. Garnish bowls with whole sage leaves and serve immediately with grated cheese passed separately.

Pureed Butternut Squash with Ricotta and Parmesan

● SERVES 4 ●

TIME: 55 minutes

BEST PASTA CHOICE: Fettuccine or other long, wide noodles

Baked butternut squash is pureed until smooth and then combined with some ricotta cheese for creaminess and Parmesan cheese for flavor. This thick, rich sauce is seasoned with nutmeg and a sprinkling of fresh chives. The squash can be microwaved on high until tender (about 10 minutes or so) to speed its preparation. *continued*

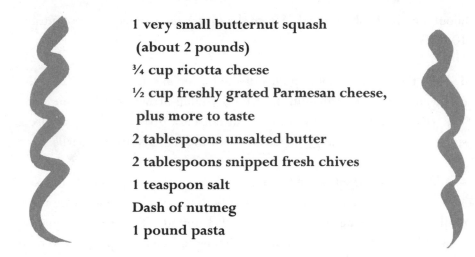

1 very small butternut squash
(about 2 pounds)
¾ cup ricotta cheese
½ cup freshly grated Parmesan cheese,
plus more to taste
2 tablespoons unsalted butter
2 tablespoons snipped fresh chives
1 teaspoon salt
Dash of nutmeg
1 pound pasta

1. Preheat the oven to 400° F. Bring 4 quarts of salted water to a boil in a large pot for cooking the pasta.

2. Cut the squash in half lengthwise and use a spoon to scrape out and discard the seeds and stringy fibers. Place the squash halves, cut side down, on a small baking sheet. Bake until the squash is quite tender (test with a fork), about 45 minutes.

3. Use a spoon to remove the squash pulp, leaving behind all traces of the skin. Place the pulp in the work bowl of a food processor and process until smooth.

4. Scrape the pureed squash pulp into a large bowl. Stir in the ricotta, Parmesan, butter, chives, salt, and nutmeg. Stir occasionally until the butter has melted. Taste for salt and nutmeg and adjust seasonings if necessary.

5. While preparing the sauce, cook and drain the pasta, making sure that plenty of liquid still clings to the noodles. Toss the hot pasta with the squash sauce. Mix well and transfer portions to warm pasta bowls. Serve immediately with more grated cheese passed separately.

Double Spaghetti with Spaghetti Squash and Spicy Tomato Sauce

● SERVES 4 ●

TIME: 50 minutes

BEST PASTA CHOICE: Spaghetti or other long, very thin shape

Spaghetti squash may look like golden strands of spaghetti, but it tastes like squash. I like to toss a combination of nutty spaghetti squash and real spaghetti with a spicy tomato sauce. The squash is cooked until tender and the strands are formed by running a fork over the cooked flesh. The thin spaghetti squash noodles are mixed with the cooked pasta and tomato sauce. Preparation time for this dish can be trimmed by microwaving the cleaned squash halves on high until tender, about 6 minutes.

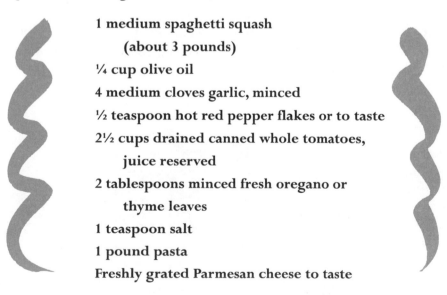

**1 medium spaghetti squash
    (about 3 pounds)**
¼ cup olive oil
4 medium cloves garlic, minced
½ teaspoon hot red pepper flakes or to taste
**2½ cups drained canned whole tomatoes,
    juice reserved**
**2 tablespoons minced fresh oregano or
    thyme leaves**
1 teaspoon salt
1 pound pasta
Freshly grated Parmesan cheese to taste

1. Preheat the oven to 400° F. Bring 4 quarts of salted water to a boil in a large pot for cooking the pasta.
continued

2. Cut the spaghetti squash in half lengthwise and use a spoon to scrape out and discard the seeds and the stringy fibers. Place the spaghetti squash, cut side down, on a small baking sheet. Bake until a metal skewer slides easily through the squash, about 40 minutes.

3. While the squash is baking, heat 3 tablespoons oil in a large skillet. Add the garlic and hot red pepper flakes and sauté over medium heat until the garlic is golden, about 2 minutes.

4. Coarsely chop the tomatoes and add them to the pan along with 1 cup of their packing juice, the oregano, and the salt. Simmer, occasionally using a spoon to break apart the tomatoes, until the sauce thickens slightly but is still a bit soupy, about 15 minutes. Taste for salt and hot pepper and adjust seasonings if necessary. Keep the sauce warm.

5. Remove the baked squash from the oven and cool it briefly. Slide the tines of a fork along the flesh to break it into thin strands. Toss the strands with the remaining tablespoon of oil in a large bowl. Season the squash with salt to taste.

6. At the same time, cook and drain the pasta. Toss the hot pasta with the spaghetti squash and the tomato sauce. Mix well and transfer portions to warm pasta bowls. Serve immediately with grated cheese passed separately.

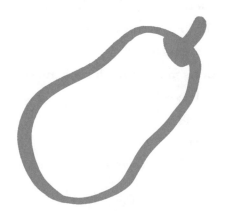

Tomatoes

No vegetable is more closely associated with Italian cooking or pasta sauces than the tomato. Of course, tomatoes are not really a vegetable but a fruit, at least according to botanists. Since an 1893 Supreme Court ruling that was made to support commercial interests, tomatoes have been considered a vegetable in this country by law and by most cooks.

Whether they are a vegetable or a fruit, tomatoes are an essential component in many pasta sauces. Several types of tomatoes are used at different times of the year in the Italian kitchen. The perfectly ripe round summer tomato, with its pleasing balance of sweetness and acidity, is the mark of excellence for all tomatoes. Unfortunately, this tomato never shows up in American supermarkets and is available only to gardeners and shoppers who patronize farm stands and urban green markets during the summer months. When local tomatoes are in season, I rely on their natural qualities and rarely cook them. Some of the best sauces I know are made with raw tomatoes, perhaps embellished with a spoonful of basil pesto or a handful of fresh herbs and a drizzle of extra-virgin olive oil.

Since the supply of ripe round tomatoes is so limited, the best bet for the off months, and whenever you shop in a supermarket, are long, thin plum tomatoes. While the flavor in even the best plum tomatoes will never rival that of a perfect summer tomato, plum tomatoes are dependable, something that cannot be said about the rock-hard, bland round tomatoes that fill supermarket produce shelves. When the quality of plum tomatoes is high, they may be used raw. More often, I use them in sauces where fresh tomatoes are briefly sautéed.

The major type of tomato, and the one I use the most in my kitchen, is canned whole tomatoes. Unlike fresh tomatoes, canned tomatoes are dependable every day of the year and they are often superior to fresh, especially in cooked sauces. California tomatoes are usually sweeter and less expensive than Italian imports, which tend to pick up a metallic flavor during their long journey across the Atlantic. While I would never consider using canned tomatoes in a raw sauce (they lack the firm texture of fresh), they can be chopped and simmered briefly with just a dash of hot red pepper flakes and garlic or maybe some chopped olives and capers for a memorable sauce.

Sun-dried tomatoes are really more of a condiment than a vegetable and are used as such in pasta sauces. For more information on this popular "gourmet" item, see page 15.

• S E L E C T I O N •

When choosing round summer tomatoes, look for ripe tomatoes that are deep red in color and have a soft but not mushy texture. If possible, try to sample a wedge (many farm stands will let shoppers taste sliced tomatoes) and move on if there is any sign of blandness or mealy texture. When buying plum tomatoes, color is usually the best indication of quality. Anemic-looking plum tomatoes never taste very good, so opt for deep-red plum tomatoes that are firm but give slightly when pressed.

As for canned tomatoes, look for California whole tomatoes packed in juice not puree. I find that the juice is a great addition to many sauces, the puree less so. Canned tomatoes should be firm but not rock hard. Very soft canned tomatoes that disintegrate in your hands should be avoided. I recommend Progresso or Red Pack tomatoes, but feel free to taste tomatoes straight from the can and find the brand you like best. If canned tomatoes do not have the proper balance between sweetness and acidity you expect in a summer tomato, choose another brand. In recipes, I have specified the amount of canned tomatoes in cups that you must measure yourself. This is because the ratio of tomatoes to juice in a particular can size varies from brand to brand. Use any extra packing juice to store opened canned tomatoes (tomatoes and juice will keep in a sealed container in the refrigerator for several days) or simply discard it.

• S T O R A G E •

Fresh tomatoes, whether round or plum, should never be refrigerated. Temperatures below 50° F. will make even great tomatoes mealy and bland. For this reason, never buy a tomato from a refrigerated produce case. Fresh tomatoes, especially those that are not quite ripe, should be left on a bright windowsill until they ripen and soften. Otherwise, store ripe tomatoes on the kitchen counter and use them as soon as they soften up a bit. Ripe tomatoes will be fine for a few days at room temperature but don't expect them to hold for much longer.

In theory at least, canned tomatoes will last for years. In general, I buy just a few cans at a time from a market with high turnover to ensure that I'm not cooking with "old" tomatoes, which may have had a chance to pick up off-flavors from the can.

• P R E P A R A T I O N •

Round tomatoes need only be cored and cut into bite-sized cubes for use in raw sauces. In some cases, you may wish to eliminate some of their liquid to prevent the sauce from becoming too juicy. Simply cut cored tomatoes in half, squeeze out the seeds over the sink, and then cut them to the desired size. Plum tomatoes are prepared in much the same way. As for canned tomatoes, I usually lift them from their packing liquid, measure them, and chop them into small pieces. If you would like to remove their seeds and make canned tomatoes less watery, simply open each tomato over the sink and push out the seeds and liquid before chopping. However, in most cases you will want some tomato liquid for a cooked sauce. In fact, in many recipes I use anywhere from ½ cup to 1 cup of the packing liquid, which is nothing more than tomato juice, to help moisten the sauce. This is especially important if a leafy vegetable will be braised in the tomato sauce.

• U S E   I N   S A U C E S •

The tomato can take on any number of guises, in part because the tomato is such a good vehicle for other flavors. However, whether the tomato is combined with a pungent black olive paste or cooked with basil and garlic, its essential characteristics will remain. For this reason, try to pick ingredients that will contrast with the sweet acidity of tomatoes. For instance, salty olives and herbaceous pestos are just two examples of the many possible partners for tomatoes.

How you cook, or don't cook, tomatoes will also affect their character in a pasta sauce. Raw sauces preserve all the nuances in flavor as well as the shape of the tomato. Sauces made with canned tomatoes rely on their watery properties as a flavor conductor. In effect, the tomato gives up its shape (but not its flavor) for the sake of the other ingredients. Cooked sauces made with fresh plum tomatoes are somewhere in between since diced plum tomatoes will soften but not lose their shape if the cooking time is brief. However, no matter how briefly they are cooked, fresh tomatoes will shed some liquid that can be used to cook other vegetables.

• RELATED RECIPES •

Raw Tomato Sauce with Avocado, Capers, and Oregano

• SERVES 4 •

TIME: 30 minutes

BEST PASTA CHOICE: Penne or other small, tubular shape

Only the ripest tomatoes and avocado and finest olive oil should be used in this no-cook sauce perfect for the sultry nights of summer. Since avocado will discolor almost immediately when cut, do not dice the flesh until the pasta is cooking. In order to keep the avocado from completely losing its shape, spoon the avocado over the pasta just before serving. Any herb can be used here but I like the floral yet spicy note that oregano adds.

4 medium ripe tomatoes (about 1½ pounds)

2 medium cloves garlic, minced

2 tablespoons drained capers, minced

2 tablespoons minced fresh oregano leaves

¼ cup extra-virgin olive oil

1 teaspoon salt

½ teaspoon hot red pepper flakes or to taste

1 pound pasta

1 medium avocado (about ½ pound)

2 tablespoons lemon juice

1. Core and cut the tomatoes into ½-inch cubes. Toss them with the garlic, capers, oregano, oil, salt, and hot red pepper flakes in a bowl large enough to hold the cooked pasta. Set the tomato mixture aside for 20 minutes to allow the flavors to blend. Taste for salt and pepper and adjust seasonings if necessary.

2. While the tomatoes are marinating, bring 4 quarts of salted water to a boil in a large pot. Cook the pasta.

3. While the pasta is cooking, peel and remove the pit from the avocado. Cut the avocado into ¼-inch cubes and toss it with the lemon juice and salt to taste.

4. Drain the pasta and toss it into the bowl with the tomato mixture. Mix well and transfer portions to pasta bowls. Divide the avocado and lemon juice mixture among the bowls. Serve immediately.

Spicy Raw Tomato Sauce with Mixed Herbs and Garlic

● SERVES 4 ●

TIME: 20 minutes

BEST PASTA CHOICE: Spaghetti or other long, very thin shape

Hot red pepper flakes and garlic give this simple summer sauce its punch. Wait for "high" tomato season to make this sauce, which depends on perfectly ripe tomatoes. Choose a variety of fresh herbs, including oregano, marjoram, basil, mint, and thyme. This sauce is fairly juicy so serve plenty of bread.

4 medium ripe tomatoes (about 1½ pounds)
¼ cup olive oil
2 medium cloves garlic, minced
1 teaspoon salt
½ teaspoon hot red pepper flakes or to taste
1 cup tightly packed mixed fresh herbs
     (see headnote above)
1 pound pasta

continued

1. Bring 4 quarts of salted water to a boil in a large pot for cooking the pasta.

2. Core and cut the tomatoes into ½-inch cubes. Toss the tomatoes with the oil, garlic, salt, and hot red pepper flakes in a bowl large enough to hold the cooked pasta.

3. Wash and dry the herbs. Keep small leaves whole and tear larger leaves (especially basil) into several pieces. Stir the herbs into the tomato mixture. Taste for salt and hot pepper and adjust seasonings if necessary.

4. While preparing the sauce, cook and drain the pasta. Toss the hot pasta with the tomato sauce. Mix well and transfer portions to pasta bowls. Serve immediately.

Italian Succotash with Tomatoes, Corn, Lima Beans, and Chives

● SERVES 4 ●

TIME: 25 minutes

BEST PASTA CHOICE: Farfalle or small shells

Raw tomatoes form the basis for this Italian variation on traditional succotash. Fresh corn kernels are blanched just until tender as are frozen (only gardeners have access to fresh) baby lima beans. Use the highest-quality extra-virgin olive oil and chives to complete this summery sauce, which can be made up to 30 minutes before the pasta is cooked. I prefer the delicate flavor of chives in this dish but more potent herbs like tarragon or basil would also be appropriate.

3 medium ripe tomatoes (about 1 pound)

2 ears fresh sweet corn

10 ounces frozen baby lima beans

Salt to taste, plus 1 teaspoon

¼ cup extra-virgin olive oil

¼ cup snipped fresh chives

¼ teaspoon freshly ground black pepper

1 pound pasta

1. Bring 4 quarts of salted water to a boil in a large pot for cooking the pasta.

2. Core and cut the tomatoes into ½-inch cubes. Place the tomatoes in a bowl large enough to hold the cooked pasta.

3. Remove the husks and silk from the corn. Stand the ears on their wide ends and carefully slide a sharp knife along the cob to remove the kernels from all sides. There should be about 2 cups of whole corn kernels.

4. Bring several quarts of water to a boil in a medium saucepan. Add the lima beans, salt to taste, and cook until almost tender, about 3 minutes. Add the corn kernels and continue cooking until the corn is cooked but still crisp and the beans are completely tender, about 1 minute more. Drain and transfer the corn and beans to the bowl with tomatoes.

5. Stir the oil, chives, 1 teaspoon salt, and pepper into the bowl with the vegetables. Mix gently. Taste for salt and pepper and adjust seasonings if necessary.

6. While preparing the sauce, cook and drain the pasta. Transfer the hot pasta to the bowl with the vegetables. Mix well and transfer portions to pasta bowls. Serve immediately.

Summer Tomato Sauce with Basil Pesto

● SERVES 4 ●

TIME: 20 minutes

BEST PASTA CHOICE: Linguine or other long, thin shape

Raw tomatoes and traditional basil pesto make a light, summery sauce. Use this recipe as a guide for other tomato and herb pesto variations with cilantro, oregano, thyme, rosemary, or mint. This pesto contains less oil than conventional recipes and is consequently somewhat thicker. However, the juices from the tomatoes thin the pesto to the correct consistency for coating pasta. Of course, only the ripest, most flavorful tomatoes should be used in raw sauces like this one.

4 medium tomatoes (about 1½ pounds)

2 cups tightly packed fresh basil leaves

2 medium cloves garlic, peeled

2 tablespoons pine nuts

6 tablespoons olive oil

½ cup freshly grated Parmesan cheese

Salt to taste

1 pound pasta

1. Bring 4 quarts of salted water to a boil in a large pot for cooking the pasta.

2. Core and cut the tomatoes into ½-inch cubes. Place the tomatoes in a bowl large enough to hold the cooked pasta and set them aside.

3. Place the basil, garlic, and pine nuts in the work bowl of a food processor. Process, scraping down the sides of the bowl once or twice, until coarsely ground. With the motor running, slowly pour the oil through the feed tube and process until smooth.

4. Scrape the pesto into a small bowl. Stir in the cheese and salt to taste. Scrape the pesto into the bowl with the tomatoes and mix well. Taste for salt and adjust seasonings if necessary.

5. While preparing the sauce, cook and drain the pasta. Toss the hot pasta with the tomato sauce. Mix well and transfer portions to pasta bowls. Serve immediately.

Spicy Tomato Sauce with Garlic and Ricotta Salata

• SERVES 4 •

TIME: 25 minutes

BEST PASTA CHOICE: Fusilli or other short, curly shape

Ricotta salata is a salted, lightly aged version of the creamy, fresh ricotta cheese that is so familiar to Americans. Although it looks like feta cheese, ricotta salata has no real substitutes since it is creamier and less salty than feta cheese. This wonderful cheese is now being imported from Italy in relatively large quantities, so look for it at Italian delicatessens and some supermarkets. The tangy, nutty flavor of ricotta salata is a perfect match for a spicy tomato sauce like this one. Use the shredding disk on a food processor or the large holes on a box grater to shred the cheese.

One 28-ounce can drained whole tomatoes,
    juice discarded
¼ cup olive oil
4 large cloves garlic, peeled
1 teaspoon hot red pepper flakes or to taste
1 teaspoon salt
1 pound pasta
½ pound ricotta salata cheese, shredded

continued

1. Bring 4 quarts of salted water to a boil in a large pot for cooking the pasta.

2. Roughly chop the tomatoes.

3. Heat the oil in a large skillet. Add the whole garlic cloves and sauté, turning them occasionally, over medium heat until golden brown on all sides, about 6 minutes. Use a slotted spoon to lift the browned garlic from the oil. Discard the garlic.

4. Add the hot red pepper flakes to the hot oil and cook for 30 seconds to release their flavor. Add the tomatoes and salt to the pan. Simmer, occasionally using a spoon to break apart the tomatoes, until the sauce thickens, about 10 minutes. Taste for salt and hot pepper and adjust seasonings if needed.

5. While preparing the sauce, cook and drain the pasta. Toss the hot pasta with the tomato sauce and the shredded cheese. Mix gently until the cheese softens slightly, about 30 seconds. Transfer portions to warm pasta bowls and serve immediately.

Spicy Tomato Sauce with Olives and Capers

● SERVES 4 ●

TIME: 25 minutes

BEST PASTA CHOICE: Spaghetti or other long, very thin shape

Spaghetti alla Puttanesca, or "whore's pasta," is a staple in trattorias throughout Italy. This dish is named for prostitutes, who perhaps were attracted to this recipe because it can be prepared with pantry items and requires little effort. These same qualities, along with the pleasant combination of salty and spicy flavors, are also responsible for the enduring popularity of this classic sauce. Although I like the contrast between black and green olives, feel free to use 16 olives (about ½ cup chopped) of a single variety.

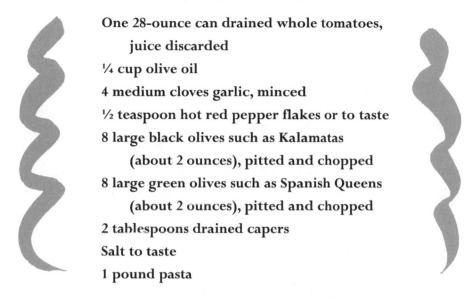

**One 28-ounce can drained whole tomatoes,
    juice discarded**
¼ cup olive oil
4 medium cloves garlic, minced
½ teaspoon hot red pepper flakes or to taste
**8 large black olives such as Kalamatas
    (about 2 ounces), pitted and chopped**
**8 large green olives such as Spanish Queens
    (about 2 ounces), pitted and chopped**
2 tablespoons drained capers
Salt to taste
1 pound pasta

1. Bring 4 quarts of salted water to a boil in a large pot for cooking the pasta.

2. Roughly chop the tomatoes.

3. Heat the oil in a large skillet. Add the garlic and hot red pepper flakes and sauté over medium heat until the garlic is golden, about 2 minutes.

4. Add the tomatoes, olives, and capers to the pan. Simmer, occasionally using a spoon to break apart the tomatoes, until the sauce thickens, about 15 minutes. Add salt to taste. (If the olives and capers are very salty, the sauce may require very little salt.)

5. While preparing the sauce, cook and drain the pasta. Toss the hot pasta with the tomato sauce. Mix well and transfer portions to warm pasta bowls. Serve immediately

Spicy Two-Tomato Sauce with Sun-Dried Tomatoes

● SERVES 4 ●

TIME: 25 minutes

BEST PASTA CHOICE: Fusilli or other short, curly shape

Sun-dried tomatoes enrich a basic tomato sauce to provide an extra jolt of tomato flavor. They also lend a meaty quality to this simple sauce. A generous amount of garlic and some hot pepper flakes give this combination of two tomatoes a nice bite. If you like milder sauces, feel free to omit the hot pepper flakes. Fresh basil can substituted for the parsley as well.

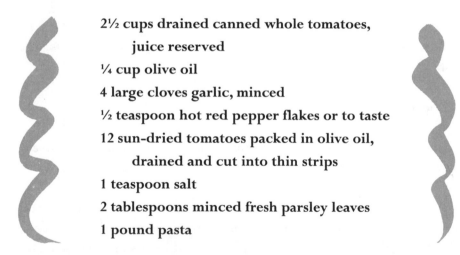

**2½ cups drained canned whole tomatoes,
   juice reserved**

¼ cup olive oil

4 large cloves garlic, minced

½ teaspoon hot red pepper flakes or to taste

**12 sun-dried tomatoes packed in olive oil,
   drained and cut into thin strips**

1 teaspoon salt

2 tablespoons minced fresh parsley leaves

1 pound pasta

1. Bring 4 quarts of salted water to a boil in a large pot for cooking the pasta.

2. Roughly chop the tomatoes and set them aside with ¾ cup of their packing juice.

3. Heat the oil in a large skillet. Add the garlic and hot red pepper flakes and sauté over medium heat until the garlic is golden, about 2 minutes.

4. Add the canned tomatoes and their juice, the sun-dried tomatoes, and the salt to the pan. Simmer, occasionally using a spoon to break apart the canned tomatoes, until the sauce thickens, 15 to 20 minutes. Stir in the parsley. Taste for salt and hot pepper and adjust seasonings if needed.

5. While preparing the sauce, cook and drain the pasta. Toss the hot pasta with the tomato sauce. Mix well and transfer portions to warm pasta bowls. Serve immediately.

Raw Tomato Sauce with Smoked Mozzarella and Basil

● SERVES 4 ●

TIME: 20 minutes

BEST PASTA CHOICE: Fusilli or other short, curly shape

The smokiness of the mozzarella contrasts beautifully with the sweet/acidic flavor of perfectly ripe summer tomatoes. A little garlic and a few basil leaves finish this simplest of summer sauces.

4 medium ripe tomatoes (about 1½ pounds)

¼ cup olive oil

2 medium cloves garlic, minced

8 large basil leaves, torn into several
   pieces each

1 teaspoon salt

½ teaspoon freshly ground black pepper

6 ounces smoked mozzarella cheese

1 pound pasta

continued

1. Bring 4 quarts of salted water to a boil in a large pot for cooking the pasta.

2. Core and cut the tomatoes into ½-inch cubes. Place the tomatoes in a bowl large enough to hold the cooked pasta. Add the oil, garlic, basil, salt, and pepper and mix gently.

3. Shred the cheese using the large holes on a box grater or the shredding disk on a food processor. Toss the shredded cheese into the bowl with the tomatoes. Mix well. Taste for salt and pepper and adjust seasonings if necessary.

4. While preparing the sauce, cook and drain the pasta. Immediately transfer the hot pasta to the bowl with the sauce. Mix well until the cheese starts to melt, about 30 seconds. Transfer portions to pasta bowls and serve immediately.

Raw Tomato Sauce with Black Olive Paste

● SERVES 4 ●

TIME: 20 minutes

BEST PASTA CHOICE: Spaghetti or other long, very thin shape

Another potent but easy-to-prepare summer sauce demonstrates the principle that great ingredients—like perfectly ripe summer tomatoes—need little adornment to make memorable meals. This rich sauce calls out for plenty of bread and a light but equally intriguing salad, perhaps roasted bell peppers dressed with a hint of olive oil and balsamic vinegar and topped with a few shavings of Parmesan cheese.

4 medium ripe tomatoes (about 1½ pounds)
20 large black olives such as Kalamatas
(about 5 ounces)
1 large clove garlic, peeled
¼ cup lightly packed fresh oregano leaves
1 tablespoon lemon juice
¼ cup olive oil
Salt and freshly ground black pepper to taste
1 pound pasta

1. Bring 4 quarts of salted water to a boil in a large pot for cooking the pasta.

2. Core and cut the tomatoes into ½-inch cubes. Place the tomatoes in a bowl large enough to hold the cooked pasta.

3. Pit the olives. There should be about ⅔ cup of pitted olives. Place the olives, garlic, oregano, and lemon juice in the work bowl of a food processor. Pulse, scraping down the sides of the bowl as needed, until finely chopped. With the motor running, slowly pour the oil through the feed tube and process until smooth.

4. Scrape the olive paste into the bowl with the tomatoes and toss gently. Add salt sparingly, especially if olives are salty, and pepper. Taste for salt and pepper and adjust seasonings if necessary.

5. While preparing the sauce, cook and drain the pasta. Toss the hot pasta with the tomato sauce. Mix well and transfer portions to pasta bowls. Serve immediately.

Spicy But Simple Tomato Sauce

• SERVES 4 •

TIME: 25 minutes

BEST PASTA CHOICE: Penne or other short, tubular shape

This tomato sauce is known as *arrabbiata* or "angry" sauce in trattorias throughout Italy. No doubt this name refers to the healthy dose of hot red pepper and garlic. However, I like to think of this modest sauce—which is nothing more than canned tomatoes, garlic, oil, hot pepper, and parsley—as a soothing and satisfying way to end a busy, even maddening, day.

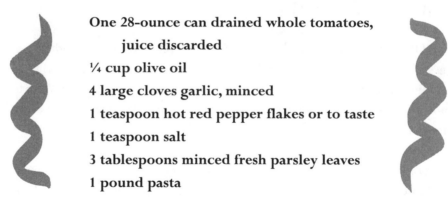

One 28-ounce can drained whole tomatoes, juice discarded

¼ cup olive oil

4 large cloves garlic, minced

1 teaspoon hot red pepper flakes or to taste

1 teaspoon salt

3 tablespoons minced fresh parsley leaves

1 pound pasta

1. Bring 4 quarts of salted water to a boil in a large pot for cooking the pasta.

2. Roughly chop the tomatoes.

3. Heat the oil in a large skillet. Add the garlic and hot red pepper flakes and sauté over medium heat until the garlic is golden, about 2 minutes.

4. Add the tomatoes and salt to the pan. Simmer, occasionally using a spoon to break apart the tomatoes, until the sauce thickens, about 15 minutes. Stir in the parsley. Taste for salt and hot pepper and adjust seasonings if needed.

5. While preparing the sauce, cook and drain the pasta. Toss the hot pasta with the tomato sauce. Mix well and transfer portions to warm pasta bowls. Serve immediately.

Quick Tomato Sauce with Fresh Basil and Garlic

● SERVES 4 ●

TIME: 20 minutes

BEST PASTA CHOICE: Spaghetti or other long, very thin shape

The simplest of all Italian pasta sauces relies on sweet canned tomatoes, a large handful of fresh basil, and a healthy dose of garlic. For this sauce, the canned tomatoes should be roughly seeded, which is something you can do with your hands while working over a sink. Seeded tomatoes make a particularly meaty, thick sauce.

3 cups drained canned whole tomatoes, juice discarded
1 cup tightly packed fresh basil leaves
¼ cup olive oil
4 medium cloves garlic, minced
1 teaspoon salt
Freshly ground black pepper to taste
1 pound pasta

1. Bring 4 quarts of salted water to a boil in a large pot for cooking the pasta.

continued

2. Working over a sink, gently open each tomato (taking care not to squirt the juices) and push the seeds and excess liquid out with your fingers. Coarsely chop the seeded tomatoes and set them aside. Stack the basil leaves on top of each other and cut them crosswise into thin strips.

3. Set a large skillet over medium heat and add the tomatoes, basil, 3 table-spoons oil, garlic, and salt. Simmer, stirring occasionally, until the liquid in the pan thickens and the tomatoes form a rough sauce, about 10 minutes. Add the pepper. Taste for salt and adjust seasonings if necessary.

4. While preparing the sauce, cook and drain the pasta. Toss the hot pasta with the tomato sauce. Mix well and transfer portions to warm pasta bowls. Drizzle the remaining tablespoon of oil over the bowls and serve immediately.

Salsa Primavera with Tomatoes, Mushrooms, and Mixed Vegetables

• SERVES 4 •

TIME: 45 minutes

BEST PASTA CHOICE: Linguine or other long, thin shape

With its contrasting flavors and colors, this sauce is the perfect way to celebrate the arrival of spring. There are several components to this dish which must be prepared separately—assorted blanched vegetables, sautéed mushrooms, and a garlicky plum tomato and basil sauce. The vegetables are blanched individually to retain their flavor and then added to the mushrooms and bound with a little cream to form the sauce for the pasta. The tomato mixture is tossed with the drained pasta to give the dish some color and provide extra moisture. Choose at least three (and as many as all seven) vegetables from the following list, using a total of 6 cups sliced vegetables:

bite-sized broccoli florets, fresh or frozen peas, thin asparagus spears cut on the bias into 1-inch lengths, small zucchini and/or yellow crookneck squash cut into thin half moons, shelled fresh fava beans, and thin green beans cut into 1-inch lengths.

6 cups vegetables (see headnote above)
Salt to taste
½ pound fresh white cultivated mushrooms
¾ pound ripe plum tomatoes
2 tablespoons olive oil
4 medium cloves garlic, minced
½ teaspoon hot red pepper flakes or to taste
12 large fresh basil leaves, shredded
Freshly ground black pepper to taste
2 tablespoons unsalted butter
⅓ cup heavy cream
1 pound pasta
½ cup freshly grated Parmesan cheese,
    plus more to taste

1. Bring 4 quarts of salted water to a boil in a large pot for cooking the pasta.

2. Bring several quarts of water to a boil in a medium saucepan. Add the first vegetable and salt to taste. Cook until the vegetable is crisp-tender, about 30 seconds for frozen peas, 1 minute for zucchini or yellow squash, or 2 minutes for broccoli, green beans, fresh peas, fava beans, and asparagus. Use a slotted spoon to transfer the blanched vegetable to a large bowl. Cook the remaining vegetables, one at a time, and transfer them when crisp-tender to the large bowl.

3. Wipe the mushrooms with a paper towel to loosen and remove any dirt. Trim and discard a thin slice from the stem end of each mushroom. Thinly slice the mushrooms and set them aside. Core and cut the tomatoes into ½-inch cubes and set them aside separately from the mushrooms.

continued

4. Heat the oil in a medium pan. Add half the garlic and all of the hot red pepper flakes and sauté over medium heat until the garlic is golden, about 2 minutes. Add the tomatoes and cook, stirring occasionally, until heated through, about 3 minutes. Do not overcook the tomatoes or they will lose their shape. Stir in the basil and salt and pepper to taste. Cover and set aside to keep warm.

5. Melt the butter in a skillet large enough to hold the mushrooms and the vegetables. Add the remaining garlic and sauté over medium heat until golden, about 2 minutes. Add the sliced mushrooms and cook, stirring often, until they release their juices, about 6 minutes. Season generously with salt and pepper.

6. Drain any liquid that has accumulated at the bottom of the bowl with the blanched vegetables. Add the vegetables to the pan with the mushrooms. Cook, tossing several times, until heated through, about 2 minutes.

7. Add the cream to the pan with the mushrooms and the vegetables. Simmer until the sauce thickens a bit, 2 to 3 minutes. Taste for salt and pepper and adjust seasonings if necessary.

8. While preparing the sauce, cook and drain the pasta. Toss the hot pasta with the vegetable and mushroom mixture, the tomatoes, and ½ cup Parmesan. Mix well and transfer portions to warm pasta bowls. Serve immediately with more grated cheese passed separately.

Zucchini

The name zucchini has the same root as the Italian word for sugar, *zucchero*. While Americans used to oversized zucchini may not make the connection, shoppers who look for small, young zucchini understand that gentle sweetness is the hallmark of first-rate zucchini. A young, thin spear of sweet green zucchini with its neon-orange blossom still attached at one end is a delicacy not to be missed by farm stand shoppers or gardeners.

Although few vegetables have a stronger association with Italian cuisine, zucchini, like all squash, has its roots in the New World and did not arrive in Italy until after Columbus's voyages. Its ability to spread like wildfire (anyone who has grown zucchini knows that this plant often overtakes the backyard garden) surely has contributed to its prominent role today. When zucchini is in season, the supply often seems endless. Luckily, zucchini and its culinary cousin yellow crookneck or summer squash take to numerous preparations.

• SELECTION •

Size and firmness are the most important factors when purchasing zucchini. In general, I find that smaller zucchini are more flavorful and less watery than larger specimens. Smaller zucchini also have fewer seeds. I look for zucchini that weigh less than 6 ounces, though 8 ounces is acceptable. Fresh zucchini will have no soft spots or obviously discolored areas and will be quite firm. Avoid any zucchini with wrinkled or pock-marked skin. Zucchini should have smooth, dark green skin. Fresh yellow squash share the same traits, except of course that their skins are yellow.

• S T O R A G E •

Firm zucchini should stay fresh in a paper bag in the refrigerator for several days. At the first signs of softness, either use the zucchini immediately or discard it.

• P R E P A R A T I O N •

As the bright orange blossoms on a zucchini plant are transformed into short and then long green spears of zucchini, the weight of the spears causes them to eventually elongate while on the ground. Thus, many zucchini have tiny bits of soil embedded in their skins. To determine how much attention the zucchini will need, simply glide your hand over the skin. If you feel small bumps, the zucchini should be briefly soaked in a bowl of cold water to loosen embedded granules of sand. If the zucchini surface feels smooth, simply rinse the zucchini and proceed with cutting directions.

The ends should be sliced off but there is no need ever to peel zucchini. Zucchini can be sliced in half lengthwise and then sliced crosswise into thin half moons, cut into long spears, sliced into thin matchsticks, or even shredded.

• U S E   I N   S A U C E S •

Because the flavor of zucchini is fairly mild, it is very versatile and takes to any number of cooking methods. Like watery eggplant, zucchini benefits from grilling since liquid in the vegetable evaporates and causes the delicate flavor to become concentrated. Zucchini can also be sautéed over medium-heat high until golden, a process that also concentrates flavor as the vegetable sheds water.

When zucchini will be the dominant flavor in a sauce, grilling or sautéing are the best options. However, steamed or braised zucchini can absorb flavors from other more powerful ingredients, acting as a vegetable sponge of sorts and making an excellent base for pasta sauces. Steamed zucchini is a nice foil for raw sauces such as pesto. Zucchini can also be slow-cooked in a rich tomato sauce; as the zucchini softens it gives up its shape and flavor to the tomato broth. One method that should be avoided for all zucchini preparation is boiling, which tends to cook out its delicate flavor.

• R E L A T E D   R E C I P E S •

Salsa Primavera with Tomatoes, Mushrooms, and Mixed Vegetables (page 298)

Sautéed Zucchini with Lemon, Pine Nuts, and Basil

● SERVES 4 ●

TIME: 30 minutes

BEST PASTA CHOICE: Fettuccine or other long, wide shape

This sauté features extra-thin slivers of zucchini highlighted by the flavors of lemon and basil. Toasted pine nuts provide a pleasant crunch. Zucchini are easily cut into thin strips that resemble matchsticks, which cook quickly and evenly.

4 medium zucchini (about 1½ pounds)
1 medium lemon
3 tablespoons pine nuts
5 tablespoons olive oil
1 medium onion, minced
20 large fresh basil leaves, shredded
1 teaspoon salt
½ teaspoon freshly ground black pepper
1 pound pasta
Freshly grated Parmesan cheese to taste

1. Bring 4 quarts of salted water to a boil in a large pot for cooking the pasta.

2. Wash the zucchini to remove any dirt that may be clinging to them. Run your hand over the skins and if they are not perfectly smooth, briefly soak the zucchini in a large bowl of cold water to loosen the embedded sand. Trim the ends from the zucchini and cut them slightly on the bias into ¼-inch-thick rounds. Stack several rounds on top of each other and cut them into very thin strips that resemble matchsticks.

continued

3. Remove the yellow skin from the lemon with a vegetable peeler, leaving behind the bitter white pith. Cut the peel into very thin strips that are about 1 inch long. Squeeze 2 tablespoons juice from the lemon; discard the lemon. Set the zest and juice aside separately.

4. Set a large skillet over medium heat. Add the pine nuts and toast, shaking the pan occasionally to turn the nuts, until golden brown (about 5 minutes). Do not let nuts burn. Set the toasted nuts aside.

5. Heat the oil in the empty pan. Add the onion and sauté over medium heat until lightly translucent, about 5 minutes. Add the lemon zest and zucchini. Raise the heat to medium-high and cook, stirring occasionally, until the zucchini has wilted, about 8 minutes.

6. Stir the reserved lemon juice, basil, salt, and pepper into the pan. Cook, stirring several times, until the ingredients are heated through, 1 to 2 minutes more. Taste for salt and pepper and adjust seasonings if necessary.

7. While preparing the sauce, cook and drain the pasta, making sure that some water still clings to the pasta. Toss the hot pasta with the zucchini sauce and the toasted nuts. Mix well and transfer portions to warm pasta bowls. Serve immediately with grated cheese passed separately.

Sautéed Zucchini with Garlic and Mint

● SERVES 4 ●

TIME: 25 minutes

BEST PASTA CHOICE: Penne or other small, tubular shape

Golden orbs of quickly sautéed zucchini blend with a healthy dose of garlic and a handful of fresh mint leaves for a light, refreshing sauce. I prefer to use very small zucchini for this recipe; if only larger zucchini are available, cut rounds into half circles so that they will be the right size.

8 very small zucchini (about 1½ pounds)

6 tablespoons olive oil

4 medium cloves garlic, minced

¼ cup minced fresh mint leaves

1 teaspoon salt

½ teaspoon freshly ground black pepper

1 pound pasta

Freshly grated Parmesan cheese to taste

1. Bring 4 quarts of salted water to a boil in a large pot for cooking the pasta.

2. Wash the zucchini to remove any dirt that may be clinging to them. Run your hand over the skins and if they are not perfectly smooth, briefly soak the zucchini in a large bowl of cold water to loosen the embedded sand. Trim the ends from the zucchini and cut them into ¼-inch-thick rounds. Set the sliced zucchini aside.

3. Heat the oil in a large skillet. Add the garlic and sauté over medium heat until lightly colored, about 1 minute.

continued

4. Raise the heat to medium-high and add the zucchini. Cook, stirring often, until the zucchini is golden and beginning to brown, about 8 minutes. Stir in the mint, salt, and pepper. Taste for salt and pepper and adjust seasonings if necessary.

5. While preparing the sauce, cook and drain the pasta, making sure that some water still clings to the noodles. Toss the hot pasta with the zucchini sauce. Mix well and transfer portions to warm pasta bowls. Serve immediately with grated cheese passed separately.

Sautéed Zucchini with Pink Tomato Sauce and Basil

• SERVES 4 •

TIME: 25 minutes

BEST PASTA CHOICE: Penne or other small, tubular shape

This elegant sauce pairs quickly seared zucchini with a tomato-cream sauce, fresh basil, and Parmesan cheese. This rich dish can be used as a first course for a formal meal or served with salad and plenty of bread for a complete weekday meal.

4 medium ripe tomatoes (about 1½ pounds)

4 medium zucchini (about 1½ pounds)

2 tablespoons olive oil

2 tablespoons unsalted butter

4 medium cloves garlic, minced

1 teaspoon salt

½ teaspoon freshly ground black pepper

½ cup heavy cream

15 large fresh basil leaves, shredded

1 pound pasta

¼ cup freshly grated Parmesan cheese,

    plus more to taste

1. Bring 4 quarts of salted water to a boil in a large pot for cooking the pasta. Add the tomatoes and turn them several times to resubmerge the parts of the tomatoes that bob to the surface. Keep the tomatoes in the water for 20 seconds. Use a slotted spoon to transfer the tomatoes to a work surface. Cool the tomatoes slightly and peel the skins with your fingers. Core and cut the tomatoes in half. Squeeze out the seeds over a sink. Cut the peeled, seeded tomatoes into ½-inch cubes. Set the tomatoes aside. Reserve the water in the pot for cooking the pasta.

2. Wash the zucchini to remove any dirt that may be clinging to them. Run your hand over the skins and if they are not perfectly smooth, briefly soak the zucchini in a large bowl of cold water to loosen the embedded sand. Trim the ends from the zucchini and cut them in half lengthwise. Slice the zucchini into thin half moons.

3. Heat the oil and butter in a large skillet. Add the zucchini and sauté, stirring often, over medium-high heat until golden, about 10 minutes. Add the garlic and cook for about 1 minute. Add the tomatoes, salt, and pepper, and cook, stirring several times, until the tomatoes are heated through, about 2 minutes.

4. Reduce the heat to medium-low. Stir in the cream and cook, stirring often, until the sauce comes to a boil and thickens slightly, about 2 minutes. Stir in the basil. Taste for salt and pepper and adjust seasonings if necessary.

5. While preparing the sauce, cook and drain the pasta. Toss the hot pasta with the zucchini sauce and ¼ cup Parmesan. Mix well and transfer portions to warm pasta bowls. Serve immediately with more grated cheese passed separately.

Grilled Zucchini with Tomatoes and Balsamic Vinegar

• SERVES 4 •

TIME: 30 minutes

BEST PASTA CHOICE: Fusilli or other short, curly shape

This room-temperature sauce is perfect on a warm summer's night when you want to keep indoor cooking to a minimum. The flavor of the zucchini intensifies over hot coals and the texture become firmer, even meaty, as the water in the vegetable evaporates. The zucchini can be prepared under the broiler, but the effect is not quite the same. This sauce can be made several hours in advance, covered, and kept on the counter until the pasta is cooked. Other fresh herbs can be added to the dressing instead of basil. Use an equal amount of parsley or half as much oregano, thyme, or mint.

5 medium zucchini (about 2 pounds)

¼ cup olive oil

Salt to taste, plus 1 teaspoon

Freshly ground black pepper to taste,
**   plus ¼ teaspoon**

2 tablespoons balsamic vinegar

2 medium ripe tomatoes (about ¾ pound)

¼ cup minced fresh basil leaves

1 pound pasta

1. Light the grill or make a charcoal fire. Bring 4 quarts of salted water to a boil in a large pot for cooking the pasta.

2. Wash the zucchini to remove any dirt that may be clinging to them. Run your hand over the skins and if they are not perfectly smooth, briefly soak

the zucchini in a large bowl of cold water to loosen the embedded sand. Trim the ends from the zucchini. Slice each trimmed zucchini lengthwise into strips that are about ½ inch thick. Lay the slices on a baking sheet and brush both sides with 2 tablespoons oil. Generously salt and pepper them.

3. Use a stiff wire brush to scrape the hot grill clean. Grill the zucchini, turning once, until both sides are marked with very dark stripes, about 10 minutes. Briefly cool the zucchini.

4. Whisk the remaining 2 tablespoons oil with the vinegar, 1 teaspoon salt, and ¼ teaspoon pepper in a bowl large enough to hold the pasta. Core and cut the tomatoes into ½-inch cubes. Toss the tomatoes and the basil with the dressing. Cut the grilled zucchini slices into 1-inch pieces. Toss the zucchini into the bowl with the tomatoes and mix gently. Taste for salt and pepper and adjust seasonings if necessary.

5. While preparing the sauce, cook and drain the pasta. Toss the hot pasta with the zucchini sauce. Mix well and transfer portions to pasta bowls. Serve immediately.

Steamed Zucchini with Basil Pesto

● SERVES 4 ●

TIME: 25 minutes

BEST PASTA CHOICE: Linguine or other long, thin shape

When tossed with pungent basil pesto, steamed zucchini wedges make a quick pasta sauce that is especially suited to a hot summer's night since it involves so little cooking. Serve with a tomato and leafy green salad and plenty of bread for a complete meal.

continued

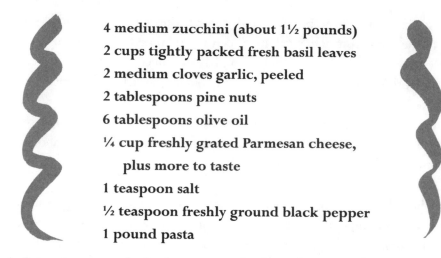

4 medium zucchini (about 1½ pounds)

2 cups tightly packed fresh basil leaves

2 medium cloves garlic, peeled

2 tablespoons pine nuts

6 tablespoons olive oil

¼ cup freshly grated Parmesan cheese,
   plus more to taste

1 teaspoon salt

½ teaspoon freshly ground black pepper

1 pound pasta

1. Bring 4 quarts of salted water to a boil in a large pot for cooking the pasta.

2. Wash the zucchini to remove any dirt that may be clinging to them. Run your hand over the skins and if they are not perfectly smooth, briefly soak the zucchini in a large bowl of cold water to loosen the embedded sand. Trim the ends from the zucchini and cut them into 2-inch lengths that are about ¼ inch thick. Steam the zucchini until just tender, about 2 minutes. Set the zucchini aside.

3. Place the basil, garlic, and pine nuts in the work bowl of a food processor and process, scraping down the sides of the bowl as needed, until finely ground. With the motor running, slowly pour the oil through the feed tube and process until smooth.

4. Scrape the pesto into a large bowl. Stir in ¼ cup cheese, salt, and pepper. Gently stir in the steamed zucchini. Taste for salt and pepper and adjust seasonings if necessary.

5. While preparing the sauce, cook and drain the pasta, making sure that some water still clings to the noodles. Toss the hot pasta with the zucchini and pesto mixture. Mix well and transfer portions to warm pasta bowls. Serve immediately with more grated cheese passed separately.

Salsa Cruda with Zucchini, Tomatoes, Red Onion, and Lemon

• SERVES 4 •

TIME: 20 minutes

BEST PASTA CHOICE: Fusilli or other short, curly shape

This raw sauce depends on shredded or grated zucchini, ripe summer tomatoes, thinly sliced red onions, and lemon juice. For added color, use two small yellow crookneck squash along with two green zucchini. Mint may be substituted for the cilantro if desired.

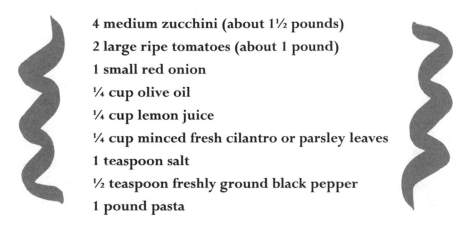

4 medium zucchini (about 1½ pounds)

2 large ripe tomatoes (about 1 pound)

1 small red onion

¼ cup olive oil

¼ cup lemon juice

¼ cup minced fresh cilantro or parsley leaves

1 teaspoon salt

½ teaspoon freshly ground black pepper

1 pound pasta

1. Bring 4 quarts of salted water to a boil in a large pot for cooking the pasta.

2. Wash the zucchini to remove any dirt that may be clinging to them. Run your hand over the skins and if they are not perfectly smooth, briefly soak the zucchini in a large bowl of cold water to loosen the embedded sand. Trim the ends from the zucchini and cut them in half lengthwise. Using the shredding disk on a food processor or a hand grater, shred the zucchini. Set the zucchini aside in a large bowl.

continued

3. Core and cut the tomatoes into ½-inch cubes. Add the tomatoes to the bowl with the zucchini. Peel and mince the onion. Add the onion to the bowl.

4. Add the oil, lemon juice, cilantro, salt, and pepper to the bowl with the vegetables and mix well. Taste for salt and pepper and adjust seasonings if necessary.

5. While preparing the sauce, cook and drain the pasta. Toss the hot pasta with the vegetables. Mix well and transfer portions to pasta bowls. Serve immediately.

Slow-Cooked Zucchini with Tomato Sauce

• SERVES 4 •

TIME: 55 minutes

BEST PASTA CHOICE: Linguine or other long, thin shape

This stewlike sauce was inspired by classic ratatouille recipes. I have eliminated many of the competing flavors in the traditional dish and focused squarely on the zucchini and tomatoes. Cooking zucchini for so long (about 40 minutes) causes it to lose its firm texture and almost melt into the tomato sauce. The effect is quite delicious so be sure to serve with plenty of bread to sop up every drop of the sauce.

4 medium zucchini (about 1½ pounds)

¼ cup olive oil

1 medium onion, minced

4 medium cloves garlic, minced

2 cups drained canned whole tomatoes,
    juice reserved

1 teaspoon salt
½ teaspoon freshly ground black pepper
3 tablespoons minced fresh parsley leaves
1 pound pasta
Freshly grated Parmesan cheese to taste

1. Bring 4 quarts of salted water to a boil in a large pot for cooking the pasta.

2. Wash the zucchini to remove any dirt that may be clinging to them. Run your hand over the skins and if they are not perfectly smooth, briefly soak the zucchini in a large bowl of cold water to loosen the embedded sand. Trim the ends from the zucchini and cut them into ½-inch cubes.

3. Heat the oil in a large sauté pan. Add the onion and sauté over medium heat until translucent, about 5 minutes. Stir in the garlic and cook until lightly colored, about 1 minute.

4. Add the zucchini to the pan and toss well to coat the cubes with the oil. Continue cooking over medium heat, stirring occasionally, until the zucchini completely loses its raw color, about 10 minutes.

5. Coarsely chop the tomatoes and add them to the pan along with 1 cup of their packing juice and the salt and pepper. Use a heavy spoon to gently break apart the tomatoes as you wait for the liquid to come to a boil.

6. Once the liquid starts to boil, reduce the heat to low, cover the pan, and simmer gently until the sauce thickens and the zucchini is extremely tender, about 30 minutes. Stir in the parsley. Taste for salt and pepper and adjust seasonings if necessary.

7. While preparing the sauce, cook and drain the pasta. Toss the hot pasta with the zucchini sauce. Mix well and transfer portions to warm pasta bowls. Serve immediately with grated cheese passed separately.

Index

~